Captive Audience

Books are to be returned on or before
the last date below.

7–DAY LOAN

23 JAN 2004

11 MAR 2005

2 7 OCT 2005

− 1 DEC 2005

LIBREX —

This book is dedicated to the memory of my grandmother,
Evelyn Jewkes, and my friend, Ros Minsky,
two woman who inspired me more than they knew.

Captive Audience

Media, Masculinity and Power in Prisons

Yvonne Jewkes

WILLAN
PUBLISHING

Published by

Willian Publishing
Culmcott House
Mill Street, Uffculme
Cullompton, Devon
EX15 3AT, UK
Tel: +44(0)1884 840337
Fax: +44(0)1884 840251
E-mail: info@willanpublishing.co.uk
website: www.willanpublishing.co.uk

Published simultaneously in the USA and Canada by

Willan Publishing
c/o ISBS, 5824 N.E. Hassalo St,
Portland, Oregon 97213-3644, USA
Tel: +001(0)503 287 3093
Fax: +001(0)503 280 8832
e-mail: info@isbs.com
website: www.isbs.com

First published 2002

ISBN 1-903240-64-6 Paperback
ISBN 1-903240-65-4 Hardback

British Library Cataloguing-in-Publication Data

A catalogue record for this book is available from the British Library

Printed and bound by T J International Ltd, Trecerus Industrial Estate, Padstow, Cornwall
Typeset by Anneset, Weston-super-Mare, Somerset

Contents

Acknowledgements

I would like to thank a number of people for the support, guidance and wisdom they have offered me during the writing of this book. First and foremost, thanks to Alison Liebling for her help, advice and friendship, all of which were invaluable in finally getting this project off the ground. Many thanks are also due to Tony Bottoms and Brian Longhurst who examined the doctoral thesis on which this book is based, and who then made constructive suggestions which helped me to conceive of it as a book. I am happy to acknowledge the financial support of the Board of Graduate Studies at the University of Cambridge whose award of a domestic research studentship made the research possible, and also to Lucy Cavendish College for the award of a small, but welcome, research grant. Thanks also go to Loraine Gelsthorpe for her support, especially in the first year of my studies, and to other staff and research students at the Institute of Criminology who, in various ways, made the research process easier and more enjoyable.

Debts of gratitude are owed to former colleagues and students at the Scarman Centre at the University of Leicester, and at De Montfort University. Both institutions provided stimulating and supportive environments in which to start this project. Special mention must go to Tim O'Sullivan and Rinella Cere who helped me to form the ideas on which this research is based and whose comments and suggestions during the early stages proved invaluable.

Thanks go to Anita Daniels and Kirsten McClymont, both of whom were generous enough to give me copies of their own work on media in prisons when little existed elsewhere. I am also grateful to the Prison Service Area Manager and the various governors who opened their doors to me, to Peter Garrett who invited me to attend Prison Dialogue and, of course, to all the prisoners who told me their stories. Rarely have I encountered a place where laughter and pathos are found in almost equal measure. I am deeply grateful to these men for disclosing their thoughts and feelings to a stranger, and for doing so with patience, clarity and passion. Their accounts made a lasting impact.

Many thanks to Brian Willan for his calm efficiency and enthusiasm, and for having the faith to publish this book. Finally, my gratitude and love go to my partner David Wright who now knows more about prisons than he probably ever thought desirable, and whose intelligent comments, keen insight and developing culinary skills have all played an immeasurable role in getting this project finished.

Yvonne Jewkes
January 2002

Introduction: prisons, media and everyday life

When I was in the Scrubs, I spent 6 months in segregation without a radio. Then the chaplain brought one in. I remember hearing a newscaster talking so fast it wouldn't go in. It blew my brain. Now I've got a TV in my cell for the first time and it doesn't seem like a prison . . . I watch more TV than I ever did outside. It's as if there's a person in the cell with you, it's company. It also gives the illusion of control. I like *Neighbours* and *Home and Away* best because it's always sunny and everyone's nice looking (Tony).

This book will explore the importance of media forms and content within a unique context: the prison. Of immense importance in their organisation of social reality and an essential part of the 'map' by which we navigate everyday life, the media are frequently taken for granted, and few of us pause to question why media matter to us in the ways they do. It is perhaps only when some problem or controversy arises that is connected to media, or when an event of national or global interest occurs, that we ask questions about the ways in which we habitually conceive of media in everyday life (Alasuutari 1999b: 86). Furthermore, it is generally when our regular media habits are disrupted by forces beyond our control that we understand how important media are to the familiar routines of our lives. The decision to research the significance of media in prisons was made precisely in order to interrogate its importance in such respects. It is hoped that by, as it were, placing a magnifying glass over this discrete, localised and usually hidden (to most of us, at least) environment, the study of media consumption among prison inmates might not only illuminate aspects of the social world of the prison, but also indicate why it is that media are so important to all of us in providing channels of communication, information and entertainment, and in forming identities, positioning ourselves in relation to others within social hierarchies, and creating a sense of ourselves in time and space.

In its consideration of media consumption patterns among the incarcerated, this book aims to synthesise, and find intellectual compatibility between, the 'classic' sociological prison studies which offer descriptive accounts of the everyday experience of imprisonment, and the media studies literature on the experience of being a consumer of media and popular culture. The dominant theme that emerges from the first body of work, and one that will provide a conceptual framework for analysis throughout this book, is that imprisonment is an inherently painful and dehumanising experience during which the inmate will experience a series of deprivations that fundamentally weaken his sense of identity. The theoretical studies of media audiences will be used to provide evidence that for such individuals, the mass media provide a key source of empowerment, offering a range of material from which individuals can create new identities or maintain pre-existing identities, explore their inner selves, form subgroups based on collective fanship, and find autonomy and self-respect in otherwise humiliating and disidentifying circumstances. The findings of the research are considered in the light of recent innovations in contemporary social theory, and analysed via a separate but integrated discussion of macro, meso and micro levels of power and identity.

The relative paucity of academic studies of prison audiences is hard to explain. The use of media by people in identity construction, and in claiming power in otherwise disempowering circumstances, was an emerging theme in studies of media audiences in the late 1980s and early 1990s and although most research concentrated on family viewing, a few studies began to address the dynamics of media consumption among so-called 'neglected audiences' (Lindlof 1987; Willis and Wollen 1990). Yet by the mid-1990s, many writers had abandoned audience research as though it were a finished project, the result of which is that little is still known about the relationship between audiences and media in contexts other than the family household. Unsurprisingly, then, the role of media in prisons has remained largely undefined. Criminology has similarly overlooked the importance of media to an incarcerated public; an oversight that may be a reflection of the low status accorded media output (and indeed media studies) in general life. The common perception that media use is mindless and trivial – an *in*activity – sits awkwardly alongside the prison service's self-proclaimed aim to engage prisoners in purposeful activity and to 'lead a good and useful life' (Prison Rule 1). Concerns about the 'quality' of media output are usually tinged with a class-based prejudice, so that anxieties about media technologies and texts – usually reductively termed 'effects' – have most frequently been voiced by the (relatively) powerful and directed at the most vulnerable: the young, the mentally ill, the poor and the criminally-inclined (see, for example, Hagell and Newburn 1994). It is somewhat surprising, then, that those class-conscious critics who claim that most media is directed at the 'lowest common denominator' of society have not turned their attention to what is arguably the most obvious candidate for the label 'underclass': the prison population.

This book will argue that to view the characteristics of television and other media as being of 'low' cultural quality misses the important point that media resources fulfil a wide range of motivations, gratifications and desires, many of which are felt acutely among the confined. Not only are the well-documented feelings of powerlessness associated with imprisonment frequently mitigated by exposure to media, but the necessary adjustments to one's identity that incarceration demands can, to various degrees, be facilitated, furthered or, conversely, hindered, by access to particular forms of media. It is the nexus of relationships between media, identity, social-psychological survival and relations of power this study seeks to address.

In setting the stage for a discussion of why media is of interest in the prison context, Chapter 1 reviews the literature on the 'effects' of imprisonment and suggests that for the majority of inmates, imprisonment is mortifying, dehumanising and painful. Confinement disconnects individuals from everything that is familiar, and effectively ex-communicates them from the world outside. Guiding the theoretical approaches to the exploration of life in prison are Sykes, Goffman, and Cohen and Taylor. From their work – and that of their followers – emerges a pattern of common deprivations that typically afflict inmates, and require carefully constructed responses, both individual and social, in order to survive with the sense of self intact. The over-riding theme of the introductory chapter is that prisoners will experience the pains of imprisonment in different ways and to differing degrees, depending on prior experiences, background and so on, but that key to social-psychological survival is their ability to adapt to life inside through a variety of coping strategies. Incorporating the literature on media consumption, the chapter highlights the gratifications sought in media content that help audience members maintain the sense of ontological security[1] necessary for the successful management of self. It is suggested that media use takes on similar, yet heightened significance in the context of the total institution because, although in some senses a microcosm of the wider society, imprisonment is none-the-less a unique social and cultural context. The regulation of access by the prison authorities, and the individual needs of the self in an environment bounded by formal (institutional) and informal (subcultural) codes of behaviour will, it is argued, intensify or otherwise alter the taken-for-granted meanings usually invested in media technologies and texts.

Having outlined the various deprivations that prisoners are subjected to, and the potential uses that might be sought in media in order to offset or compensate for them, Chapter 2 aims to relate prisoners' individual experiences of imprisonment to the enveloping social and structural conditions. Giddens' theory of structuration and Bourdieu's notion of habitus are introduced in order to gain insight into the relationship between identity and power in prisons. Specifically, it is argued that the means by which inmates adapt to the rigours of incarceration can only be understood in relation to outside contacts, social networks, the overtly masculine inmate culture,[2] the biography and history of the prison they are confined in, and the wider practices of the prison service, criminal justice system, incumbent government and prevailing social attitudes towards criminals. Structuration theory is viewed as an important counter to the deprivation literature, arguing that subordinates are never entirely powerless even in the most bounded of locales. But in a refinement of Giddens' work, this account highlights the importance of culture, arguing that the forms and codes of overtly masculine behaviour that characterise the inmate culture are dangerously self-perpetuating. In a spiral of self-destruction, criminal behaviour in society may be regarded (at least to a significant degree) as a learned response to the imperatives of masculine hegemony, while in prisons, masculinity and machismo may be seen as a learned response to the imperatives of the criminal inmate culture. In other words, it is in the realms of the masculine cultural milieu that structure is internalised by human agents who act back on, and shape, future processes, ensuring the reproduction of social disadvantage and, ultimately, of prisons.

Chapter 3 provides a methodological context for the empirical analysis, describing how the research was carried out and giving an account of the prisons in which the fieldwork was conducted. The chapter also reflects on some of the ways in which the subtle, intimate and reflexive qualities of ethnography made me sensitive to the role of my own gendered identity as a female researcher in a predominantly male and overtly masculine field. Chapter 4 is the first of the three empirical chapters which collectively take us from the intimate 'micro' sphere of prisoners' lives, via the intermediate or 'meso' social environment of the inmate culture, to the macro structures that determine prisoners' access to media. Developing the issues raised in Chapter 1's review of the 'coping' literature, Chapter 4 argues that the primary resource required to survive a prison sentence relatively intact, and to be able to revert to one's pre-prison identity on re-entering the community, is the facility to 'be oneself', a process which is explored in relation to media resources as technologies of identity, agency and memory.

Chapter 5 moves from the microsocial sphere of prisoners' media use to the intermediate realms of prison communities and cultures, arguing that the prison society is infinitely more complex than the classic prison studies imply. In addressing the tensions between structural demands and the needs of the self, this chapter argues that in public at least, prisoners must suspend their pre-prison identities and construct social identities that will conform to the expectations and demands of the performative and excessively masculine prison culture. Media forms and content play a significant role in this respect, and the research process uncovers some of the specific and varied uses to which media resources are put in constructing identities and negotiating power in the social and public prison environment.

Finally, in its examination of the macrosocial processes that determine prisoners' access to media and constrain their autonomy, Chapter 6 explores in more detail the complex question of where power lies in prisons and the extent to which media can be said to be a primary locus of power and control. The aim of this chapter is to determine the extent to which the issue of media availability in prisons is shaped by the requirements of the institution or, alternatively, by the needs of inmates. The chapter thus draws together some of the theoretical issues arising from the methodological account in Chapter 3 and explored throughout this empirical section; not least the paradox of media's role as both a transformative resource and source of empowerment on the part of inmates, and as a structural device to limit or close down their agency on the part of prison staff and authorities.

Notes

1 'Ontological security' refers to a person's elemental sense of safety in the world, including a basic trust of others. It is an essential ingredient of human existence and is necessary in order for a person to maintain a sense of psychological well-being. Ontological security is important in Anthony Giddens' theory (see Chapter 2) but originates from the work of Laing (1960), who argues that mental illness derives from the lack of such security.

2 A point that should be established from the outset is that this study focuses exclusively on men's prisons. Traditionally, prison societies have overwhelmingly been studied from the viewpoint of male inmates, reflecting the fact that across almost all countries, some 90 per cent of prisoners (96 per cent in England and Wales) are male (Newton 1994) but, unlike the majority of studies which fail to address or problematise the gender of their male subjects, this study will treat it as a key variable. An investigation of prison audiences with different demographic profiles (and here we might include inmates of various racial and ethnic origins, young offenders as well as adult prisoners, and women) is beyond the scope of this project, but may be a suitable area for future study.

Chapter 1

Prison, pain and identity: a review of the literature

Before embarking on a review of the potential harms that imprisonment can afflict on the confined, and how individuals might use media resources in their responses and adaptations to such harms, it is first necessary briefly to outline what is meant by 'self' and 'identity'. A central tenet of this book, and one that will be explored fully as the chapters unfold, is that personhood is composed of both a personal identity, informed by largely unconscious process – which from here on will be termed 'self' – and a social identity attuned to the value judgements of others – which shall be termed 'identity'. It is anticipated that, through a primary investigation of the construction of gender, but also taking into account issues of class and economic marginality, the notion of identity may be deconstructed in order to explore and account for discrepancies between the *ascribed* identity and the *experienced* identity of the 'prisoner'. In order to account for these personal and individual experiences, a model of identity will be established which takes into account biological determinants, social constructions of class and gender *and* psychoanalytic insights into unconscious elements of experience. It is hoped that by adopting such an eclectic approach this study will shed light on the extent to which individual personality is constructed within, and contingent upon, its biological 'essence', its social, economic and political context, and its unconscious and irrational drives.

A concern with external structures, internal psychic development, *and* social, ideological and discursive aspects of gratification, is necessary in order to explore the full range of media-related coping and adaptation strategies adopted by prisoners in response to their enforced confinement. Following the example of prison researchers in the USA, the UK and Europe, this chapter will propose a pattern of deprivations that typically afflict inmates. The first and most fundamental is the loss of liberty, which will be explored in relation to its three core components: the transition from the 'free' community to the prison; confinement of movement *within* the institution; and rejection by the community at large. Following this discussion, the remainder of the chapter will consider a further six deprivations which, it will be argued, potentially inflict severe psychological harm on the inmate. Throughout this discussion, the prison deprivation literature will be interwoven with evidence that access to media resources can mitigate, alleviate, or subjugate the pains described.

The loss of liberty

Since the end of the eighteenth century, when the object of penal repression moved from the body to the mind, and prison replaced corporal punishment as the favoured form of state-sanctioned penalty, loss of liberty has generally been regarded as central to the act of punishment (Foucault 1977; Ignatieff 1983; Garland 1990). The nature of this loss can be regarded as threefold. First, and most obviously, the inmate is removed from his normal environment, incarcerated in an unfamiliar and largely hostile institution and allowed only limited access to the outside world. The reception of new inmates into prison has provided a special focus in the prison literature, particularly the formal and informal processing and induction procedures which take place. Goffman (1961b: 23) describes the processes through which the new inmate is 'shaped and coded into the kind of object that can be fed into the administrative machinery', a metaphor taken up by Caird, an ex-prisoner who defines reception as the most aggressive part of the prison; a 'sophisticated sausage machine' into which newly convicted prisoners are fed at one end and fully fledged inmates, stripped of 'every connection a man has with the outside world' are led out at the other (Caird 1974: 9). A former prison governor, meanwhile, describes reception as 'one of the most traumatic experiences any individual can undergo' (Coyle 1994: 27). So, although newly incarcerated prisoners often attempt to prepare for what awaits them, the shock of entering such an austere and depersonalised environment, together with the sudden and enforced separation from family and friends, can result in severe trauma. Withstanding 'entry shock' is, then, the first of many psychological assaults which the new inmate has to face, and attempts at suicide and self-harm, and the onset of self-destructive psychiatric disorders are most prevalent in the initial phase of confinement (Gibbs 1982; Sapsford 1983; Zamble and Porporino 1988; Liebling 1992; Liebling and Krarup 1993).

Although the passage through the 'barrier' from the outside

community into the world within involves many necessary administrative procedures, its symbolic significance goes well beyond the bureaucratic requirements of the establishment. Described by Goffman (1961b: 25) as a 'civil death', entry into the total institution involves being subjected to a series of social and psychological attacks which undermine the sense of self:

> The recruit . . . comes into the establishment with a conception of himself made possible by certain stable social arrangements in his home world. Upon entrance, he is immediately stripped of the support provided by these arrangements . . . [and] he begins a series of abasements, degradations, humiliations and profanations of self. *His self is systematically, if often unintentionally, mortified* (Goffman, 1961a: 23, emphasis added).

This dehumanising process may make it easier for staff to carry out their tasks effectively, and in the new generation of prisons, greater efforts have been made to be sensitive to the needs of the new inmate as well as to the bureaucratic demands of the system. But it is nevertheless arguable that the demands of efficiency are incompatible with the concerns of the individual who, when he most needs it, is given no opportunity to discuss the reality of the world he is entering or his fears concerning any unresolved problems on the outside. These opportunities might come eventually, but at the point of greatest stress to the new inmate, the needs of the system come before the needs of the individual (Coyle 1994).

The second aspect of loss of liberty is that the inmate is further confined *within* the institution and his movements severely restricted. With some inmates still spending the majority of their time in cells their sense of restriction might be exacerbated by their close proximity to other inmates, especially in prisons that are overcrowded. Adaptation to these conditions takes many forms, and a general overview of the inmate culture is undermined by the fact there is no singular pattern of adaptation which describes all types of inmate responses. However, many studies of inmate societies have used Goffman's typology – or slightly modified variations of it – in order to make some general observations about behavioural responses. Goffman (1961b) identifies four basic adaptive stances. The first is 'colonisation' whereby the prisoner minimises contact with the outside world, preferring to concentrate on making as full and comfortable a life for himself as possible within the institution. He tends not to make long-term plans and the extent of his horizons is to advance within the hierarchy of the inmate society. In extreme cases, he makes such favourable comparisons between life in the

3

institution and life on the outside that he plans ways of getting readmitted after release. Goffman's second category of inmates is those whose primary mode of adaptation is 'situational withdrawal'; that is, the drastic curtailment of involvement in association with both fellow inmates and those outside the prison. Situational withdrawal may involve escaping from one's immediate environment by daydreaming or fantasising. Cohen and Taylor (1972) note this mode of adaptation among life-sentence prisoners, and recall Farber (1944; cited in Cohen and Taylor 1972: 72), who found evidence of prisoners cutting off all contact with those outside in an attempt to minimise their suffering. 'Intransigence', Goffman's third category, involves setting a lower limit to attacks on one's self, below which the inmate will resort to retaliation or non-compliance. It may thus be regarded by the inmate as a way of maintaining a degree of self-esteem and independence. The fourth of Goffman's categories is 'conversion' whereby the inmate comes to reject his own values and adopt those of the staff, becoming a 'model inmate'.

The final aspect of loss of liberty to be considered here is the most enduring. Gresham Sykes (1958: 65) characterises confinement as a 'deliberate moral rejection of the criminal by the free community', a theme taken up by Goffman who states that this rejection amounts to profound stigmatisation. Thomas Mathiesen (1965: 73) suggests that the majority of inmates feel they belong to the 'very bottom floor' of society, and the description of prisons as the 'garbage-cans of society' is frequently to be found in the literature. Ericson (in Ericson *et al* 1987) argues – after Durkheim – that any form of deviant behaviour marks the outer edges of a community or society, and gives an inner strength to its core. So, by publicly condemning through the courts those who have committed a deviant act, and confining them in an institution resonant with symbolic moral censure, a consensus is achieved in the rest of society. The rejection by the community of those who are labelled 'deviant' is further enforced by the architecture and geographical location of many institutions. In England and Wales many prisons were built in the early to mid-nineteenth century and resemble fortresses with castle turrets, watchtowers and high wire-topped outer walls. They were also, until recently, usually prominently located in the centre of towns and cities, thus standing as a symbolic reminder to the rest of the community of the potential consequences of deviance.

But although the physical appearance of prisons can be austere, many writers have criticised Goffman and his followers for placing too much emphasis on the 'totality' of total institutions (Irwin 1970, 1980; Jacobs 1977, 1983; Meyrowitz 1985), arguing that prison walls are inherently more permeable to external forces than Goffman implies.[1] Arguably the most regular, sustained and influential of the external forces that have penetrated, and thereby altered, the prison environment in recent years, are the media of mass communications. Giddens (1991a) suggests that the media provide alternative 'life-worlds' – a means of escape from everyday life – and come to form a kind of paramount reality, supplementing or replacing the 'significant others' who in 'normal' life mediate to the individual the cultural values and meanings of the world he or she inhabits. For many, mass media can facilitate the retreat into an inner psychological state of mind, a world of fantasy and imagination that provide a powerful route to the inner self. For those who have had their liberty taken away from them, fantasies and daydreams provide an inner sanctum where private emotions which otherwise have to be kept hidden in the over-riding macho environment – grief, sadness, frustration, poor coping and so on – can be expressed and worked through in safety. They can also consist of thoughts that must be kept secret from the prison authorities; for example, a common form of daydream is that of escaping – literally – from the prison.

Media-assisted fantasies and daydreams are common among the population at large. Media provide a flow of images and experiences which are used by individuals in their everyday lives as a means of escape; a flight of fancy from day-to-day existence (Lefebvre 1991; Abercrombie and Longhurst 1998). Broadcast media are of particular importance in this respect because they allow the audience member to be in two places or even in two times simultaneously. For media commentator, Paddy Scannell (1996: 91), this facility is 'truly magical': 'it is not just that radio and television *compress* time and space. They create new possibilities of being: of being in two places at once, or two times at once.' In the confined context of the prison, the illusion of escaping to another place takes on even greater intensity:

> The sense of radio [and television] as magical, as lighting up lives bound by monotonous and narrow routines is palpable. Whereas the public world beforehand was over the hills and far away, now it is close at hand and graspable. Its eventfulness enters into uneventful lives giving them new texture and substance (ibid.: 90).

Related to daydreaming and fantasy in its facility to ward off insecurity is memory. Although long established in psychology, only recently have sociologists begun to acknowledge the importance of memory as a faculty which locates the individual in space and time, and gives a sense of both structural location and personal biography within particular historical and cultural norms:

> Memories – sudden sharp ones and generalised amorphous ones –
> are integral to every moment of our being . . . [and] constitute part
> of contemporary temporal existence. Contents differ but the
> principle remains the same: we are temporally extended in time and
> space. We transcend not just our present but our historical, socio-
> cultural and geographic location (Adam 1995: 14–15).

The role of media in furnishing individual and collective memories is still
a relatively new area of academic interest, but it is increasingly being noted
that individual life histories are structured, shaped and made sense of
within frames of reference provided by the mass media (O'Sullivan 1991;
Spigel and Jenkins, 1991; Scannell 1996). In particular, media serve to give
individual biographies a place in the collective, shared experience of public
life, thus making individuals feel connected to a wider community. As
Scannell (1996: 91) notes, 'big' events such as coronations, royal weddings,
state funerals and assassinations become part of a collective memory
through mass media; 'marked up not only on the public calendar of
"history" but also on the private calendars of people's lives'.

It is not just momentous events of national or global significance which
give generations a sense of shared cultural experience, however. The
temporal framework of broadcast media gives a common structure and
substance (what Scannell calls a 'texture of relevances') to people's lives,
so that a common, yet largely unspoken, sense of cultural identity and
national unity is formed by memories of particular TV and radio shows
and their associated viewing and listening contexts. Of particular
importance in this context are the television and radio programmes we
consumed as children and adolescents. As signifiers of leisure time spent
in casual relaxation with friends and family, memories of watching *Doctor
Who* on a Saturday tea-time or listening to *Two-way Family Favourites* on
the radio at weekends not only provide many of us with nostalgic
memories of times gone by but also foster a sense of 'imagined
community' which binds us with others of the same culture and
generation. The extent to which collective mediated events give those
who are confined within total institutions a sense of common experience
with the wider community, or serve only to make them feel even more
marginalised, will be discussed in Chapter 4, but Silverstone (1999: 92–93)
suggests that memory and home are crucially inter-related, and that when
we cannot go home, the pictorial stories we carry around in our minds
are shaped by media images:

> Think of your own childhood and adolescence . . . I think of mine.
> A black and white television screen in the front room. The
> Coronation of Elizabeth II. Transistor radio under the pillow.

The programmes of childhood: *Journey into Space. . . Quatermass. . .* the Potter's Wheel, Radio Luxembourg. To share that world with one's contemporaries, to reflect on the past it evokes, is to connect with the other, to domesticate a shareable past. But it is also to include memories of media into one's own biography, into memories of home, good, bad and indifferent. These are the shaping experiences: of home as a mediated space, and of media as a domesticated space. Secure in them we can dream. Without them we are bereft.

Spigel and Jenkins (1991) explore this theme in their essay on American audiences' memories of the 1960s television series *Batman*, in the light of its resurrection as a Hollywood movie in 1989. They explain *Batman*'s enduring appeal in terms of its positioning as an integral part of American culture's past: '*Batman* seemed a point of entry into children's culture of the 1960s, and it also provided a clue to yuppie culture of the late 1980s because these memories seemed to constitute a common heritage of a particular adult generation' (ibid.: 119). Memory, then, is linked to fantasy and, for Spigel and Jenkins, the revival of *Batman* can be seen as a deliberate evocation and celebration of childhood fantasy; 'an invitation to turn the present into the past' (ibid.: 1991: 130). They found that when remembering the *Batman* series, people tended to construct vivid images of themselves watching the programme as children; 'remembering *Batman* brought back a situational context, a scene that painted a rough sketch of places in the house, times of the day, and childhood relationships with family or friends' (ibid.: 134). Mediated recollections of television viewing can also act as a catalyst for more wide-reaching explorations of the social context in which the viewing took place:

> Remembering *Batman* meant remembering themselves, and that dialogue between programme and self continually framed the stories they told about the past. Memories fluidly moved from personal to collective consciousness as people weaved histories around themselves, while at the same time imbricating themselves into the wider social fabric. Indeed, this matching of personal and public pasts became a strategy for understanding the relationship of self to society, and within this matching process television memories served a key role ('when I go back and see something from that long ago, I tend to remember who I was when I first saw it, how I thought the world was'). These memories are not simply the residue of earlier times; instead they are a resource people use to think about the world and their position within it (ibid.: 137).

In addition to radio and television broadcasts, music can also evoke powerful memories. In an ethnographically rich study of music in everyday life, Tia DeNora (2000: 67) demonstrates how, for many people, 'the past comes alive to its soundtrack'. Central to people's reminiscences of former lovers, deceased parents, times past, the power of music to evoke the emotional content of relationships can be painful. But reliving experience through music is also '(re)constituting past experience, it is making manifest within memory what may have been latent or even absent' before (ibid.: 66). It is, moreover, 'part of the work of producing one's self as a coherent being over time. . . which in turn fuels the ongoing projection of identity from past into future' (ibid.). DeNora's study of music consumption thus shares with Spigel and Jenkins' analysis of fans of *Batman* an interest in how media texts function as 'a point of symbolic, biographical reference, representing some aspects of the difference perceived between identity or circumstances "then" and "now" ' (O'Sullivan 1991: 163). Popular memory is thus based on the dialectic between autobiography and the description of public events, past entwined with present, so that individuals have a sense of themselves in history and continually use the past as a way of understanding the present and constructing their future identities. As mass media increasingly come to form part of our historical consciousness, so memories evoked and shaped by particular media texts have to be seen as an important part of the routine, politics and spectacle of everyday life. To those who are confined within total institutions, the facility of mediated memories to ground notions of personal identity within the contexts of national community and historical contingency may be especially significant.

The individual human desire to feel part of a wider community is also addressed by uses and gratifications research, a methodological approach to media audiences that turned on its head the question that had dominated the largely psychology-orientated agendas of mass communications researchers ('what do the media *do* to people?') and asked instead from a sociological perspective, 'what do people do *with* the media?' The most famous 'uses and gratifications' study was arguably that conducted by McQuail, Blumler and Brown in 1972. Respondents were given a questionnaire listing possible uses and gratifications and asked whether any of the examples given were the motives behind their television viewing. Although examples of possible satisfactions were chosen after focus groups had been conducted, the limitations of this closed-question approach offering a definitive set of motivations are obvious. But in its resistance to the idea of an all-powerful and homogeneous media, and in its rejection of the establishment view that television was essentially a trivial leisure activity in which viewers sought shallow, undemanding escapism, McQuail *et al*'s study represented a watershed in media research. Deliberately avoiding the language of functionalism which had dominated since the late 1940s, and emphasising gratifications *sought* rather than gratifications *obtained*, the researchers outlined a typology of media–person interactions which amounted to four main 'needs' sought in television viewing. The first is 'diversion', encompassing retreat from the immediate environment, deviation from the constraints of routine, escape from the burdens of problems and emotional release. The second is a need for 'personal relationships' whereby – in a process known as 'para-social interaction' (Horton and Wohl 1956) – companionship is provided by television personalities who become media 'friends', counteracting feelings of loneliness and isolation. In addition, television may provide a social utility function, giving people a source of conversation with others in 'real' life. Thirdly, 'personal identity' was identified as a key factor in programme choice; television can be seen as a reference point for one's own life, allowing viewers to compare their experiences with those of people – real or fictional – on screen. Television also contributes to the reinforcement of ideas and opinions, and may play an important role in identity formation and maintenance. Finally, 'surveillance' was identified as a primary motivation whereby viewers use television as a means of keeping informed about the world, and particularly the events most likely to affect them. Although these responses were drawn from a 'normal' sample of citizens, the uses and gratifications approach is of interest when considering the viewing habits of prison inmates. All the categories of motivations found amount to a need to be 'connected', and are therefore particularly apt in the context of media use in a controlled and restricted environment, where a greater level of sensory deprivation and disconnection with conventional domestic life might be expected. Furthermore, although dependence on media varies greatly across different social groups, it is generally recognised that those with the greatest levels of attachment to all media are people who are confined to the home, on low incomes and suffering from some kind of stress (McQuail 1994). All these variables clearly have parallels among the prison community.[2]

However, the primary drawback of the uses and gratifications approach, other than its implicit prescriptiveness, is that its emphasis on agency excludes any real consideration of social context or the actual source of the needs sought in television consumption. For example, it would be naïve to assume that individual media consumption does not change under prison conditions. Furthermore, the classic uses and gratifications model concentrates on personal uses, ignoring *inter*personal and social (i.e. structural or relational) uses. Even before the 1972 study,

McQuail (1969: 71) had already recognised that its 'guiding assumption of utility' led uses and gratifications research to draw conclusions which were not necessarily self-evident, but one of its most vociferous critics is Phillip Elliott (1974) who states that the findings of uses and gratifications research only add up to generalisations about aggregates of individuals and cannot be converted into social structure and process in any way which is not theoretically reductive and empirically meaningless. This problem is further highlighted by Katz *et al* (1974), who note that not only are the gratifications associated with exposure to the media *per se* ignored, but the audience member is generally regarded in individualistic terms, devoid of his or her place in the social structure, and seeking gratification only of individually experienced needs. The combined product of psychological dispositions, sociological factors and situational context that determines the specific uses of media by audience members has thus been completely overlooked. Given its inability adequately to conceptualise relations of power, I propose adopting a refined version of the uses and gratifications model. In an attempt to embrace a more situated theory of subjectivity that can offer insights into the role of the media in expressing identity, identification and difference, this study will therefore seek to explore the *meanings and motivations* that prison inmates seek from media resources (see Chapter 4).

The problem of time: 'doing' time, 'killing' time and 'marking' time

Related to the loss of liberty is the notion of time. Usually characterised as being both quantitatively and qualitatively different inside prison, concern for time is 'almost a constant and painful state-of-mind' for some prisoners (Galtung 1961: 113). Matthews (1999: 39) maintains that time served in prison is not so much 'spent' as 'wasted' while other writers have likened imprisonment to being in 'cold storage' or 'frozen in time'. Ruggiero (1991: 74) sums it up thus: 'Prison distorts time, it deprives it of its use-value while riddling it with an institutional, alienated and amorphous rhythm. Stress, tension, nervous and psychosomatic diseases all derive from this institutional imposition of time.'

Doing time

The notion of *doing* time is problematised by the fact that the judicial system views time taken from the prisoner as being both an objective entity and a ratio-scale starting at an absolute zero point. In other words, as far as the criminal justice system is concerned, time means the same thing to all of us, and punishment is measured by a commonly understood scale whereby a ten-year sentence is regarded as doubly punitive as compared to a five-year sentence. But to view time in this way qualitatively ignores or negates the actual 'doing' of time, with all its pain and frustrations. The meaning of time is relative and is dependent on the individual's propensity to cope with his state of enforced cryogenic suspension. While it is undoubtedly true that long-term prisoners face a very particular set of stresses (Cohen and Taylor 1972; Flanagan 1982; Sapsford 1983) the implication that the pains of imprisonment can be measured in relation to the amount of time spent in prison is far too simplistic a pretext to warrant serious attention and its quantifiable demonstration has been described as a 'methodological nightmare' (McKay *et al* 1979: 4). Most notable in this respect is von Hirsch (1992) who argues that lengths of sentences do not necessarily correlate in a relationship of proportionality, and that the effects of confinement will be a function of the individual's personal perception of time and his ability to 'use' or 'fill' time. It is perhaps more useful in this context to employ King and McDermott's revised definition of Downes' (1988) concept of the 'depth of imprisonment' – that is, the degree to which a prisoner is embedded into the security and control systems of imprisonment – or King and McDermott's (1995) own notion of the 'weight of imprisonment' – the extent to which the heavy and oppressive nature of confinement seems literally to bear down on the inmate like a millstone around the neck – rather than thinking simply in terms of the length of prison sentence.

Studies of unemployment have demonstrated that those who lack a clear time structure are often chronically deprived of meaning in their lives.[3] Bostyn and Wight (1987) note that when men lose the temporal pattern which is provided by regular work, the significance that different time-bands had for them (as work time, leisure time, week and weekend, holiday or retirement) is lost, and their sense of purpose, of feeling *in control* is diminished. This loss of temporal rhythm, combined with the lack of money with which to confirm one's status through symbolic consumption can lead to an 'impoverished' and 'passive' group (Bostyn and Wight 1987: 153). Prisoners share with the jobless feelings of disempowerment and purposelessness at the lack of temporal structure which employment provides and, although work is provided in most prisons, it is usually repetitive, monotonous and fragmentary.

Killing time

An ironic term in a context where time is often regarded as being already 'dead', *killing* time is one of the biggest practical problems facing the inmate and explains why a high premium is placed on 'removal' activities which fill lengthy periods of time. Most prison sociologists have alluded to the deadening monotony of prison routine and the serious lack of constructive and purposeful activities for inmates to engage in but, perhaps most famously, Irwin (1970) identifies three principal adaptive strategies which have some bearing on the passing of time. For those prisoners able to regard incarceration as a comparatively short-lived interruption in their usual way of life, the 'doing time' mode might prove the most effective way of coping, whereby the prison is evaluated in terms of whatever non-demanding benefits and privileges can be had from it, and association with other inmates tends to be casual and impermanent. The second adaptation strategy in Irwin's typology is the 'jailing mode', whereby inmates remain relatively unaffected by the temporal structure of prison life, and deal with the inherent routine and boredom by immersing themselves in the inmate culture, forming cliques with like-minded individuals and openly exploiting the indigenous economic and sexual trades. Alternatively, inmates might adopt the third mode, 'gleaning', which involves accepting the institution's incentives for rehabilitation and passing the time by seeking out programmes and relationships which can be expected to lead to some kind of educational, vocational, psychological or spiritual improvement.

Of course, Irwin's categories, like other typologies, presuppose that prisoners *do* cope. But the literature on breakdowns, self-harm and suicide in prison reminds us that prison research can only take account of the *survivors* of the prison experience, and that those inmates who have thought about taking their own lives while in prison (17–18 per cent of the total inmate population) report higher-than-average feelings of apathy, boredom and lethargy (Liebling 1992). When compared to the prison population as a whole, significantly fewer suicide attempters are able constructively to occupy themselves or relieve their considerable sense of boredom and most are locked in their cells for considerable periods of time (ibid.). Both assaults upon the self, and more widespread disruptions involving a number of inmates, can be seen as a means of withstanding the psychological stress brought about by the dull grind of prison routine; as Cohen and Taylor (1972: 64) rather poetically put it, 'every total institution can be seen as a kind of dead sea in which appear little islands of vivid, encapturing activity'.

Marking time

The ability to *mark* time is also a problem in an environment where the loss of liberty is central to daily existence, and the available means of distinguishing weekends from weeks, summers from winters, or the end of one year and the beginning of the next, are a pale imitation of 'normal' life. Galtung (1961) somewhat contentiously implies that the inmate whose minimum sentence exceeds his probable lifetime has something of an advantage over the majority of prisoners in that he can adapt himself fully to institutional life without having to preserve an identity appropriate for life outside when release comes. Most prisoners, however, are painfully aware of the necessity of maintaining an identity relevant to the world beyond the institution, and the notion that life-tariff inmates are at an advantage because they do not have to worry about their non-prison selves is contradicted by Cohen and Taylor (1972) who claim that few prisoners are able to come to terms with the possibility that they will die in prison. Institutionalised for many years and facing an abundance of time to fill, the lack of traditional benchmarks with which to divide or differentiate time can result in severe psychological stress for long-term prisoners: 'Each minute may be marvellously – or horribly – profound. . . There are swift hours and very long seconds. Past time is void. There is no chronology of events to mark it; external duration no longer exists' (Serge 1970: 56–57).

But mass media, by their very 'dailiness' (Scannell 1996), give time a sense of order, routine and rhythm. The development of the mass media in Western society reflects the industrial segmentation of time into specific bands, and virtually all established media are implicated in the routines and restrictions of industrial 'clock-time' (Brittan 1977; Adam 1995). The cost of using a telephone is cheaper outside working hours; newspapers are distinguished by what time of the day or week they are on sale; radio and television programmes become part of the routine of people's daily work lives and leisure time, so that particular programmes will invariably accompany other, routine activities. Television and radio schedules generate a degree of dependence, security and attachment through the regularity of their scheduling and through the familiarity of certain genres, narratives and personalities; daily newspapers also help to give everyday life its seamless flow, and further reassure that however bad the news, some sense of normalisation can be achieved in the routines and customs associated with reading a regular newspaper (turning to the sports page, browsing the television schedules, doing the crossword, etc.); weekend newspapers, with their obligatory 'lifestyle' supplements, mark the end of the working week and signify a time for relaxation and private space. The continuing, cyclical nature of most media is at the heart of their role in facilitating ontological security and, for Scannell (1996), it is imperative to explore the temporal arrangements of media if we are to understand how they matter for us in the ways that they do.[4]

The importance of material possessions

The deprivation of goods and services is manifested in the fact that, although inmates' basic minimum requirements are met, a standard of living constructed in terms of calories per meal, hours out of cell per day, cubic feet of space per inmate and so on, does little to address the way that an inmate actually *feels* about his deprivation (Sykes 1958). Even in the very early days of the overt consumerism generated by advanced capitalist societies, Sykes recognised that a minimum standard of living might be hopelessly inadequate to a prisoner used to the 'subtle symbolic overtones which we invest in the world of possessions' (ibid.: 68). Furthermore, even for those prisoners who experienced a similar or even greater level of poverty *before* entering prison (as found by, for example, Morris and Morris in their study of Pentonville Prison, 1963) it is the systematic deprivation of goods and services, and the fact they are so tightly controlled by staff which amounts to an attack on the individual's self-perception. Of great frustration is that many seemingly trivial goods and services are restricted and can be awarded or withdrawn at the discretion – or whim – of staff. In fact, the formal implementation of a service-wide incentives scheme (see Chapter 3) has gone some way towards reducing feelings of discontent, but there is still a perceived unfairness regarding the regulation of many of the goods and services permitted in prison, especially those considered too trivial to warrant formal attention. Sykes can again be called upon in this context; he notes that when chronically deprived of one's liberty, material goods and so forth, the minor pleasures which *are* granted can take on a heightened significance which few of us in the free community can appreciate (Sykes 1958: 50). Goffman (1961a: 49) endorses this with a graphic description of how material possessions can become objects of 'desire, fantasy and conscious concern', causing the inmate's attention to be fixed on them so that 'he spends his day like a fanatic, in devoted thoughts about the possibility of acquiring those gratifications or in contemplation of the approaching hour at which they are scheduled to be granted'.

The suggestion that material goods can make a positive impact upon a person's well-being conflicts with the views of many cultural commentators who take their cues from the tradition of cultural pessimism founded by the Frankfurt School. For example, in *The Privatised World* (1977), Brittan argues that the picture of social reality which many of us hold on to is the fraudulent product of the media industry and that the conspicuous consumption which marks modern life is a new and vicious form of alienation which has supplemented and, to some extent, replaced the alienation of the factory. Where once all human relationships were conceived of as extensions of the labour market, now individuals are defined not by what they do (i.e. produce) but by what they *own*. Consequently, we all exist not only as consumers but as audiences to the spectacle of others' consumption. The consumer has replaced the 'active man' as the possessor of happiness (Lefebvre 1971: 56) and in this new configuration, 'capitalism manages to maintain its hold on the masses' (Brittan 1977: 32).

Not only is this formulation overtly structuralist in essence, but it neglects the very real impact of conspicuous consumption on many people's sense of self. Group affiliations are frequently organised around media images of style, personality, clothing and music, which – in addition to being sources of individual gratifications – also act as powerful articulators of culture (Tudor 1979). The adoption of particular designer clothing and footwear by large sections of the working classes (including prison inmates) may be seen – in Brittan's terms – as a symbol of exploitation of mindless conformists at the hands of powerful manufacturers and marketers, but that should not necessarily deflect from the positive self-image that such symbolic gestures can generate in structural environments where self-esteem and aspiration are under constant assault. Bostyn and Wight (1987: 140) understand this relationship well, arguing that 'consumer goods provide materials with which to represent one's self-identity, create or confirm particular social relationships, and provide the ritual marking of time'. Moreover, '[t]he goods people choose to buy are a physical expression (often not conscious) of their characters, or at least what they want to project as such' (ibid.). Recalling the work of Barthes, Bostyn and Wight highlight what they see as the intrinsically masculine attributes of many commodities, and suggest that one's identity as an adult, a father, and a man, are inextricably bound up in commodities such as meat, machines and alcohol. The deprivation of such items – particularly when associated with the inability to purchase them with a 'man's wage' – emasculates the individual and attacks his sense of self-worth.

In prisons the deprivation of a wide range of material goods similarly heightens the need for, and value of, consuming and spectacle, both as a restorer of the embattled and emasculated self and, more fundamentally, to bring colour into an otherwise drab and uniform environment. Prison cells might be furnished with the aspirational symbols of media-saturated consumer capitalism – posters of glamour models and pop stars, pictures of expensive sports cars, hi-tech audio equipment and, increasingly, televisions – but to reduce these symbols to mere products of an exploitative media's desire to take advantage of passive dupes who know no better, negates the real sense of agency and empowerment which the choice, purchase and use of these consumables can produce, albeit that it is within a structure of domination and exploitation. Cultural theorist Dick Hebdige (1989) discusses the social significance of efforts to construct new identities through conspicuous consumption and develops a 'sociology of aspiration'; less concerned with what people *are* or even what they *want*, but much more interested in what people aspire to *be*. While he does not make any claims for it being a substitute for class analysis, Hebdige believes that aspiration is an important dimension of social stratification none-the-less. Market research, packaging and presentation have cut across the old social–sexual polarities so that 'lifestyle' has become a social phenomenon no less real than previously privileged sociological categories such as class. Unlike Brittan, Hebdige is optimistic about the postmodern condition; in addition to constructing new identities through consumption fuelled by media industries such as advertising, he suggests that another important means by which people form aspects of their identity is through active use of media forms and texts. In other words, far from being passive dupes, people as individuals and as groups *use* the media in positive, constructive ways to develop new identities. As indicated above, the culture industries, including the mass media, serve not simply to sell people their products, but to allow them to buy into wider forms of community and alliance. Within the context of the total institution, the desire to feel connected to a wider community is easily understood.

Autonomy, choice and personal responsibility

Allowing 'choice' in any significant sense is very difficult in prisons because of the classification system which lumps together prisoners perceived to be of similar security risk, regardless of the differences between their crimes or their personalities. However, the ability to make even the smallest choices fosters the illusion of control that is a basic human need (McKay *et al* 1979) and the prisoner's frustrations at not being able to make even minor decisions for himself are found in many personal accounts of inmate life (e.g. Caird 1974; Boyle 1977; Shannon and Morgan 1996). The loss of autonomy in prison is usually total and, again, the issue of self-identity is central, as the prisoner is reduced to the weak, helpless, dependent status of a child who is unable to contest parental power other than by reference to a generalised, and frequently flouted, expectation of 'fairness' (Sykes 1958; Mathiesen 1965). Vagg (1994) notes that this state of 'infantilisation' is created by the need to ask permission for virtually everything one wishes to do and is further enforced by the manner in which permission is sought; one has to ask 'correctly' in order to avoid conflict with staff. 'Infantilisation' also points to the rigidity of staff control over inmates and encapsulates the notion that the creation of dependence is also the creation of a means of control. If inmates depend upon staff to facilitate, for example, extra visits, the threat of refusal to allow visits is a means of ensuring compliance and good behaviour.

One of the ways in which autonomy is preserved in prisons is through performance, which is often subtly linked to prior media consumption. The characterisation of everyday life as performance or spectacle has dominated the cultural studies tradition, and a large body of work has been generated concerning people's collective and individual involvement in majority cultures, minority cultures, fan cultures and subcultures. An especially productive focus within this body of research has been the relationship between subjectivity and power, and the extent to which they are to be found in the realms of the everyday (de Certeau 1984; Fiske 1989; Silverstone 1994; Miller and McHoul 1998). Abercrombie and Longhurst (1998) coin the term 'diffused audience' to encapsulate the combination of performance, spectacle and narcissism that constitutes modern social life. They argue that the omnipresence of media in everyday life has led to a general 'heightening' of behaviour which 'carries with it some sense of specialness, a moment of being transported out of the mundane, even if the transportation is brief and slight' (ibid.: 40). In prison societies, it is the public self which most obviously constitutes performance, but equally, private actions can be described as performances. From the overtly masculine posturing that can be seen in the gymnasiums and on the sports fields, to the act of watching television or listening to music in one's cell; every element of life which in some way transcends the paramount reality of being inside prison is invested with a sense of 'the sacred and the extraordinary' (ibid.: 41) and thus constitutes performance. As Abercrombie and Longhurst state, 'all performances involve a degree of ceremony and ritual' (ibid.) and in an environment where one is effectively stripped of choice and autonomy, the most mundane practices (reading, listening to music, cleaning one's teeth, even using the toilet) can be accompanied by an acute sense of sacredness and ritual not experienced in the execution of such mundane tasks in 'ordinary life'. As such, performance can be regarded as one of the primary loci of agency and empowerment in the face of potentially overwhelming structural demands.

The deprivation of heterosexual relationships and notions of masculinity

One of the most striking features of men's prisons is the relative scarcity of women. This represents a problem for the presentation of the robust sexual appetite normally associated with manhood among this group, to the extent that some researchers have likened imprisonment to physical castration (Sykes 1958; Segal 1990). Others maintain that even in the highly constrained environment of the prison there exists the possibility for men to fashion a 'way of being' (Pronger 1990) as an adaptive stance to the patterns imposed on them by their environment. Indeed, an emerging theme in the literature on constructions of masculinity that is reviewed in Chapter 2, is that many social institutions organise masculine power through constructs of sexuality, socialising their inhabitants in the ways of 'doing' heterosexuality as a means of validating their masculinity and gaining acceptance to the group (studies of sexuality in families and in schools are especially prominent in this respect; see Mac an Ghaill 1996; Messerschmidt 1999). Most obviously, an exaggerated version of heterosexuality is maintained discursively through story-telling and banter, both of which may contain an element of embellishment and exaggeration (Thurston 1996). For example, boasting about sexual conquests is common and, in an environment where misogyny and homophobia go hand in hand with proof of one's own 'normal' masculinity, the number of children fathered, usually with more than one woman, is frequently viewed as a favourable criterion (Mathiesen 1965). Yet in a seemingly intractable contradiction, homosexuality – the subject of much scorn and derision among prisoners and officers – is an abiding feature of prison life. Actual homosexual encounters and relationships are commonplace and can, for some individuals, take the place of heterosexual relations in a way that is relatively normalised, and amounts to an act of resistance. Furthermore, in a bizarre mutation of sexual power relations, a man who rapes another man can be a symbol of superordinancy, signifying him as a 'double man' (Scacco 1975). However, the notion of the subject as consumer, freely choosing their identity from a vast array of commodified choices, may be problematic in this context as it ignores the complex interaction between biological determinants, psychological processes and social expectations. While it may be the gift of some men to play at will with the conventions of gender, many others will be constrained from doing so by a variety of psychological and cultural impediments. Despite the relative normalisation of homosexuality in prisons, many inmates strenuously resist homosexual advances, and the existence of sexual predators can make the prison world extremely unpredictable, frightening and alien, especially to the new or vulnerable inmate (King 1992).

A common response among lower working-class men to the requirement of presenting an overtly masculine facade is to take up bodybuilding, which may serve the purpose of attracting a mate or, conversely, of warding off potential advances.[5] In prison, keeping physically fit is understandable given the level of fear among inmates and prison officers. More than that, however, the serious pursuit of an excessively muscular physique is significant in terms of the presentation of self as a powerful and self-controlled individual. The body is constructed as a site of difference in relation to others who are physically less strong, and is a key performative device. In institutions where standard prison clothing is issued, remodelling the body may be the primary means of asserting one's individual personality and gaining ground in an overtly competitive environment. It is a statement of presence and of power (which obviously makes it attractive to those who are marginalised or disempowered) and it represents the ultimate achievement of self-control and agency. Not only do individuals form an understanding of themselves by continually re-working their sense of self as they go through life, but their personal biography is also constructed partly through the systematic ordering of the body through fitness, shape and diet (Giddens 1991a). Put simply, the constructed, laboured-over body is the locus of an under valued presence in the world, albeit one which is open to reconstruction and the pleasures of narcissism. It also accords with the ideology of the 'time-doer' who wishes to use the institution for whatever benefits might be available (Irwin 1970) and the 'withdrawer' (Cohen and Taylor 1972) who is attracted to a solitary, narcissistic pursuit which entails no relation to other inmates (Ward Jouve 1988).

Media and popular culture provide much of the substance from which prisoners construct their masculine identities, and a number of observers of prison inmates have testified to the importance of role models from the worlds of sport and entertainment. Both participation in sporting activities, and engaging in discourse which demonstrates knowledge and opinion about sport, are powerful indicators of one's masculine credentials. Moreover, sport acts as a routine everyday leisure activity, yet also acts as a release from the daily grind and transcends the everyday via media entertainment networks (Miller and McHoul 1998). In both professional and amateur circles, performance and spectatorship are central, and nowhere is the aestheticisation of the human body more obvious. In the last few decades, during which the culture industries have taken narcissistic body development to new heights, it is likely that a large proportion of male inmates – like the wider social stratum from which they are drawn – have equated 'making it' with achieving the tough, seemingly indestructible physique of Schwarzenneger or Stallone. But as the following chapter will demonstrate, contemporary society is marked by the superordinancy of a particularly aggressive kind of masculinity, and the heroes identified as inmates' role models in much of the prison literature ('tough guys' such as John Wayne and Clint Eastwood) have been superseded by more violent characters played by the likes of Jean-Claude Van Damme and Stephen Segal, whose status as good guy/bad guy is frequently ambivalent.

Fear of contamination and assault

The precedence of security, the temporal structure of prison life and the spatial arrangements of much prison architecture leave the prisoner with few opportunities for privacy. The deprivation of security and fear of assault are correspondingly among the biggest problems associated with imprisonment (Sykes 1958; Toch 1975; Kalinich 1980; Adler 1996). With less evidence of the solidarity and comradeship found by Sykes, most subsequent studies are in agreement that one of the worst aspects of imprisonment is having to live among other prisoners, and accounts of inmates who request periods in solitary confinement are common. Brittan (1977) pre-empts more recent commentators on the nature of risk by suggesting that for all of us in late modern society, the ebb and flow of everyday life involve consciousness of differences between the boring present and the threatening future, the possibility of pain and suffering, and the actuality of personal troubles. But for those who live and work in prisons, the need to be attuned to risk is especially acute, and both *actual* risks, and the ever-present awareness of *possible* risks, shape and determine many aspects of life, both structurally and culturally. In addition, prisoners live under almost constant surveillance, subject to staff members who may periodically, and without warning, expose them to sudden searches, cell checks or interrogations by drugs officers. Goffman (1961a, 1961b) argues that this aspect of mortification has a contaminative element whereby the threat of assault or invasion of one's personal territory by staff or fellow inmates is not just of a physical or superficial nature but has a deeply penetrative psychological impact because the agency of mortification is another human being. While the most profound case of interpersonal contamination in our society is rape, Goffman (ibid.) reports that there are many less severe examples of the penetration of the private reserves of the individual in environments where privacy is all but non-existent.

But while a heightened awareness of potential risks might be the paramount reality in which many prisoners and prison officers (and, arguably, most of us in general life) conduct their everyday lives, an unremitting atmosphere of risk and fear would result in inoperative institutions. Consequently, the construction of alternative life-worlds (Brittan 1977; Giddens 1991a) which privilege other emotional qualities – intimacy, companionship, humour, learning, relaxation, competitiveness, boredom or whatever – is a primary means of coping with an otherwise potentially overwhelming paramount reality. Such alternative life-worlds frequently involve popular culture and, in prison, perhaps even more than in general life, the media provide a refuge from the demands of public presentation and the rigours of social life. In an environment where everyday life is sometimes described in terms of its 'thinness' (Sapsford 1983), media can provide a richness, colour and texture that are, in some way, comparable to life outside.

Fear of personal deterioration and breakdown

Anxiety about personal deterioration has two elements. At one level, prisoners are concerned about being cut off from the outside world to an extent where they fear that on release they will be as aliens in an unknown world. The benefits of having wide access to the media of mass communications hardly need explaining in this context. But at a more fundamental level some inmates serving long sentences may fear the possibility of 'turning, or being turned, from a live person into a dead thing, into a stone, into a robot, an automaton, without personal autonomy of action, an *it* without subjectivity' (Cohen and Taylor 1972: 109). Johnson and Toch (1982) surmise that the main factors which give rise to this fear are the inability to counter the unfavourable definitions of oneself which are continually offered; the decreasing ability over a long period to 'mark time', resulting in a fear of losing other cognitive faculties as well; and the dependency which long-term imprisonment instils in inmates, so that they assume an uncharacteristically passive role and fear losing the capacity to think and act for themselves. One might expect that education could provide a way out of this state of immobilisation, but among a population whose literacy levels are poor, education provision is frequently rejected. So humiliating and alienating have been previous experiences of the education system that, like their lower working-class counterparts on the outside, the thought of returning to education can induce a 'kind of post-traumatic stress' accompanied by 'intrusive recollections and the kind of intense psychological distress that is characteristic of disorders like agoraphobia' (Charlesworth 2000: 252). For these inmates, access to mass media may take on a heightened significance as a means of staying attuned to issues of local and global relevance and of keeping mentally alert.

Contextualising the importance of media in everyday life

It can be seen from the discussion thus far that for most inmates of total institutions, everyday life is something to be got through, to be survived, with the sense of self intact, and it is not difficult to imagine how media resources can alleviate some of the discomforts and hardships encountered in prison. But a number of writers have recently argued that the relationship between everyday life and media is in fact more than this and that media *is* everyday life (Altheide and Snow 1979; Morley and Silverstone 1991; Abercrombie and Longhurst 1998; Silverstone 1994, 1999;). The perceived centrality of media in daily life is partially explained by their facilitation of a sense of security, grounded in familiar spatial and temporal rhythms. Many commentators share Brittan's belief that lived experience is fraught with anxiety, risk and the breakdown of interpersonal trust. The argument is that where once our ability to trust in the continuation of predictable and routinised activities was upheld by face-to-face encounters, increasingly social and technological developments have extended the parameters of our knowledge, so that ontological security is now a function of space–time distantiation (Giddens 1990). Modern societies are no longer reliant on kinship relations or locality but on wider processes which lie beyond the physical space and time that we, as individuals, occupy. Our collective horizons have broadened, so that the knowledge and information required in order to alleviate our fears are now global in scope. Not only does much media content address these concerns directly, but television and other media provide a predictable temporal flow that contains and controls the management of otherwise unmanageable anxieties (Silverstone 1994).

These views might, however, seem a little overstated. The characterisation of media as central to everyday experience and at the core of our capacity to make sense of the world in which we live could be countered by the argument that there are alternative forms of experience – not least that of face-to-face interaction – which are arguably at least as important in the formation of self and identity. Furthermore, there are many everyday activities – such as going to school or work – that contribute to our sense of spatial and temporal awareness, and foster ontological security. However, even in more moderate analyses lived experience, while remaining fundamental, is increasingly recognised as being supplemented or displaced by mediated experience, which in turn impacts upon processes of self-formation and ontology. Thompson comments (1995: 233) that 'individuals increasingly draw on mediated experience to inform and refashion the project of the self', and there can be little doubt that contemporary society is a truly media-saturated society:

> The media, in all their forms, have worked their way into daily life on an unprecedented scale. . . Besides being regulative or constitutive of everyday life, the media also provide images, models of performance, or frameworks of action and thought which become routine resources of everyday life. People, in other words, *use* what the media provide in daily life (Abercrombie and Longhurst 1998: 104).

This reflection on media audiences *using* the media is important. Whether or not one follows recent commentators' views of the media's omnipresence in modern life, the potential use of media as a primary means of exerting one's agency and autonomy is central to contemporary media and cultural studies. For example, a number of writers have noted that audiences are extremely selective in what they take from the vast range of media messages available:

> People relate to the media on the basis of personal identities and then use media as sources of information and situations to play out those identities. Media's influence is that it serves as a repository of information and situations for voluntary action by audience members. Therefore, media influence should be understood not as a cause beyond an individual's control but as something consciously used by people to varying degrees. The media world can become an environment for total immersion, a world tempered by critical evaluation, or an aspect of culture almost totally rejected by an individual (Snow 1983: 62).

Indeed, much of the intense and infinite 'mediascape' (Appadurai 1993) which is modern life is disregarded or rejected by audiences: not all

23

media products are meaningful to audience members, and most people will select images and meanings from the media and combine them with other experiences connected with work, family and social relationships to form particular imagined worlds and maintain an ontological sense of self (Snow 1983; Hermes 1995; Thompson 1995). A very recent development in media studies has been an increased interest in exploring what happens to notions of self in the context of changing and proliferating systems and forms of mediated communication (Grodin and Lindlof 1996). For Grodin and Lindlof, it is not just media content that affects identity, but also the presence of media technologies. This will be an important point in the context of the prison: in common with the placement of television in public spaces such as shopping centres, restaurants and pubs, its instalment in prisons changes the nature of social interaction and the ways individuals experience themselves in relation to others. Grodin and Lindlof believe that the increase in numbers of mediated experiences that individuals are having, in conjunction with the mobility and interactivity of media technologies, are serving to undermine many notions of self and identity that have endured through the modern period. They ask: (ibid.: 6)

> What does it mean for self-experience that we can now form relationships over electronic mail with those whom we may never meet? Do we think of ourselves differently than those of the previous century because we are exposed to multifarious personalities and lifestyles through use of television, radio, and newspapers (Gergen 1991)? What images of self are portrayed in film, television and magazines, and to what ideological perspectives are these images aligned? For example, are we a culture dominated by images of self as autonomous and self-determining, or are other images emerging and in what contexts? What do talk shows and other media that focus on self-expression and healing tell us about the condition of self and identity in contemporary times?

Renewed interest in audience studies has resulted in reception analysis becoming increasingly global in outlook over the last decade. Yet simultaneously, there have been calls for a return to local 'community' studies of media use in order to examine in detail the kinds of microsocial contexts in which most media use takes place (Jensen and Rosengren 1990). There has also been a developing interest in accounting for the actual unfolding of everyday interactions with media within the contexts in which they are consumed. In part, this new focus has answered criticisms that the developments in media technologies have weakened or even made obsolete the notion of audiences. For example, despite his early pioneering work on media audiences, McQuail (1994) has more recently suggested that the notion of audiences is untenable. He points to four developments in support of this view: an abundance of supply and increased media choice; the increasingly individualised nature of media which encourages 'narrowcasting' to smaller, niche audiences; a more versatile media based on interactive computer technology; and a growing internationalisation of transmission and reception so that audiences are no longer confined within temporal, spatial or cultural boundaries. All these factors, according to McQuail (and others: see, for example, Allor 1988), make the idea of the audience as an identifiable social collectivity unknowable and irrelevant.

While this view is hypothetically valid in so far as no one is obliged to accept the same package of information or entertainment at the same time as anyone else, in practice this is not very close to realisation. Audiences are a product not only of technological and industrial development, but of social and behavioural forces which generate strong social and normative ties among otherwise diverse groups. In the specific context of the prison, new information and communication technologies tend to be relatively restricted to inmates and therefore have a less profound impact on this group of media consumers than in society at large. Arguments about greater choice, more autonomy, multiplication and fragmentation of the audience, and audience behaviour being more selective and interactive than previously, are also of less consequence in this environment. Even in society at large, McQuail's comments seem overstated. The received notion of a *mass* audience may arguably have less relevance for the reality of contemporary mediated communication than it once did, but live coverage of major world events such as royal weddings and funerals, and global musical events, attract billions of viewers, and even British television serials such as soap operas regularly attract domestic audiences of around seventeen million. Moreover, time spent watching television is the third most common activity behind work and sleep. The notion of audiences is thus central to understanding the ways in which mediated communication is organised as a practical activity in local, private and familiar settings which themselves shape the selection and use of media by specific individuals and groups. Indeed, if Abercrombie and Longhurst's (1998) notions of performance and the diffused audience are adopted, the concept has more relevance than ever before.

In any case, the academic study of audiences is far from redundant and a new generation of researchers has retained the uses and gratifications' premise of an active audience, but adopted a more sociocultural approach to studying the conditions of media reception. Emphasising the

25

polysemic nature of most media texts (that is, their 'meanings' are not given and obvious, but are open to several different interpretations or decodings), they have emphasised the need for detailed ethnographic descriptions of particular audiences in specific kinds of contexts. This has most often resulted in a commitment to qualitative research which seeks to understand media use as a significant element in everyday life in relation to four main categories of users: the family or household (Lull 1980; 1988; Ang 1985, 1991; Morley 1980, 1986, 1992); subcultures and fan cultures (Hebdige 1979; Tulloch and Jenkins 1995); women (Radway 1984; Gray, 1987, 1992; Hermes 1995); and children (Hodge and Tripp 1986; Buckingham 1993a, 1993b).

One of the most important audience studies in the early phase of their development was David Morley's *The Nationwide Audience* (1980) which he followed up with the equally influential *Family Television: Culture, Power and Domestic Leisure* (1986) and *Television Audiences and Cultural Studies* (1992). Concerned with the 'increasingly varied uses to which the television set can now be put' (Morley 1986: 8) his work draws upon a range of theoretical frameworks including symbolic interactionism and psychoanalysis. Morley's approach is also firmly rooted in cultural studies and takes as its starting point the premise that although audiences are active producers of meaning, media discourses will none the less be decoded in accordance with the broader societal and cultural practices in which the viewer is situated. Although Morley's focus, like that of most reception analysts, is the domestic household which he takes to be the 'dynamic unit of consumption' (ibid. 15), his approach is of interest because it allows him to analyse individual viewing activity within its social context, and to study television as a source of unallocated power by some individuals over others.

Through a series of interviews with lower working-class families, he gathered evidence about who watches television; how; at what times; in relation to what other activities; and in conjunction with which other family members. He found that even in the busiest households, television can provide an environment for privacy and personal space, functioning as a way of avoiding conflicts or reducing tensions in lieu of spatial privacy (Morley 1986: 21). Conversely, television may also be used as a method for engaging in shared experience and social interaction with others (ibid.: 20). His most interesting finding, however, is that use of television is strongly gendered and that through the operation of power over this media technology, the dominant social group (men, or when they are not present, male children) restrict the range of material and symbolic options open to the less powerful members of the household (women and girls). On the whole, according to the findings of *Family*

Television, men enjoy uninterrupted access to the kinds of television they designate as important and have no qualms about using it as a primary means of relaxation in what they regard as their leisure time. Women tend to watch in a much more haphazard and distracted fashion, frequently combining the viewing of their favourite programmes with attending to the needs of other family members. In contrast to their male partners, women are still to be seen at work within the domestic sphere (even if they have paid employment outside the home as well) and consequently their viewing preferences are frequently overlooked.

The position of power that working-class men occupy in relation to media technologies will inform much of the empirical analysis of media use in prisons. Spigel and Jenkins (1991) note that competence of media technologies can start early in life for males, and they quote one respondent, Dan, whose parents attempted to prevent him from watching *Dallas* by pulling out the cord from the back of the set: 'I was the one who figured out how to fix the TV. And to this day, they always give me the clicker [at family gatherings]. It's like I'm the master of the TV' (ibid.: 139). For Dan, not only does this small act of childhood resistance to adult control mark out his placement in the family structure, but it also demonstrates that where masculine power is the ultimate determinant on occasions of conflict over viewing choices ('We discuss what we want to watch and the biggest wins. That's me. I'm the biggest' is a typical comment from a male respondent in Morley's 1986 study), it is even more profoundly displayed where there is a remote control device, which is usually the symbolic possession of the father of the household (or the son in the father's absence) and frequently sits on the arm of 'Daddy's chair' to be used exclusively by him. This use often takes the form of obsessive channel-hopping across programmes, which is one of the biggest complaints of women who are trying to watch a single programme. The main exceptions to this general pattern are to be found in households where the man is unemployed and the woman working. Here Morley found that men are slightly more likely to give way to the viewing preferences of their partners, although their more flexible timetables mean they can video their choice of programming and watch it alone the following day. As Morley points out, this would seem to suggest that the position of power assumed by men in this context is not based on biology, but is culturally determined and linked to the socio-cultural definition of being the 'breadwinner'. When this aspect of traditional masculinity is felt to be absent, the man may be prepared, or feel compelled, to give way to the demands of other family members. However, other unemployed men in Morley's sample had no such compulsion and felt it necessary to exert their masculinity even more forcibly in monopolising the TV. One striking example is the unemployed man who had the television set switched on virtually all the time and insisted on watching it in uninterrupted silence. Such was his feeling of control in the domestic setting (presumably one of the few areas of his life where he experienced a sense of authority) that he became reluctant to leave it to pursue other activities outside the home for fear of losing his 'total power' (Morley 1986: 70).

But the fact that audience research has been confined to the domestic sphere means that there is currently very little understanding of how mediated communication is organised as an everyday activity in other local environments and how it is shaped and determined by those locales. Despite the acknowledgement on the part of a number of writers that television changes its meaning from context to context (Morley 1986, 1992; Silverstone 1994), these authors' persistence in limiting both the social dimension of context to the domestic setting, and the technological dimension of context to television, has severely restricted the field of enquiry. One writer who has attempted to build on the work of other cultural theorists, but extend their analysis to the study of a wide range of popular cultural forms and sites of cultural reception, is John Fiske, whose perspectives on audiences will be apparent in the discussion of prisoners' responses to media in the later chapters of this book. Drawing on the work of de Certeau (1984), Fiske (1989) argues that it is through everyday practices that cultural goods and services are transformed, and identities are constituted. Popular culture may be produced by the culture industry, but it is *made* by the people (ibid.). Inherent in the 'popularity' of popular culture is not only the notion that commodities have to be mass produced for economic profit, but that they must be potentially transformable into subversive readings and practices of resistance by consumers. Summing up the approach of de Certeau and Fiske, Stevenson (1995: 90) says:

> Everyday life has to operate within the instrumental spaces that have been carved out by the powerful [but t]o read a fashion magazine, listen to a punk album, put on a soccer supporter's scarf, or pin up a picture of Bruce Springsteen, is to discover a way of using common culture that is not strictly prescribed by its makers. The act of consumption is part of the 'tactics' of the weak that while occupying the spaces of the strong converts disciplinary and instrumental time into that which is free and creative.

To illustrate the ways in which media texts can be used as a form of resistance, Fiske draws upon the research of Hodge and Tripp (1986) who are concerned with how children and parents read television differently, and who, coincidentally, remind us of the similarities between different types of 'total institution'. In an analysis of the popularity of the soap opera *Prisoner Cell Block H*, Hodge and Tripp found that the schoolchildren psychically identified with the prisoners in the TV series. They explain this by reference to the structural similarities of the position of the pupils within the school and those of the fictional prisoners. Both live under a single authority, are subject to a tightly scheduled order imposed from above, and have their activities co-ordinated by the rational plan of the institution. The schoolchildren recognised that the prisoners in the show were reduced to 'childlike' roles, and they drew parallels between their teachers and the prison officers. They also voiced a number of similarities, as they saw them, between themselves and the inmates: they were often shut in, separated from friends, felt they had no rights, were only there because they had to be, and had to keep rules they felt were pointless. But they also recognised and attempted to emulate strategies of resistance in the soap; for example, the prisoners were adept at communicating under the eyes of their guards with a secret language of gestures and slang. For Fiske (1987: 132), the popularity of this programme is explained by the children's understanding that schools are like prisons and they use *Prisoner Cell Block H* to articulate and make sense of their experience of subordination and powerlessness within an institutional social structure.

However, despite his claims to the contrary, the micro-politics of audience consumption are not convincingly positioned within macro-social relations in Fiske's work, and his approach has been criticised for, among other things, concentrating on text at the expense of context (Stevenson 1995). One of the problems facing audience research in its current phase, then, is accounting for the influences of media on both macro and micro levels of analysis. As McQuail (1994: 320–21) puts it:

'Media use can. . . be seen to be both limited and motivated by complex and interacting forces in society and in the personal biography of the individual. This is a sobering thought for those who hope to explain as well as describe patterns of audience behaviour.'

In the light of this recognition, and mindful of the fact that this study follows conventional audience research in isolating gender as the key variable in relations of power as they are reinforced by media use, it is important to emphasise that it does not do so at the expense of other factors such as class, race, status and physical location. Above all else, this work is predicated on the assumption that media use will take on heightened significance, and may serve different purposes, in the context of the total institution. The aim of this investigation is not simply to recognise the structural and ideological functions of media in a given locale, nor to investigate individual or social consumption, nor even to understand the media's role in the ritual or social organisation of everyday life. Rather, it is to understand all these dimensions as they interact with, and act back on, each other. With this in mind, the following chapter will introduce two important theoretical perspectives from sociology. Giddens' theory of structuration will provide a counter to the deprivationist thesis, the former arguing that subordinates always have *some* resources at their disposal with which they can alter the balance of power, and Bourdieu's notion of 'habitus' will be employed further to explore constructions of masculinity in the prison setting.

Notes

1. Certainly, the prisons that have been built recently bear great similarities to other public sector buildings such as modern hospitals and schools. However, although 'total institution' might be deemed inappropriate in relation to modern prisons, the term conjures up an imagery whose topic is not really institutions but confinement (Sparks *et al* 1996: 60). In its evocation of the 'role-stripping' procedures of bureaucratisation, the inherent deprivations of incarceration, and the substitution of institutional values for human ones, 'total institution' is a compelling empirical description (Jones and Fowles 1984: 22) and one that will be used throughout this book.
2. Although most studies of media uses have focused exclusively on television, some have considered other media. One of the earliest uses and gratifications studies was Herzog's (1944) analysis of radio listening while, most recently, the ways in which music is used in the constitution of self has been an emerging theme (DeNora, 2000).
3. Analogies between long-term unemployment and long-term imprisonment are evident throughout this study, and striking parallels can be found in unemployment studies by Bostyn and Wight (1987), Fineman (1987), Fryer and McKenna (1987) and Burman (1988).
4. Interestingly, Cohen and Taylor and a number of other writers (Caird 1974; King and McDermott 1995; Sparks *et al* 1996) note the importance of mealtimes as significant landmarks in the day, week and year (with 'special' foods being allowed at weekends and Christmas), but fail to appreciate that media play a similarly important role in the marking of time.
5. King and McDermott (1995) report an 'astonishingly high' concern about physical condition in prisons, which inversely corresponded to actual sports and recreational facilities. Thus, in prisons where inmates spent most time locked up in their cells and had little opportunities for sport, or where there existed long waiting-lists for physical education, concern about physical well-being exceeded 65 per cent. In prisons where there were no barriers to the pursuit of physical activities, the proportions dropped to between 45 per cent and 51 per cent (ibid. 181).

Chapter 2

Identity, self and constructions of masculinity

One of the most enduring legacies of the sociological prison literature reviewed in Chapter 1 has been its success in highlighting the institutional pressures that bear upon inmates, especially as they enter prison for the first time or come to terms with a long sentence. Deprivation theory, and the numerous studies that have applied it over the last fifty years, have been invaluable in building up a coherent picture of the pains of imprisonment in a wide variety of penal establishments across the world. They have also helped to counter the more recent view of psychologists that prisons do an adequate job of containing society's criminals and that the psychological effects of incarceration are minimal (e.g. Bukstel and Kilmann 1980; Sapsford 1983; Zamble and Porporino 1988). As Caird (1974: 98) remarks: 'If you set up a twenty-foot fence around a man's body it would be naïve to say: "But I didn't mean to affect his *mind*"'.

But the findings of deprivation studies are incompatible with the notion that prisoners' responses to their circumstances may be partly located outside the prison walls. In other words, prisoners' coping strategies may be to some extent dependent upon social and cultural factors and learned responses to structural inequalities. This study aims to integrate creative human responses with encompassing structural determinants, and is predicated on the assumption that the psychological survival of a prison sentence may rely on inmates' potential to construct two separate identities. First, they must maintain a private sense of self that pre-exists and is entirely divorced from the socially sanctioned identity of 'prisoner'; and, secondly, they must be capable of drawing upon a range of strategies, resources and prior experiences to provide the material from which they can construct a public identity that enables them to 'fit in' with the social environment of the prison. It is proposed that without a stable sense of self *and* the necessary 'macho' credentials, many inmates find the prison culture merciless and intolerable. Later chapters will explore how the media can help individuals in both these endeavours, and the particular properties of media as a means of establishing and exerting unallocated (gendered) power over others will be a salient theme. But before considering in more detail the role media plays in the prison culture, it is first necessary to explore the social and environmental factors that shape this overtly masculine environment. Chapter 1 established that the deprivations suffered by prisoners, and their responses to such hardships, are in many ways unique. But equally, the norms and values of the prison society intersect with, and are mediated through, the belief systems and modes of behaviour commonly associated with the backgrounds of the majority of inmates. Consequently, an adherence to lower working-class masculine codes of behaviour is not only a typical response to imprisonment, but is arguably also one of the main factors in the social reproduction of class disadvantage, crime and imprisonment.

The cultural milieu of the prison

Prisoners are overwhelmingly young, male, unemployed and drawn from the lower working classes (Walmsley *et al* 1991). Explanations of why the working classes have seemingly colluded in perpetuating and reproducing their disadvantaged class position have been a perennial concern of sociologists since the publication of the first volume of Marx's *Capital* in 1867 and, more recently, the penal system's central role in the emergence of capitalism has preoccupied a number of prison commentators (Rusche and Kirchheime 1939/1968; Foucault 1977; Ignatieff 1978; Howe 1994). These writers have claimed that since imprisonment was introduced as the primary means of punishment in the eighteenth century, a move which coincided with a surplus of labour and a corresponding devaluation of human life, prisons have essentially been used as human warehouses designed to remove from society a subclass of people who are disenfranchised, disaffected and economically unproductive. But while undoubtedly providing a sense of the pivotal importance of social, historical and economic contexts in the continuation of imprisonment, these studies have tended to be overdeterministic in their approach, and have failed to allow for the relative autonomy of individuals even in highly regulated environments. On the question of agency – particularly the importance of resistance – even Foucault is found wanting (Giddens 1984; Howe 1994). So, in order to assess culturally attuned models which privilege the experiences of individuals and the cultural meanings they attach to structural determinants, it is necessary to go beyond prison studies and consider the findings of researchers from other fields of academic enquiry.

In *Learning to Labour*, one of the most influential sociological studies of working class male culture, Paul Willis (1977), himself working within a broadly Marxist/Weberian tradition, reminds deterministic Marxists that although class is significant in shaping a person's life chances (determining, as it does, a range of factors including geographical location, local opportunity structure, job market and availability, educational aspirations and so on) these structural elements are none the less acted through, and mediated by, their cultural surroundings:

> For a proper treatment of [the reproduction of social disadvantage]. . . we must go to the cultural milieu. . . and accept a certain autonomy of the processes at this level which defeats any simple notion of mechanistic causation and gives the social agents involved some meaningful scope for viewing, inhabiting, and constructing their own world in a way which is recognisably human and not theoretically reductive (ibid.: 172).

Willis' strength, then, is in recognising that structural forces and individual experience are linked by, and through, the *intermediary* cultural sphere so that culture is central to both the production of meaning and the reproduction of social relations.[2] Thus, although manual labour and relative poverty are the incontrovertible destiny of boys born into the working class, they are not simply passive or indifferent towards socio-economic pressures; at a personal and cultural level they respond with contestation, resistance and compromise (MacLeod 1987). Yet, while these responses give back a sense of personal agency and sovereignty, perversely they also serve further to weaken the individual in relation to structural power and to reproduce disadvantage and discrimination. As Foucault (1980) suggests, resistance is assured given the range and diversity of sites of power in late modern society. But inevitably, resistance simply reinforces the need for subjugation and discipline.

The reasons why groups of people who face structural discrimination do not take collective action to improve the conditions of their lives, but seemingly collude in their subordination by accepting the meaningless and often restricted life choices available to them, is a complex area of analysis. Simon Charlesworth (2000) has provided a recent exposition of this question in a phenomenological account of working-class lives in a town in northern England. Among the factors he highlights as being integral to the reproduction of disadvantage are the presentation of a heavily managed 'front' indicating a potential capacity for aggression that must be constantly maintained in the face of systemic disrespect and stigmatisation; lives lived in the context of circumscribed horizons and minimal expectations; and an inability to look beyond government institutions to broader structures of inequality when apportioning blame for the pain and degradation routinely suffered. All these factors are potentially found among prisoners. However, there are arguably a number of additional reasons why prisoners apparently contribute to the reproduction of their circumstances and only infrequently collect together to challenge the structural authorities which contain them. First, they are a diverse and heterogeneous population whose concerns do not necessarily constitute a 'common cause'. They are an aggregate, rather than a group, who happen to share a derived status (Mathiesen 1965). Secondly, because of the stigma attached to being a prisoner, they have no *positive* common social identity on which to base a call for collective action (Goffman 1961b). Thirdly, because of the deprivations attached to the experience of imprisonment, they lack resources and feel themselves to be impotent or even invisible, both within the prison and in the wider political and cultural spheres (Sykes 1958). Given these obstacles to collective organisation it is perhaps not surprising that prisons are relatively ordered environments.

But imprisonment is nevertheless a *lived experience* and must be managed in terms of the exigencies of everyday life by those inside. Consequently, small but significant acts of resistance are common, and in their study of prisoners at HMP Durham, Cohen and Taylor (1972) graphically demonstrate that inmates do not passively experience imprisonment: they live, negotiate and resist it, even if in doing so they sometimes suffer predictable but undesirable consequences which merely reproduce the situation in which they find themselves (for example, a relatively minor act of intransigence may lead to the withdrawal of privileges, extension of tariff or temporary removal of the prisoner from his cell into segregation). The psychological survival of a prison sentence is therefore probably best thought of as a delicate balancing act between prisoner demands (that is, the demands of the self) and staff discretion, involving a degree of compromise on both sides and negotiated against a backdrop of institutional regulations, expectations and sanctions. Traditionally, sociology has tended to adopt an 'over-socialised' image of the human subject as a passive conformist who eagerly co-operates with others but, as Wrong (1967) points out, people are also confrontational and their elemental impulses and motivations constantly jostle with the requirements of social conformity and discipline. Prison researchers Sparks *et al* (1996) further discredit the notion that people are basically 'acceptance seekers' passively conforming to an imposed regime, and highlight the balance that prison authorities must achieve between situational and social control methods. If all forms of imprisonment implied the unrelenting use of force as some commentators suggest, prisons would have no genuine internal sense of order and little sense of legitimacy on which to base the maintenance of order. Either scenario – a muted and fragile order sustained by an enforced compliance, or a bedlam of violent and desperate prisoners with nothing to lose – is too crude an analysis, and places undue focus on the processes of structure and agency working as independent forces (ibid.: 1996).

For many cultural theorists the division between structure and agency in accounting for social reproduction is an ongoing concern, but it is increasingly recognised that to view the two forces in a dichotomous fashion amounts to a crude reductionism that either suppresses the significance of individual autonomy or ignores the structural processes that lie outside the immediate experience of human actors (Giroux 1983a; Giddens 1984; Layder 1994). In the work of Foucault – a 'central reference point in the sociology of imprisonment' (Garland 1990: 131) – we find an attempt to resolve the structure/agency and micro/macro dualisms by joining together discourse, practice, power and knowledge at the intermediary, impersonal and institutional levels (institutions such as prisons, factories, schools, asylums being the channels through which power is circulated). However, Foucault remains trapped in an intermediate vacuum in which he can neither take full account of the 'macro' features of power, including state power, which he characterises as amorphous and disorganised (Poulantzas 1978), nor the micro, individual aspects of power, because throughout his work he retains the idea that power is an impersonal and anonymous force which is exercised outside the actions and intentions of human subjects (Best and Kellner 1991; Layder 1994). Although in his later work he recognised that his early emphasis on the 'technology of power and domination' had all but eliminated the active subject altogether, and he then proceeded to compensate for this oversight by concentrating solely on individuals as creative agents who can overcome socially imposed limitations (the 'technology of self'), he never attempted to connect the two phases of his work. Consequently scant regard is paid to the constitutive relationship between the active human subject and the circulation of power and production of social life.

The project to integrate structure and agency was taken up by Giddens, who was receptive to, but who ultimately rejected, much of Foucault's work. Of particular importance to the current study is his attempt to demonstrate how social production (the way in which social life is produced by people as they go about their day-to-day activities) and social reproduction (the way in which social life becomes patterned and social institutions are reproduced over time, providing order and continuity in society) are inextricably interlinked. It is this attempt to link social practices – the intended and unintended consequences of social activity – with social conditions – the practices, knowledge and resources which underpin the fabric of society – that lies at the heart of Giddens' theory of structuration; arguably the most sustained attempt to theorise human social activities in a way which avoids the conventional dualisms of subject and object, agency and structure, and structure and process (Bryant and Jary 1991). Specifically, structuration theory attempts to show how social structures are both constituted *by* human agency, and yet at the same time are the very medium of this constitution; what Giddens (1977: 121) terms a 'duality of structure'. Thus, in the current context, the penal system is both the *medium* in which the practices of the prison inmates and staff are shaped, and the (partly unintended) outcome of those human, minded practices as they act back on, and shape, future environing processes. Foucault (1977) demonstrates that people in all areas of everyday life are subject to the patterns, discourses and logic of organisations and institutions. But the reverse is also true, and life (in any sphere, but not least the prison), although immensely routinised and structured, only 'happens' because 'real-life, flesh-and-blood people make it happen' (Sparks *et al* 1996: 72).

Giddens' attempt to account for human agency in even the most restricted structural environments is a significant theoretical break-through. Its rejection of the implicit (and sometimes explicit) portrayals of prisoners as having been 'mortified' is an important development because the majority of prison research characterises power in prisons in a rather crude, one-dimensional way, and has arguably been guilty of the very thing it has accused the prison system itself of; that is, stripping inmates of their personalities and individual identities, and replacing them with crude typologies which lump them all together in stereotyped categories of predictive behaviour.[3] Even though Giddens devotes little attention to the prison *per se*, his criticism of Foucault is particularly relevant in this context. Foucault's conceptualisation of the power of carceral organisations is rigid and mechanistic and those who are subject to forms of discipline are rendered acquiescent and anonymous. As Giddens (1984: 154) says, 'Foucault's bodies do not have faces'. Even the most rigorous forms of discipline cannot dissipate human agency altogether. Although there are circumstances in which autonomy is severely limited, it is 'rarely negated entirely' (ibid.: 156).

Another aspect of Giddens' theoretical approach which is of particular interest here is that he is alert to psychoanalytic theories and the role of unintended and unconscious actions in the production and reproduction of social systems. Thus in addition to the two conscious levels of action which he refers to – reflexive monitoring of action (what actors are able to say about the conditions of their own action) and rationalisations of action (what actors know tacitly about the conditions of their own action, but are unable to articulate) – he also proposes a third, motivational, level of action which involves processes largely barred from consciousness (Giddens 1977). This is important because it is frequently the knowledgeability of agents at the core of Giddens' thesis that is used by his critics to undermine it (see, for example, Boyne 1991). It has been suggested that Giddens' stress on individuals' knowledgeability and reflexive monitoring 'tilts the balance of structuration theory towards subjectivism' and gives 'vaunting power to human agency' (Kilminster 1991: 96; see also Johnson *et al* 1984; Thompson 1989; Sparks *et al* 1996; Vaughan 2001).

Certainly, an over-emphasis on knowledgeable reflexivity might lead to an over-assertion of the power of agents to shape the social structures around them and exercise undue control over their futures. But three points pertain. First, much action is unconsciously driven and produces unintended or 'perverse' consequences (Giddens 1984: 13). Secondly, human agency – both conscious and unconscious – will nearly always be in conflict with the actions of other humans, as well as with structures, and is therefore usually a site of contestation, negotiation and compromise. Thirdly, although Giddens is frequently contradictory about the role of the unconscious, believing that the infant is, from the very first days of his or her life, able consciously to influence interaction with others (Giddens, 1976), he also states that the routine activity which shapes everyday life gives, at a psychological level, a necessary and desirable sense of ontological security, and that society needs a concept of the unconscious to represent that knowledge which is known to, and applied by, the actor, but which he or she is not able to formulate discursively (Giddens 1976, 1979, 1984). Consequently, despite accusations that Giddens' subjects have the ability to create meaning and to pursue purposes seemingly unhindered by larger structures of domination, there is nevertheless implicit in his theory the suggestion that there are social structures and systems which exist independently of the *conscious* motivations and reasons people give for their actions.

In any case, while it is perhaps fair to criticise Giddens on the grounds of over-asserting the role of action in social processes and underplaying the notion of constraint in social life, the introduction of a model of human agency which takes into account both unconscious drives *and* knowledgeable choice is a refreshing development, and counters the prevailing view of prisoners as passive subordinates. Even the acts of 'withdrawal' noted by Goffman and Cohen and Taylor, while they might in some circumstances be motivated by unconscious triggers, are often strategic and 'knowing' acts of resistance, rather than passive admissions of defeat. Similarly, and perhaps more controversially, attempts at suicide and self-harm may be seen as acts of resistance, an assertion of agency over the body and the self (Liebling and Krarup, 1993) and, as such, may be more accurately thought of as a response rooted in 'moral and political indignation' rather than in psychological dysfunction (Giroux 1983b: 289). 'Resistance' encompasses small, personal acts of defiance, more significant assaults on the self and, more rarely, large-scale eruptions of disorder. As a means of 'keeping one's head above the mire of institutionalisation' transgressing rules becomes 'part of the survival kit' (Caird 1974: 62). Resistance is, by its very nature, a dynamic and active strategy, requiring insight into the structural constraints being resisted. In other words, the violation of a rule does not in itself constitute resistance, unless committed by someone who sees through the institutional ideology and knowingly acts on that basis (Willis 1977; Giroux 1983a, 1983b; MacLeod 1987). It is this knowingness and sense of being wise to the ideological structures of the prison which help many inmates to maintain a stable sense of identity inside.

A number of writers have compared Giddens' theory with Bourdieu's (1977) notion of 'habitus' (MacLeod 1987; Layder 1994). Habitus is 'the basic stock of knowledge that people carry around in their heads as a result of living in particular cultures or subcultures' (Layder 1994: 143). It therefore corresponds with the work of Willis and other cultural theorists in that a person coming into prison from a particular class background will carry the 'influence' of that environment into his behaviour in the new setting. For example, an inmate from a lower working-class background might bring with him a type of knowledge, speech pattern, attitude and so on which will enable him to fit in to the inmate culture more easily than his middle-class counterpart. But a middle-class prisoner might feel more comfortable when dealing with figures of authority in the penal system, because of shared values, life experiences and educational background.

Habitus, then, is the 'set of "dispositions" that feeds into a person's anticipations about what they want and what they can achieve in their interpersonal relations' (Layder 1994: 144) and therefore bears similarities to Giddens' 'rules and resources'; the 'mutual knowledge' that people draw upon which inform their behaviour in any particular encounter (Giddens 1984: 17 *ff*).[4] Like Giddens' concept of structure, habitus is the means through which people produce and reproduce the social circumstances in which they live. The issue of resistance is missing from Bourdieu's theory, but what makes it of particular interest in the current study is that he retains the idea of an objective world which is different from the world of situated behaviour, whereas Giddens maintains they are simply different aspects of the same thing (the duality of structure). Similarly, Bourdieu underplays the aspect of Giddens' work which is most troubling to many commentators; that is, that people are free and unfettered by social conditions. For Bourdieu, human behaviour is always conditioned by habitus and, while this study understands human agency – an ability to 'make a difference' – to be crucial to the psychological survival of a prison term, it is reluctant to go as far as Giddens in elevating the power of the individual creative subject over the structures that contain him.

Another criticism of structuration theory pertinent to the current context is that it fails properly to account for 'social interconnectedness' (Kilminster 1991: 99) and 'flattens out' the ontological terrain of society (Layder 1994: 146). Giddens concentrates on the consequences of individual actions and broad social structures, but overlooks the complexities of the collective actions of the *interdependent* individuals and groups who make up societies (Willis' 'cultural milieu'). In other words, there is a missing area of analysis *between* the micro and the macro. Interdependence is a complicated, multifaceted, relational structure wherein the balance of power is subject to significant shifts over time, and a complex relationship exists between interpersonal networks and society as a whole (Kilminster 1991). Consequently, although it is true that when certain practices and institutions are highly co-ordinated towards their own reproduction, as prisons are, they tend to achieve a relatively high level of fixity (Sparks *et al* 1996), none the less the actions of the various human beings who make up the prison society will be inscribed with so many different influences that the social practices shaped by them will be unique. Broad structures, including structural inequalities, are reproduced by human action over time and space but, because human beings are unpredictable and conditioned by the prevailing culture at any given time, the flow and structure of social practices will never quite be a perfect repetition of what went before. A study which has overcome these limitations is Burman's (1988) investigation of unemployment,[5] an example of a successful attempt to apply structuration theory to the complex interaction between the 'microsocial sphere' (individuals, families, groups, friends), the 'intermediate community sphere' (social networks such as clubs and local enterprises) and the 'macrosocial sphere' (large organisations including state bureaucracies). Burman's schema will provide a framework for analysis in the empirical section of this study, which will broadly argue that despite the macro, structural constraints they face, inmates construct their identities and assert their agency through a nexus of micro and meso associations.

Self and identity

According to the social psychologist Richard Jenkins (1996), the study of identity became one of the unifying frameworks of intellectual debate in the 1990s, and is the most effective device for bringing together what C. Wright Mills calls the 'private troubles' of milieu and the 'public issues' of social structure, encouraging us to use one in order to make sense of the other. Although individual identities and social identities are often regarded separately, this study follows Jenkins' belief that each is routinely related to, and entangled with, the other, and that in the context of prisoners' identities, a necessary precursor for the creation and maintenance of a convincing public persona is the construction of a healthy, private, interior sense of self, and *vice versa*. Perhaps the most significant distinction between individual and collective identities, and one that will be evident in the empirical section of this study is that the former emphasises difference, while the latter stresses similarity (ibid.: 19). In both cases, prisoners may call upon the wide range of external resources and experiences that constitutes their habitus, drawing on the specific interpersonal relations (family, work, style, cultural preferences and so on) that mark them out as being different from the rest of the inmate population and, at the same time, hailing the dispositions and resources that enable them to engage with, and integrate into, the prevailing culture.

On entering prison, the individual is – to the outside world – immediately labelled a 'prisoner' (along with other labels, such as 'criminal' or 'deviant'). His ability to resist that identification, rather than internalising it, may be critical in determining how successfully he accommodates the pains of imprisonment. Put simply, public image may become self-image (ibid.: 57). For some, this is not necessarily problematic; indeed the strategy of 'prisonisation'[6] is a device that provides the aculturised inmate with the status and power necessary to absorb any sense of social rejection implicit in the label 'prisoner'. Most inmates, however, view the labels ascribed to them negatively, and fear that the carrying of the ascription 'prisoner' diminishes or even subsumes all other aspects of their identities. Consequently they spend much of their prison sentences trying to hold on to their pre-prison selves, through contact with friends and families, the continuation of occupations or hobbies, or through consumption of popular cultural artefacts that were important to them on the outside. In addition, many inmates construct new identities inside, such as a student identity or that of a particular tradesman. For Sapsford (1983) the adoption of such identities nourishes the self and is typical of working-class cultures, particularly among the working-class un-employed. He asserts that prison is a form of unemployment for men inasmuch as work is traditionally what gives men status, and that what passes for work in prison is actually more akin to occupational therapy. Pre-empting much of the 'underclass' literature, Sapsford argues that stripped of their work identities and concomitantly their status, individuals experience a loss of any marker by which to locate themselves within the social world. The adoption of work-related roles by prisoners represent 'escape' identities: for example, the two most common – 'student' and 'craftsman' – are usually regarded as prestigious in working-class company and offer the possibility of mobility upwards (ibid.: 1983: 104–105). Other roles adopted by prisoners may include 'artist', 'musician', 'writer', 'bodybuilder' or 'sportsman'; all of which might be said to be traditional routes out of the working-class.

All these adopted roles might be interpreted as positive adaptations to confinement. They recall Irwin's 'gleaners' and represent ways of self-improvement which may enhance the individual's public presentation of self, providing an opportunity to flaunt oneself symbolically; a kind of 'psychological one-upmanship' (Cohen and Taylor 1972). But more importantly, such roles work to sustain and nurture the personal, interior, psychological self. There may, however, be conflict between the public and private aspects of these identities; for example, student inmates sometimes face ridicule or hostility from fellow inmates and especially from staff. In a society where advanced levels of education are at odds with the habitus of the majority, and where a disproportionate number of the population are illiterate, education does not always have a high premium placed on it. Other factors – for example, the relatively low educational attainment required by the prison service of its officers, and the pressure on governors to reduce non-essential costs – combine to thwart prisoners' efforts to study. The fact that most inmate students persevere is a powerful testimony to the significance that the formation of such identities has on their sense of selves (usually characterised as self-worth, self-esteem, self-importance and so on).

The self, then, might best be conceptualised as the emotional 'core' which people carry with them from context to context. It represents a place of retreat: when the public work of identity management becomes

Jewkes (2002)

too arduous it is important to have a private place where the public façade can be put aside and one can 'be oneself'. This distinction between the private sense of self and the public presentation of identity is usually conceptualised in terms of their 'backstage' and 'frontstage' settings respectively (Goffman 1959; see also Giddens 1984). On the whole, the social aspect of one's identity will be presented frontstage in social engagement with others. Backstage is where one's basic, personal ontological security system is restored, and where the tensions associated with sustaining the particular bodily, gestural and verbal codes that are demanded in this setting are diffused. Imprisonment may involve disruption of the equilibrium between the two spheres, resulting in further damage to the individual's sense of well-being. If forced to share a cell with one or more other inmates, the prisoner may be continually in an enforced state of 'frontstage' with little opportunity to restore his sense of self. If locked up on his own for prolonged periods, however, he may suffer equally in his inability to engage in activity frontstage. In prison, the boundaries between frontstage/backstage and personal/ social identities may not be clear cut, and the pressure for conformity and compliance may undermine the inmate's personal and social identities, preventing both from functioning as they would in other circumstances.

The public identities adopted by inmates depend upon two things: first, they correspond to the cultural conventions of the immediate prison environment (which vary from institution to institution but share certain characteristics); secondly, they depend upon the repertoire of roles which the larger culture makes available (Sapsford 1983). In both cases, identities are not forced upon inmates, but are adopted by them through a process of social learning or socialisation. This calls to mind the postmodernist view that the subject can assume different identities at different times in a perpetual act of self-creation. Limitations of space prevent a full analysis of the ongoing debate concerning whether we are witnessing the emergence of a new era of 'postmodernism' replacing and leaving behind the three-hundred-year period of modernity which went before, and for the purposes of this study, the term 'late modernity' will be used, suggesting certain important continuities as well as discontinuities with the modern project (Giddens 1991a; Hall 1992). The importance of the debate for this study is twofold. First, there is a suggestion that while there has been a general trend towards bureaucratic management and rationalisation over the last two decades (Feeley and Simon 1992), in very recent years we have seen a concomitant 'refiguring of the penal spectrum' resulting in a resurgence of 'emotive and ostentatious' punishment (Pratt 2000: 417) in the form of correctional initiatives designed in part publicly to stigmatise and shame the offender

– community sentences, electronic tagging, and the like – and in the form of public involvement in the surveillance of released sex offenders, vigilantism, and so on. This supports Garland's (1990) view that the language of prison service accountability and prisoners' rights masks a corresponding change of tone regarding the 'expressive' function of the prison which appears to be returning to a site of public revenge (see also Liebling 2000).

The second point about postmodernist theory which makes it of interest in the current context is its suggestion that media-inspired and consumer-driven aspirations have started to merge and collide with traditional identifications (such as those based on class, race, gender, nationality) resulting in what cultural optimists might see as a greater awareness of the endless possibilities that the global market has to offer for constructing the self (Jenkins 1996), and what cultural pessimists characterise as an 'unstable amalgam of self' (Giddens 1991a; Hall *et al* 1992). But whether positive or negative in essence, the postmodernist assumption that we are continuously confronted by a 'bewildering, fleeting multiplicity of possible identities, any one of which we could identify with' (Hall 1992: 277) overlooks the structural and institutional constraints that most of are bound by in at least some spheres of our lives, and ignores social theories of learning. In the context of the prison, a postmodern analysis would not be able to account for either the social roles that inmates import into prison from outside, or for the socialisation processes they go through inside the institution. This is important, for it is through socialisation that the individual acquires the knowledge, skills and dispositions that enable him or her to function as an effective member of a group. Without the conscious and unconscious assimilation of the ideologies of the prison culture – a society where individuals are subjected to influences and sanctions in roughly equal measure – and the ideologies of the lower working-class culture from which the majority of prisoners originate – the individual inmate would be subjected to immeasurable, and inescapable, role expectations (Bondeson 1989).

Another weakness of postmodernism is that although it can certainly account for the 'public' identities which we present to others, it is less convincing when it comes to the deep-seated sense of self that we internalise and that may impact upon our feelings, emotions and behaviour at a subconscious or unconscious level. Most of us maintain a sense of being 'more or less unitary selves' (Jenkins 1996: 45), despite the enacted roles which various situations demand primarily through the construction of a personal ontological narrative; a story one tells about oneself, which can be altered and modified in accordance with different situations and periods in one's life and with different 'audiences' in mind, but which essentially enables one to make sense of – in order to act in – one's life. In any case, the key point here is that while it may be possible for prison inmates to assume certain outward characteristics in order to help them to fit in with aspects of the prison culture, such traits are likely to be little more than a façade, constructed to mask the real personality beneath. Furthermore, while it is true that popular cultural forms and new communication technologies support the postmodern thesis in allowing us to inscribe different characteristics on the identity which we present to others, and to conceal elements of 'ourselves', it is a way of being which, as Craib (1998: 7) puts it, 'can bear little contact with an external reality, and cannot outlast anything but the most cursory human contact'. But more fundamentally than that, cultural identities – whether they are based on 'fixed' components such as class, gender and race, or on less stable aspects such as occupation, leisure interests, social status, group membership and subcultural affiliations, or a combination thereof – represent only half of the picture, and miss entirely what goes on 'inside' their bearer: 'Social identities can come and go but *my* identity goes on as something which unites all the social identities I ever had, have or will have. . . [it] overflows, adds to, transforms the social identities that are attached to me' (ibid.: emphasis added).

The notion of identity is thus underpinned by a range of powerful unconscious as well as conscious processes, which are shaped and directed in various ways according to the disciplines and discourses of the time, resulting in a plurality of parts which go to make up the 'whole'. As stated earlier, although personal and collective identities form a synthesis, one way in which they can usually be distinguished is by the former's appeal to difference, individualism and uniqueness, and by the latter's appeal to similarity or sameness. However, the picture is complicated by the subject's unconscious which, at the levels of both private self and public identity, can create desires and fears which may merge or conflict with the various discourses and structures in which they are situated. Identity and self converge with power and discourse in defining us, not only by who we *are* but also, crucially, by what, or who, we are *not* (Hall 1992, 1997; Craib 1998; Minsky 1996, 1998). Identities are often characterised by polarisation and by the discursive marking of inclusion and exclusion within oppositional classificatory systems: 'insiders' and 'outsiders'; 'us' and 'them'; men and women; black and white; 'normal' and 'deviant' and so on, so that it is primarily a sense of 'difference' which is crucial to an understanding of the ways in which identities are shaped. In particular, it is the notion of difference which has not only been put forward as a theory of crime, but which is crucial to understanding the relationship between identity and power in the generally disempowering world of the prison.

In a psychoanalytic interpretation, 'difference' involves the denial of large parts of ourselves, or the projection of those parts of ourselves which make us feel vulnerable, on to 'others' in the external world. Stemming from the Oedipal conflict which arises when the infant begins to have sexual feelings and desires towards the opposite-sex parent, and at the same time has accompanying feelings of resentment and jealousy towards the same-sex parent, this perspective helps to explain the persecution of the 'other' throughout history. Put simply, in the case of the male child, he has previously seen himself as sharing an identity with his mother, but is suddenly confronted with the reality of her sexual difference. This induces a fear of castration and a masculine identification with the father, not only physically, but also as a source of cultural power and moral authority. In the context of this discovery, culture (i.e. the Law of the Father) wins over individual desire, and the child 'succumbs to a destructive unconscious solution' (Minsky 1998: 83) in which he expels or externalises the part of himself which he finds intolerable – in other words, the painful 'victim' feelings of humiliation and vulnerability – and projects them on to his newly discovered 'other', his mother. In this way he is able to disown the harmful feelings which interfere with his newly discovered sense of power and project them on to 'woman', who is now defined as 'different and therefore bad' (ibid.: 84). 'Subsequently, women, femininity or passivity wherever it exists may be deemed contemptible and feared because it represents a despised, castrated part of the self' (ibid.).[7]

For post-Freudian writers such as Minsky, the victimisation of feminised 'others' helps to explain sexism, racism, nationalism, tribalism, homophobia and religious persecution: implicit in all these forms of intolerance is the notion of a despised 'other' as the means to maintaining an idealised self. Symbolic cultural representations are intuitively 'picked up' by individuals, identified with at a psychical level, and then played out within social relations, thus reinforcing and reproducing divisions and inequalities (Messerschmidt 1986; Giddens 1991a; Craib 1998; Minsky 1996, 1998). It is the interplay between unconscious fears and culturally reinforced prejudices which defines who, at any given time, is designated 'the scapegoat "other"' against whom we bolster our own individual sense of identity (Minsky 1998: 2). In the prison world, otherness is most evidently conferred on sex offenders. In a study of a Vulnerable Prisoner Unit (VPU), Richard Thurston (1996) notes that not only does the categorisation of inmates in the VPU as 'different' and 'feminine' represent a process of objectification, but it also works to sustain the acceptability of violence against them on a routine basis.[8]

Although generally regarded as a contemporary concern, as long ago as 1955 the sociologist Albert Cohen was moving tentatively towards an integrated theory of identity (in this case, criminal identity) as the construction of conscious and unconscious processes in his ground-breaking analysis of delinquent boys, a study which is greatly acknowledged by later researchers such as Clarke (1975), Willis (1977) and Corrigan (1975 1979) in their studies of male subcultures:

> Because of the structure of the modern family and the nature of our occupational system, children of both sexes tend to form early feminine identifications. The boy, however, unlike the girl, comes later under strong social pressure to establish his masculinity, his *difference from* female figures. Because his mother is the object of the feminine identification which he feels is the threat to his status as a male, he tends to react negativistically to those conduct norms which have been associated with mother and therefore have acquired feminine significance. Since mother has been the principal agent of indoctrination of 'good', respectable behaviour, 'goodness' comes to symbolise femininity, and engaging in 'bad' behaviour acquires the function of denying his femininity and asserting his masculinity. This is the motivation to juvenile delinquency (Cohen 1955: 164).

This quotation is important for three reasons. First, it provides an early model for the connection of conscious and unconscious motivations for behaviour. Secondly, it unites personal and social identities and alludes to the ways in which individual agency, both conscious and unconscious, correlates to patterns of interaction learned through processes of socialisation (the 'social'). As will be demonstrated later, individuals are constantly engaged in these two interlocking forms of emotional endeavour: 'the "internal" work of coping with contradiction, conflict and ambivalence, and the "external" work of reconciling what goes on inside with what one is "supposed" or "allowed" to feel' (Craib 1998: 113). Thirdly, Cohen draws our attention to the importance for males of constructing and maintaining a culturally acceptable 'masculine' identity. Nowhere are the tensions between conscious and unconscious drives, private and social identities, and acceptable or unacceptable masculinities more evident than in the predominantly male locale of the prison.

The social construction of masculinity

In order to examine the relationship between institutional demands and the individual motivations which enable inmates to survive imprisonment, it is necessary to consider what many prison sociologists regard as the defining characteristic of the social life of prisons. Of all Sykes's 'pains of imprisonment', the deprivation of security is probably the least studied, yet the fear for personal safety which is engendered in every direction between inmates and staff is arguably the over-riding feature of life in most institutions.[9] For most inmates, peer group respect, individual status and access to scarce resources all rest upon a reputation for aggressiveness and physical strength. As in any organisation a climate of fear is bound to lead to the exploitation of weaker individuals by more powerful ones and, in prison, the illusion of power often rests on outward displays of intimidation and violence. It is necessary, then, to explore what has been described as the prison-coping strategy *par excellence*; 'manliness' (Toch 1975: 146), first in its broadest social context, and then within the specific context of the prison.

That prisons contain violent men is hardly a revelation, but the exact nature of the 'macho' culture, the extent to which it emerges as a result of the deprivations of imprisonment or is imported into prison by inmates (and therefore simply represents a microcosm of the lower working-class culture from which most inmates originate), and the precise means by which hierarchies of domination are created and maintained among groups of male inmates, have yet to be thoroughly explored. Indeed, despite the fact that men comprise the vast majority of prisoners worldwide, hence the concentration of research on male prisons, most studies treat the gender of their subjects as more or less incidental (Gelsthorpe and Morris 1990; Sim 1994). This is perhaps not surprising when even the emergent literature from gender studies concentrated for decades on the subordination of women under a global system of patriarchy; only relatively recently has the notion of 'masculinity' been problematised in any meaningful way (Newton 1994). So, while ethnic and generational differences among prison inmates have been studied (Genders and Player 1995), the assumption among criminologists has tended to be that, in the mainly male world of the men's prison, the normal rules of patriarchy do not apply. However, the notion of patriarchy (as it is commonly used) although simplistic, is *not* irrelevant to the predominantly male environment and it is now widely accepted that men can be its victims as well as its perpetrators.

'Patriarchy', 'fratriarchy' and the study of masculinity

Despite its wide usage, however, 'patriarchy' is somewhat misleading. Its meaning has been corrupted in the wake of the feminist women's movement, so that it is now popularly used to describe what might more properly be termed 'androcracy' – rule by men (Remy 1990). 'Masculinity' first became the subject of academic study in the mid-1970s, and it is therefore unsurprising that it was substantively constructed as a problematic from within a feminist framework (Kimmel 1990). The result of this was that in the early days of gender studies, dimensions of division and oppression other than those imposed by white, middle-class, heterosexual men on women were largely ignored (ibid.). This changed with the publication of Tolson's *The Limits of Masculinity* in 1977 which was arguably the first work to analyse in detail the social construction of masculinity as it pertains to relationships between powerful and (relatively) powerless men, as opposed to simply the general domination of men over women. A combination of personal accounts of his own childhood, anecdotal evidence gathered from acquaintances, and qualitative data based on conversations with young gang members, brought together and interpreted through a social constructionist framework, it was the first attempt to define a 'problem of masculinity' involving an adjustment to disintegrating images of self, and was pivotal in encouraging the previously female-dominated and feminist gender studies to embrace the study of men and masculinity.

Building on Tolson's work, a small number of gender theorists have argued that masculinities are numerous, ephemeral, contested and highly problematic. Thus, in the process of deconstructing masculinity, recent writers, notably Brittan (1989), Hearn and Morgan (1990), Connell (1987, 1995), and Jefferson (1997), have suggested a more complex conceptualisation of masculinity than had previously been employed, the most significant aspect of which is a shift to the notion of multiple masculinities. To talk of 'masculinity' in the singular is now regarded by these writers as crude biological reductionism, and their emphasis is much more focused on the interplay between different *forms* of masculinity. This has led to a reconceptualisation of the structure of gender relations and a recognition among some commentators that the term 'patriarchy' has entered academic debate and the popular consciousness as a kind of short-hand ascription which grossly oversimplifies the structures of gender (Connell 1987).

One way of overcoming the ambiguities inherent in the term 'patriarchy' (the rule of the fathers) is to consider, instead, the merits of 'fratriarchy' (the rule of the brothers); a mode of male domination which, while sharing some of the origins of patriarchy, is none the less concerned with a quite different set of values, and which seems more appropriate in an analysis of a predominantly male environment. Although it does not appear to be in common usage, and certainly could not be said to be a sharply defined analytical tool, the term 'fratriarchy' is used by Brod (1990) and Remy (1990) to account for the disjunction between the facts of public male power and the feelings of individual male powerlessness. It thus explains how, within a broadly patriarchal society, in which the oppression and subjugation of women is well documented, superordinate notions of masculinity serve to weaken – for want of a better word, 'feminise' – the authority of some men. Where patriarchy is a father-to-son transmission of authority, and is therefore intergenerational, the dimension of temporal continuity is rendered more problematic in the intragenerational relationships of the brotherhood: 'As opposed to the patriarch, who embodied many levels and kinds of authority in his single person, the brothers stand in uneasy relationships with each other, engaged in sibling rivalry while trying to keep the power of the family of man as a whole intact' (Brod 1990: 133).

Furthermore, while the brothers may share the desires of the patriarch in matters of paternity and parenting, it is a concern largely fuelled by self-interest. Elsewhere, Gilmore (1990: 223) states that the three core elements of manhood are impregnating women, providing for one's dependants and protecting one's kin. While these codes of behaviour are undoubtedly characteristic of men across the socioeconomic strata, it is arguable that in the lower working classes these ideals are transmuted according to the demands of association with other men and the 'freedom' to do as one pleases and 'have a good time'. As such, even men who marry and/or have children may permanently remain psychologically trapped in the fraternal fellowship, eschewing all responsibilities and thriving on the conflict and aggression which are characteristic of most male associations. As Remy (1990: 45) demonstrates in the parlance of the 1970s, this generally amounts to 'causing a bit of bovver'.

Remy (ibid.) uses the term 'men's hut'[10] as a metaphor for the public institutions beyond the private world of the home, where men go primarily to associate with other men: 'this is. . . where those males who have earned the right to call themselves *men*, or are in the process of attaining this emblem of privilege, gather'. 'Men's huts' for the middle classes are institutions such as golf clubs, 'gentlemen's' clubs and Freemasons' lodges, while working-class manifestations include pubs and betting-shops. Male bonding has also, of course, found its expression in a highly visible form in political arenas, including the House of

Commons and extreme fascist organisations such as the Nazi movement (ibid.). The interesting aspect of men's huts, from the perspective of the current consideration of unequal power relations among men, is that they not only emphatically exclude women, but also those males who have, as Remy says, not yet earned the right to call themselves men. This form of 'social closure' (Weber 1964) operates through a number of mechanisms, including exclusion of those who have not yet passed the requisite rites of passage, those who are either too old, or too young, to be fully respected by their peers, and those who are not versed in the special language or 'argot' which frequently characterises these groups. In all these respects, prison societies can be said to resemble men's huts and can be seen as a continuation of practices adopted in the working class world of manual labour where male ascendancy over other men on the basis of age, authority and peer group credentials is frequently evident. Apprenticeships and probationary training periods are commonly remembered in terms of drudgery and shame; a humiliating induction into masculinity as well as trade. Yet once the training has been successfully completed, the apprentices are generally accepted as 'brothers' (Cockburn 1986). Similarly, the new prison inmate will frequently have to undergo a period of testing, involving some kind of initiation which may entail physical assertions of strength (McDermott and King 1988). Young offenders institutes are particularly notorious for the bullying which takes place on induction, but in all custodial settings, if the victim succeeds in defending himself and asserting his autonomy, he will often be accepted, at least by some sections of the prison fraternity (Sykes and Messinger 1960; Newton 1994).

A recognition of the disparity which exists between the structural dominance of patriarchy, and individual feelings of powerlessness among the fratriarchy, has led many writers to claim that the women's movement has left men feeling confused by the wide range of diverse and often contradictory imperatives placed upon them. In particular, the frequently invoked 'crisis' of masculinity has brought to the surface the need to reconceptualise masculinity in terms of its dominant, hegemonic representation, and other, subordinated versions of it. Bearing similarities to the 'myth of manliness' (Toch 1975) and the 'masculine mystique' (Miedzian 1991), the term 'hegemonic masculinity' (Connell 1987), encapsulates the social ascendancy of some men over other men and women, but goes one step further than 'fratriarchy' in identifying its deeply embedded, structural character. It recognises that men, too, can experience subordination, stigmatisation and marginalisation at every level, as a consequence of their sexuality, ethnic identity, class position, religious beliefs or some other 'difference' (Hearn and Morgan 1990).

Using 'hegemony' in much the sense that Gramsci (1971) intended, Connell (1987) is clear to point out that hegemony in this context is not ascendancy based on the use of force: indeed coercion is rarely required given that hegemony is achieved in social forces which extend beyond contests of brute power into the organisation of public and private life. However, he also emphasises that hegemony and force are not incompatible, and that the two often go hand in hand. Sim's (1996) study of vulnerable prisoners demonstrates that violence frequently endorses dominant cultural patterns. The fact that assaults on some inmates (by both fellow inmates and by officers) occur and are tolerated by those with the authority to intervene demonstrates that hegemonic values based on physical coercion are part of the complex horizontal and vertical relationships instituted between prisoners and prison officers, and between these groups and what Sim (1994: 102) calls the 'technocrats who occupy powerful positions as governors, area managers and state bureaucrats in the Home Office'.

Hegemonic masculinity is clearly, then, a structural device which understands the production and re-production of masculine attributes, attitudes and behaviours as outcomes of social processes and inequalities which are upheld at every level of society. It is therefore not surprising that many of the dominant features of the prison society (intergroup loyalty, adherence to a 'code of honour', a distinctive jargon, displays of aggressive toughness, passing initiation rites, opposition to authority and so on) can be found in many underclass[11] cultures. Studies of lower working-class culture have provided an important focus in academic sociology since the 1970s and have undoubtedly done much to popularise and give credibility to ethnographic research methods, as well as providing some of the impetus for the emerging studies of masculinity. In Willis' 1977 study of school-age boys in the Midlands, he found a construction of masculinity based on machismo and bonding with other 'lads' which effectively prepared them for a later life of repetitive, manual labour. The macho solidarity of the 'culture of work' which found its genesis in the 'lads' subculture at school produced an extreme form of masculinity ('machismo') which compensated for their social subordination to other men, enabling collective resistance to authority and self-respect (Tolson 1977).

Of course, since *Learning to Labour* was published, long-term employment in industry has become less of an option for male school-leavers in Britain and, while the image persists of a working-class masculinity bound up with the requirements of hard manual labour, young men are growing to maturity with an increasingly weak attachment to the world of work (Wilson 1987). In an ever more competitive and 'feminised' labour market, those without qualifications and other advantages clearly have their life chances diminished, but in many areas of high unemployment, young men are second- or even third-generation unemployed, and therefore have simply never been socialised into the world of work. Seemingly condemned to failure from the day they were born, these males have little to give them a sense of self-worth other than their ability to exert power over others through bullying and intimidation. In creating a macho façade they are attempting to transmute the qualities of hegemonic masculinity – power, control, authority, respect and so on – to give them meaning within their own culture. Unlike women (for whom no equivalent 'hegemonic femininity'[12] exists) being a man of whatever class, age or ethnic background, involves constantly proving that you are a man: 'Masculinity is something you can never feel at ease with. It is always something you have to be ready to defend and prove. You have to prove that you are as much of a man as everyone else. Often this means putting others down. . .'[13] (Seidler 1991: 132).

Hegemonic masculinity is, however, very different from the notion of a biologically determined male sex role, and the ideal of masculinity most prized by a culture may not correspond to the actual personalities of the majority of men. Indeed, the winning of hegemony often involves the creation of models of masculinity which – if not what powerful men *are* – nevertheless are what they are motivated to support in the interests of maintaining their power. These models are frequently fantasy figures, or real people whose image is intrinsically bound up in a somewhat exaggerated media persona; for example, footballers, pop stars and 'action movie heroes'. Furthermore, the fact that the comparatively few female counterparts of these embodiments of a masculine 'ideal', with all its connotations of power, wealth and success, are frequently treated with hostility or resistance by the culture industries and the public at large is an indication of a patriarchal system which finds its cultural expression in hegemonic masculinity.

All forms of masculinity inevitably involve a certain degree of putting on a 'manly front', and it therefore seems reasonable to consider the outward manifestation of all masculinities as 'presentation' or 'performance'. This dramaturgical conception of self, made famous by Goffman (1959), once again recalls the interplay between structure and agency. Tolson (1977) takes up the dramatic motif and gives it a class-based edge, arguing that the working class boy 'expresses himself, not so much in an inner competitive struggle for achievement, as through a collective toughness, a masculine "performance" recognised and approved by his "mates" ' (ibid: 43). Although it is not being suggested here that middle-class boys do not share this need to live up to certain idealised representations of masculinity in order to gain the respect of their peers (based predominantly on educational and sporting achievement, perhaps), the concern here is with underclass males for whom masculinity is a kind of ritualised dramatic enactment; generally mundane and predictable, but punctuated by sporadic bursts of excitement. In a study of Sunderland street-corner culture, Corrigan (1975) testifies to the intense activity which is involved in the common pursuit of 'doing nothing', echoing other commentators' observations concerning passing time in prison. Occasionally, confrontations or 'contests of honour' between rival gangs have to be fought and within in order to preserve a masculine reputation (Newburn and Stanko 2004). Such contests are usually fought over territory and the communist districts of the working class is the inter[...] ly loyalty to the local districts, neighbourhoods, streets and even [...] patches [...] that are closely marked by gangs and gua[...] to apparent absurdity) (Tolson 1977: 42).

Although the ability to 'prove oneself' by physical means is essential in hegemonic, underclass culture, another important aspect of the lower working class male's existence is the ability to 'talk up' his physical prowess. Even if an individual rarely has the need to engage in actual combat, he must impress his 'audience' with his repertoire of stories and jokes. The stories do not have to be true necessarily, but they must be as interesting as possible, and meaningful to the story-teller's 'public'. Within his peer group he is socialised into this mode of behaviour, learning at an early age that bravado is a key element in gaining membership of the fratriarchy. Not only do the stories serve the important function of filling time, but they are also youthful versions of the *Männerbünde*, underlining the group's collective identity and internal solidarity (Tolson 1977; Corrigan 1975, 1979).

Ironically, it is the very existence of male subcultures which weakens the hegemonic notion of masculinity to which they are culturally encouraged to aspire and ensures the social reproduction of disadvantage and marginalisation. Gender is constructed as a situated social and interactional accomplishment; it grows out of social practices in specific social structural settings and, at the same time, serves to inform such practices in reciprocal relation (Messerschmidt 1999: 199). Inside the locally constructed working-class world there is little room for deviation from the prescribed norms which characterise this group, and conformity is paramount. But while collective allegiance to the locality provides the group with some of its internal cohesion, the overwhelming price which the young working-class boy has to pay is conformity to the monotony and routines of working class culture (Tolson 1977: 44). In this context, then, it would appear that Bourdieu's (1977) concept of habitus is more convincing than Giddens' theory of structuration. As Layder (1994: 157) notes: 'Bourdieu makes clear distinctions between the external context of activity, the immediate situational circumstances, and the habitus which acts as a conduit between them'. The compliance which group membership demands is imposed at all three levels of social interaction (micro, meso and macro) and always involves compromise in the face of restraints. It is at the intermediate level where habitus is key; it represents the 'resources that people draw on to make activity happen, but at the same time limits its potential' (ibid.). The importance attached to 'putting on a front' in order to adjust to the disintegrating sense of self, and the engagement in gratuitous violence which is characteristic of much underclass masculinity, masks the overwhelming sense of futility and disappointment which many disadvantaged youths feel. What characterises their 'performances' is a sense of fatalism, of 'taking the world as you find it' (Tolson 1977: 43) but this prevents them from doing anything to overcome the structural disadvantages they face; indeed, it frequently serves to perpetuate their marginalisation.

It is thus reasonable to suppose that male aggression, much of which is 'acted out' in a stylised fashion, is the human response to structural inequalities. Without the sense of incorporation which the traditional world of work facilitates, young people are less apt to form their identities on the basis of occupation and life chances, and are more likely to get their sense of self through football, music or some other 'fanship'. The difficulty which faces them is that all these identifications require conspicuous consumption of designer-label clothing and accessories, and it may be that young men in today's anomic society are fostering at an early age, not the skills necessary to prepare them for a mundane working life in industry but, rather, the wells of ungratified desire which instil a sense of dissatisfaction with the gains to be made through legitimate means. Although it is not being suggested that all lower working-class males are unable to find ways of accomplishing masculinity in ways that do not involve crime, it might reasonably be assumed that those who *do* offend bring into prison with them a masculine ideology and commitment to a criminal subculture which prepares them for life inside. For men with few material advantages, the rewards of reproduction, provision and protection may only be securable by conflict and struggle; and marginalisation, whether it is along economic, class or racial lines (or all three) is likely to lead to clashes for personal power with rivals from a similar background (Messerschmidt 1986). The intensity of the desirable male image would appear, therefore, to be linked strongly to social organisation, environment and productivity: as Gilmore (1990: 224) notes, 'the harsher the environment and the scarcer the resources, the more manhood is stressed as inspiration and goal'. Few environments offer a more intensely harsh, un-productive and impoverished set of circumstances than the prison.

Hegemonic masculinity in prisons

The desire to prove one's manhood which frequently leads to criminal behaviour, conviction and imprisonment may itself, then, be a pre-requisite to a successful adaptation to life inside. This may be particularly true of those who have committed very serious offences, who might be said to import with them into prison the ideology of aggressive macho values which precipitated their crimes in the first place. Indeed, feminist writer Nicole Ward Jouve, in her account of the circumstances surrounding the crimes of 'Yorkshire Ripper' Peter Sutcliffe (1988: 144), argues that 'the whole aura of. . . aggressive maleness that surrounded Sutcliffe made his murders possible'. This aura was provided partially by a father who, Ward Jouve suspects, would rather have a mass murderer for a son than a closet homosexual, and by friends of the offender, who 'regarded prostitute-bashing as a joke' (ibid.). Yet macho values are not the preserve of the underclass, or the psychopath. Even though the likelihood of them becoming prisonised or actively seeking to adapt to prison life is arguably less probable, white-collar criminals and inmates from an ostensibly middle-class background will have their masculinity tested in various ways during the course of their sentences by the deprivations of imprisonment, all of which – in enforcing a state of infantilised dependency – attack the very core of hegemonic masculinity which men of all social classes are culturally encouraged to aspire to.

Ward Jouve's (ibid.) exploration of Sutcliffe's relationship with his father reinforces the point that hegemonic masculinity is not achieved solely through domination over women, but is also constructed in relation to subordinated or less powerful men. Hegemony does not mean total or uncontested dominance; it is not fixed, but may alter over time, and it is achieved within a balance of forces so that other forms are subjugated, not eliminated altogether. But achieving hegemony may depend on preventing alternatives from gaining cultural definition and legitimacy. For example, in the context of the prison, the power achieved and held on to by those at the top of the prisoner hierarchy is to some degree legitimised, normalised and sustained by its opposite number at the bottom. Put simply, the hegemonic masculinity at the apex of the hierarchy of power – represented most strongly by the professional criminal and armed robber – is culturally reinforced by its opposite number at the bottom – the rapist and paedophile who deviate from conventional heterosexual masculine norms.

An interesting aspect of the prison hierarchy is that, although it has always existed, it has changed in recent years to the extent that there are now many more prisoners prepared to inflict physical violence on those who languish at or near the bottom (Coyle 1994). One of the most significant factors in the increase in interpersonal violence right across the prison population is the drugs culture which is evident in all British prisons. According to Coyle, however, it is also partially explained by the role of the tabloid press who give a high profile to criminal cases involving certain kinds of offences, encouraging other prisoners to place themselves in the role of vigilantes on behalf of society at large. The fact that the tabloids enjoy the highest circulation figures among the British press while reporting the lurid details of crimes against the most vulnerable members of society, yet frequently fail to report subsequent assaults by some prisoners on their fellow inmates, is perhaps a further indication of the implicit sanction society places on the exertion of hegemonic masculine values over weaker, subordinated ones.

Hegemonic masculinity in prisons, then, is clearly as bound up with aggression and violence as it is on the outside. That is not to say that the most violent men (in respect to their crimes or to their behaviour in prison) are the most powerful inside; indeed the volatile offender is more likely to be marginalised than respected. Nevertheless, a certain degree of 'controlled aggression' is required in order to survive the psychological and physical rigours of imprisonment. Ascendancy achieved by means of threats, bullying and predatory aggressiveness is *not* hegemony, but the necessity of establishing a no-nonsense, tough reputation on reception into a new institution is well documented in personal accounts of life inside (e.g. Boyle 1977; Probyn 1977; Shannon and Morgan 1996). Indeed, as in the world of manual work, the successful completion of 'initiation rites' is frequently an important element of establishing one's masculine credentials, and guaranteeing some acceptance by, and solidarity with, other men, in the hope of ensuring a relatively trouble-free passage through one's sentence (Grapendaal 1990). Conversely, if an inmate 'fails' his initiation test, or is for some other reason labelled as weak, he must live with the knowledge his reputation for weakness will spread, and that he may be targeted by his more aggressive peers. Such physical jostling for positions of power and status are common among lower working-class groups of males, but it is perhaps especially visible in prisons because they are such blatantly status-depriving environments and therefore create a particularly acute need for indices of relative status

(Toch 1975: 64). Of course, even after a tough façade has been established, it has to be maintained and this in itself can be a great source of pressure. Toch reminds us of the analogous nature of self and identity in his comment that some inmates go to extraordinary lengths to accommodate an image of themselves which conforms to the hegemonic ideal, but that their manly self-portraits crumble, indeed are 'relinquished with gratitude', during conversations with researchers (Toch 1975: 15).

Concluding thoughts

This chapter has demonstrated that the overt masculinity evident in so many studies of imprisonment has parallels in the wider culture beyond the prison walls. The explanation of aggressive masculinity in purely biological terms is problematic, but even if it is accepted that aggression has a biological basis, it is none the less also dependent on culture in so far as violence takes social forms and is therefore historically conditioned and culturally determined. In short, violence, whatever its roots, is generally enacted with knowledge of the rules and norms which govern the expression and control of aggression in any given time and place (Dunning *et al* 1988). Many studies have suggested that the criminal life of the offender begins with some degree of contact with delinquent or offending peers, through whom a criminal identity and perspective are acquired. Echoing Goffman's use of the term, Irwin (1970) states that any new phase of the offender's 'career', including the frequently cyclical path through arrest, sentencing, imprisonment and release, is structured by meanings and definitions brought to the phase from perspectives gathered earlier. Criminality as a learned response to the imperatives enforced by hegemonic masculinity is suggested in a number of inmates' autobiographical accounts, and sociological studies of lower working-class culture show the excessive display of one's masculinity, including aggressive and violent behaviour, to be a central feature of working-class life. It hardly needs to be stated that any previous contact or involvement with criminal perspectives and behaviour systems prior to arrest will inevitably shape the new inmate's over-riding prison identity and coping strategies.

But given the evidence already cited for the brutalising and psychologically damaging effects of imprisonment on all but the most 'prisonised' inmates, it would be naïve to suggest (as do Irwin and Cressey 1962, and Irwin 1970) that the prison is simply one functioning part of a wider criminal mechanism, and that inmates only adapt to incarceration to the extent of it being another integrated episode within a long criminal career. Indeed, to suggest that the social life of a prison revolves entirely around essentialist male beliefs and criminal ideologies not only presupposes that the inmate culture is virtually identical across all male prisons regardless of category, physical location and management policy, but is also tantamount to blaming the victims of the bullying, oppression and fear which characterise many prisons (Stevens 1994). Whatever their circumstances, individuals are not mere bearers of structure but are complex amalgams of several influences, responding to their life experiences with greater or lesser degrees of compliance and confrontation, and defining their own individuality in terms of both cultural conformity and resistance. As Layder (1994: 210) comments: 'unique psychobiographical experiences will intersect with the dynamics of particular situations and the influence of wider social contexts to determine a person's behaviour'. In prisons, as in other spheres of life, the marking of 'sameness' and 'difference' is crucial to the construction of identity positions and both may be reproduced and mediated through a range of symbolic systems and through forms of social inclusion and exclusion. For example, individuals may be marginalised (or accepted) on the basis of the crimes for which they are serving a prison sentence, or for their stance on a particular aspect of the prison culture such as drugs use, or indeed 'otherness' might be conferred on much more mundane and spurious grounds. Hyper-masculinity as an identity position can counter *some* aspects of marginalisation and is one of the most common responses to the imperative to conform to the lower working-class dominated prison culture. It is thus simultaneously a reflection of wider social norms and a response to the specific, unique properties of imprisonment. But not every inmate will conform to the hegemonic masculine ideal; as already demonstrated, hegemonic masculinity carries no intrinsic meaning without the subordinated versions against which it is pitched.

In its more general analysis of identity and the extent to which the self can retain a sense of agency in the most structurally restraining of environments, this chapter has made reference to a number of meta-narratives which have advanced social theory. Marxism, in putting social relations rather than an abstract notion of the individual at the centre of its theoretical system, displaced the view there is a universal 'essence of man' at the core of each subject (Bocock and Thompson 1992). Freud 'discovered' the unconscious, undermining the traditional Enlightenment view of the individual as a wholly rational being, capable of calculating the consequences of his or her actions. He also offered the first insight into gendered relations and the human fear of the 'other'. But psychoanalysis is almost entirely unable to account for the importance of

social, political and economic factors in constructing individual personality. Feminism's achievement was in politicising identity and shifting the
emphasis on how individuals are formed as gendered subjects, a theme
taken up by a new generation of gender theorists concerned to investigate
the origins, relations and forms of masculinity which are privileged in
late modernity. Finally, late modernity (or postmodernism) heralds a
period of significant social change which may have a profound impact
upon individual and collective identities, but whose long-term trajectory
remains uncertain.

Foucault is perhaps the most striking example of the rejection of grand
theory with its analysis of momentous historical individuals and events,
preferring to concentrate on the smaller narratives which analyse power
among groups who have been marginalised, stigmatised or neglected in
conventional historical accounts. However, Foucault ignores what Layder
(1994: 112) calls the 'interactive dimension of meaning'. While he is right
to highlight the socially constructed production of meaning at the level
of discourses, practices and power relations, he overlooks that element
of meaning that is produced through the 'inter-subjective processes of
negotiation, definition and general forms of creativity that are brought
into play whenever and wherever human beings mix socially' (ibid.).
Furthermore, his historical emphasis prevents him from analysing
everyday, situated behaviour, and even though his later work claims to
focus on 'everyday life', he remains strangely unconcerned with actual
face-to-face encounters or the minutiae of day-to-day interaction. This
omission of the intersubjective sphere weakens an approach which
otherwise succeeded in disclosing new dimensions of power and
alternative ways of investigating its effects (ibid.). The quest to look for
power at every level of society has led Bourdieu and Giddens (among
others) to reassert the importance of analysing everyday life, and to
revive the notion of human beings' inclination to be affected by, and
affect, their social environment. Influenced by Garfinkel and Goffman, it
is unsurprising that Giddens asserts that it is in the ordinary spheres of
mundane, trivial or fleeting interaction that institutions, organisations
and cultural patterns are reproduced over time and space. However, this
study accords the intermediate level of culture and interpersonal relations
a level of importance not found in Giddens' work, and will therefore use
Bourdieu's notion of habitus as a complement to structuration theory.
While the macro picture – the Home Office, prison service and wider
culture – is important to an understanding of media provision, access and
regulation, and the micro level – the personal use of media by individuals
– will illuminate the specific meanings and motivations sought by
prisoners from media resources as a means of overcoming the pains of

imprisonment, the meso level of the prison culture can also contribute to our understanding of prison life, particularly in relation to the construction and maintenance of identity. Following the example set by Burman (1988), this study is concerned to interrogate the concept of identity as it is defined and mediated through the microsphere of the individual, and the intermediate and macrocultural spheres beyond individual, private experience. The 'dialectic of control' present in all social structures encompasses a range of possible means of exerting power in the everyday context of the prison. The situational and social controls implemented by prison authorities and staff are well documented elsewhere (see, for example, Sparks *et al* 1996), but the opportunities for inmates to exert *their* agency – over each other and over the 'system' – are also numerous and varied, and will be investigated in relation to media access and consumption in the remainder of this book.

Notes

[1] The deprivation thesis - emphasising the degradations *indigenous* to the experience of imprisonment - has been challenged by the 'importation' model (Irwin and Cressey 1962); a social learning perspective that stresses pre- and extra-prison influences that shape inmate adjustments. Long regarded as competing perspectives, they are now generally regarded as complementary and the current study recognises that while inmates clearly import with them into prison diverse experiences, belief systems and moral standpoints (far wider indeed than one easily identifiable criminal subculture), none the less, the experience of confinement unites them, to some degree, in a shared experience of, and response to, pain and deprivation (Grapendaal 1990).

[2] 'Culture' is used by Willis in the sense that Mary Douglas (1966) uses it (itself a development of Durkheim's work), i.e. the public, standardised values of a community.

[3] A failing that Cohen and Taylor recognise of themselves in their later reflection on their research (1977).

[4] Although Giddens' term also incorporates the *formal* rules and resources that govern institutional conduct and is therefore of wider relevance in the prison context.

[5] Which Giddens highlights as being of particular interest to him (in Bryant and Jary 1991).

[6] 'Prisonisation' is a much-used term coined by Clemmer in 1940 (2nd edn 1958) to indicate the process of socialisation or assimilation which takes place when the prisoner enters an institution. Although often characterised as a destructive process, prisonisation is not simply a form of 'institutionalisation' as described by some (Zamble and Porporino 1988; Morgan 1997). Like institutionalisation, prisonisation may involve the acceptance of inferior roles and a large degree of passivity in relation to the formal structures of the institution. But it also indicates a positive willingness to accept the mores of the primary inmate group and is a rather more proactive survival strategy by which inmates learn how to 'play the system' and use the proliferation of underground economies, and the existence of subcultural gangs and hierarchies, to their advantage. These illegitimate activities, far from grinding down the inmate, actually provide him with the status and power necessary to ameliorate the sense of social rejection and loss of status inherent in the label 'prisoner' (Kalinich 1980).

[7] Two of the most compelling explorations of masculine violent crime that address psychoanalytic factors are case studies of the same man: serial killer, Peter Sutcliffe (Ward Jouve 1988; Smith 1993). The strength of these studies lies in their recognition of Sutcliffe's repeated failure to live up to social expectations of manliness, leading him first to blame the feminine in himself, and then to externalise the hatred and project it on to women (Jefferson, 1997).

[8] Interestingly, even prison officers actively colluded in this demonisation of sex offenders, and expressed surprise that the researcher wished to talk to prisoners in the VPU about male violence, the implication being that these were not 'real' men (Thurston 1996).

[9] Adler (1996) reports that 51 per cent of prisoners and 67 per cent of prison officers admit to feeling scared, while Scraton et al's (1991) study of Peterhead finds that 86 per cent of prisoners interviewed felt unsafe. Given the prevailing 'macho' culture, these figures are likely to under-represent actual feelings of fear.

[10] From the German '*Männerbünde*', or 'men's league', coined by early German sociologists to denote the kind of fratriarchy described here. Although, like 'fratriarchy', the notion of the *Männerbünde* is relatively under-used, it has been taken up in various guises by feminist writers, notably Millett (1971), Cockburn (1983; 1986) and Hey (1986).

[11] The underclass literature is too extensive, and the precise meaning of the word too contested, to explore thoroughly here, but 'underclass' will be used throughout this book in addition to the synonymic 'lower working class' because, with its subterranean connotations, in both left-wing and right-wing accounts it encapsulates the prison population, the *potential* prison population and, most importantly, the authorities' attitudes towards them.

[12] According to Connell (1987: 183), there is 'a bewildering variety of traits considered characteristic of women' but there is no superordinate version of femininity which is deemed more structurally powerful than others. *All* versions of femininity are subordinate to the patriarchal power of men, rendering any jostling for positions of power among women ultimately futile. There does exist, however, an 'emphasised femininity', constructed around compliance with the global subjugation of women, and organised at an individual level around the accommodation of men's interests and desires. There is thus likely to be a kind of 'fit' between hegemonic masculinity and emphasised femininity, which may help to explain why many women remain in violent relationships (ibid.: 185).

[13] The need to 'prove' one's 'womanhood' does not exist in the way that some males deem it necessary to prove their manhood, thus making the notion of hegemonic femininity even more untenable.

Chapter 3

Research context and methodology

In its consideration of micro, meso and macro forces, the empirical section of this book aims to take both audience studies and prison research in a new direction. To these ends, this chapter describes the research methodologies used to study the impact that the introduction of media resources into prisons has had on those environments, and on the people who live and work in them. The role media play in the negotiation of power and construction of inmate identities will be an important and innovative focus for, despite the extensive literature on audience behaviour, our knowledge of individual motivations and of the social constitution of mediated communication in localised, private, community-based settings remains at a primitive level, and there is currently little understanding of how identity develops from both selective and fortuitous uses of media resources (Lindlof and Meyer 1987).

Taking its lead from uses and gratifications research, but in a refinement of the model as outlined in Chapter 1, this analysis will try to account for the motivations *sought* rather than those gained and the meanings *desired* rather than those achieved. That is not to say that a study of needs *met* by various media is unlikely to shed light on people's perceptions of themselves, but illumination of the inner self is inclined to be more successfully achieved with an open-ended, discursive approach exploring motivations and aspirations, rather than measuring actual results observed as is characteristic of more positivistic studies. Of course the reasons why prisoners watch certain television programmes, listen to specific radio stations and read particular newspapers, magazines or books are broadly dependent on the same over-riding factors as those governing any other audience members. Above and beyond personal preference is habitus; age, family background, education and general cultural context all have a bearing on the media habits of individuals. Such personal factors may intersect with the policies of media producers so that viewers will frequently be 'interpellated'[1] according to their sociodemographic profile; hence the increasing output targeted at children, teenagers, young men, middle-aged women, specific geographical regions and even those inside or with a professional interest in prisons.[2] Availability and routine are also important factors; people are likely to develop loyalties towards particular media or channels which, in the first instance at least, are dependent upon the availability of reception. In terms of specific content preferences, most people will form early patterns of likes and dislikes for broad kinds of content (sport, news, comedy, soaps), although personal taste is, to some extent, always governed by awareness of alternatives (McQuail 1994). Most importantly, given the new direction in which this study is attempting to take audience research, individuals' media use will always be affected by social context, especially where viewing, listening or reading are shared – and thus may have to be negotiated or modified – with other, non-related, individuals.

All these factors have to be considered carefully when approaching the study of media consumption in prisons, for it is not being argued that media use takes a fundamentally *different* form within the context of a total institution. On the contrary, it is suggested that the reasons why people inside prison seek gratification from mass media are similar, yet intensified, when compared to those experienced in ordinary life. Prisons are both part of society and yet, at the same time, are extraordinary social environments. Consequently, media – while fundamentally fulfilling functions similar to those found in the domestic sphere and elsewhere – nevertheless may take on an elevated significance in a semi-closed institution. Arguably even more central in the unfolding of everyday life, media resources may give structure and purpose to otherwise unfulfilling existences, and give back to prisoners a sense of identity the institutional system has systematically violated. As with 'normal' viewers, readers and listeners, media use among prisoners might be largely a second choice activity when compared to 'real' social interaction with others, and similarly it may be the case that media are *used* far more than they are valued (Himmelweit and Swift 1976). But like the unemployed, prison inmates are likely to have a far greater degree of attachment to and appreciation of media as a source of entertainment, escapism, identity and opinion reinforcement, social interaction, or simply a means of enduring painfully slow-moving periods of time.

In accepting the basic premises of the uses and gratifications approach – that audiences actively use media resources for a number of identifiable purposes – this study is nevertheless predicated on the belief that individuals are not the sole initiators of action and that locus of control issues may lie beyond the individual user. Furthermore, the research methodology of uses and gratifications – which may include open-ended methods of inquiry, but also embraces survey reports, highly structured interviews and multiple choice questionnaires – is problematic, not only because of its implicitly prescriptive and positivist nature, but because of what Lindlof and Meyer (1987: 3) term the 'ambivalent, happenstance, routinised and class-determined character' with which such information-seeking is riddled. Their recommendation for researching the relationship between mediated communication and specific cultures is to adopt interpretative qualitative methods or, what is conventionally termed, 'ethnography', a research strategy that encompasses seven methods of analysis: participant observation, observation, 'just being around', group discussions, recorded discussions, informal interviews and use of existing sources (Willis 1974: 12–14). Although each of these methods is distinctive from the rest, they share a logic of discovery and alertness to the diverse forms and details of social life which means that, when used in conjunction with each another, they provide a holistic description of cultural membership (Lindlof 1995). As Willis (1982: 78) himself puts it: 'An ethnographic argument shouts at us that however persuasive and inclusive some of the theoretical arguments concerning the formation of the subject may be, they can by no means fully account for real, solid, warm, *moving*, and *acting* bodies in actual situations.'

The particular advantage of ethnographic inquiry for my purposes was that it implicitly understands Giddens' (1984: 285) assertion that we cannot adequately describe social activity 'without knowing what its constituent actors know, tacitly as well as discursively'. It thus allows the researcher to look beyond the obvious uses of media resources (those which are self-evidently reported by the respondent or which are easily observable to the outsider) to those less apparent uses and the meanings generated from them, many of which are embedded in the taken-for-granted contexts of everyday social usage. Ethnography is therefore an approach that can study local realities and needs without imposing the value assumptions of traditional media 'effects' research. Furthermore, with its complex layers of rules and behavioural codes that permeate the multifarious subcultures, the prison provides a fascinating and challenging environment for ethnographic study. Although direct observation of prisoners interacting with media in their cells is mostly prohibited, access to information about media use is freely available and, unlike conventional ethnographic audience research which, by its very nature, intrudes on the most private sphere of an individual's life – the home – the prisoner's access to media is, in some respects, much more openly displayed, whether he likes it or not. Rosters listing the names of inmates whose 'turn' it is to receive one of the wing newspapers are posted up on the wing office wall; prison librarians are only too happy to show the researcher the records of magazines and journals subscribed to by individual prisoners; radios and sound systems blare out of cell windows; and talk about television provides much of the substance of social intercourse. In fact, the boundaries between public and private are blurred to the extent that the deprivation of private space suffered by most prison inmates, together with the general level of mistrust accorded other inmates and staff, and the essentially punitive attitude of society at large, result in most prisoners being only too glad to talk to a non-judgemental 'outsider' about virtually any topic arising from their experience of imprisonment. All these factors combine to make ethnography a 'natural' choice and, relative to the audience research described earlier, prisoners are a willing group of informants less likely (indeed, less able) to keep some areas of their lives hidden from a stranger.

Despite observation of most interactions with media being impossible, observation of the wider context is relatively straightforward, and both prisoners and prison staff get used to an 'outsider's' presence very quickly.[3] Furthermore, observation is far from casual or detached; indeed, in a reflexive account of the research experience in prison, Alison Liebling favours the term 'reserved participation' (first coined by Tony Bottoms) to capture the sense of activity involved in what is otherwise sometimes assumed to be a passive role:

> [T]he term 'observation' does not adequately capture the process of being present in others' worlds. We see, observe, but inwardly (subjectively) digest scenes and encounters; our inner lives inter-playing with the lives of others. We watch, hear, take notes, drink tea, chat, experience periods of engagement, distraction, warmth, sadness or fear; we are entertained, frustrated, fascinated, puzzled – we are no more 'passive' agents in our research than our research 'partners' are (Liebling 1999a: 160).

In addition to undertaking this type of 'reserved participation', collecting interview data, predominantly from prisoners, but also from officers and governors, became the main objective of this part of the study. I administered a questionnaire on in-cell television to ten governors and seven other professionals working within the prison service (see Chapter 6) and informally interviewed several officers and at least one governor grade in each establishment. This multidirectional approach ensured that not only was detailed information about media access and availability in prisons gained, but also a great deal of data was collected concerning the individual and collective motivations that inmates bring with them to the viewing, listening or reading context. This correspondingly allowed interpretative conclusions to be drawn about the subjective meanings generated from media texts and resources, and the relationship between these meanings and the processes of identity adjustment that the experience of imprisonment entails. Before the interview schedule could begin, however, a period of detailed observation of the research context had to be undertaken. Extensive reading of existing literature on prisons was helpful in preparing for entering a total institution, but I felt it important to spend a reasonable amount of time actually inside a prison, interacting with prisoners and staff and observing at first hand the demands on the inmates' sense of self. The empirical study was undertaken between November 1998 and June 1999 at four men's prisons (with supplementary visits to two further men's prisons) of different security categories in central England.[4] The main and most intensive period of research took place at two Category C prisons, but prior to this I spent varying amounts of time (ranging from a few hours to five days) at the other four prisons, which allowed me to become acclimatised to what is, after all, an unusual environment. These visits also enabled me informally to test some of my general hypotheses relating to media consumption and identity.

Pilot phase

My first research site was Gartree, a Category B lifer establishment. In November 1998 I was invited to give a paper at a conference organised by the Gartree Debating Society on 'Prisoners and the media'. I followed up my paper with a visit to the Gartree Debating Society in the following January, and in February I spent a further five days at Gartree accompanying a new recruit to the prison service on an induction week for trainee officers. This was a fascinating insight into the expectations and fears of a young, female graduate recruit with no previous experience of prisons. It also enabled me to familiarise myself with the field, accustom myself to its unfamiliar practices and routines, and do some initial hypothesis-testing. Following my five-day induction, I returned to Gartree to take two GCSE sociology classes while the regular teacher was on holiday. Subsequently, I attended weekly meetings of Prison Dialogue[5] for three months early in 1999, at Whitemoor, a maximum-security Category A 'Dispersal' prison, and chaired a meeting of the Lifer Discussion Group there on one occasion. I also attended Prison Dialogue at Blakenhurst – a local, privately run prison – for two full days in March.

Finally in this early phase, I visited Leicester, a local jail, where I was shown round the prison by a training officer. Although much of this period was spent conducting preliminary investigations and was intended as an extended pilot exercise, there was never a point at which I felt one stage of the research had finished and the next had begun. Rather, it was a continuous process of exploration and discovery, in which a holistic approach was taken. As time went on I refined my questions and my selection of respondents probably became more astute, but there was no clearly defined point when I could claim the 'real' research began.

The main phase of research

The main research sites, where the most intensive period of investigation was carried out, were HMP Ashwell and HMP Stocken, two Category C training institutions separated by less than ten miles in the English East Midlands. These two prisons were chosen at the suggestion of the Prison Service Area Manager because of the 'open' and progressive outlook of their management teams, their contrasting style and features, and their geographical proximity to each other. Prior to my fieldwork, the Governor and Head of Inmate Activities gave me a comprehensive tour of both prisons, respectively. This had the advantage of giving my presence some sense of legitimacy in the eyes of the prison staff, which eased the research process later on when I was largely relying on officers to introduce me to willing inmates. I was also allocated keys in both prisons, which similarly appeared to authorise my presence in the eyes of both staff and inmates. Indeed, in both these establishments my stays were marked by a remarkable level of co-operation and interest in my research, and the relatively relaxed regimes ensured I quickly felt part of the conceptual and social furniture.

It soon became clear, however, that 'fitting in' to the everyday rhythms of a prison culture – to the extent where inmates and staff equally accept one's presence and legitimacy – is a delicate balancing act. While it is important that a certain amount of approval is given (and, more significantly, is seen to be given) by both parties, it is also critical the researcher should not be seen by either group as over-identifying with the other. Thus, while maintaining good relationships with the prisoners and protecting their confidences, I simultaneously had to work at sustaining cordial relations with staff, many of whom were keen to know what inmates had said to me. However amicable the relations are between staff and inmates (and I believe Ashwell and Stocken to be quite good in this respect) there is always a degree of 'them' and 'us', and I

67

sometimes found myself treading a fine line between upholding the relationships I had formed with inmates, and keeping 'on side' with the staff who view security as their highest priority and are obliged to write reports on the minutiae of their charges' lives, however trivial it might seem to an outsider. So emphatically drawn are the lines of demarcation between officers and prisoners that I found myself subconsciously devising a number of strategies for distancing myself from the discourses and symbolic practices of the prison staff when with my inmate respondents. These strategies ranged from wearing clothing which could not be semiotically construed as any kind of uniform (in the way that even suits can be 'read' in terms of their signification of power and status) and using prison vernacular or 'argot' when appropriate, to making clear to participants at the outset of each interview that I was a university researcher, independent of the Home Office and prison service, and with no particular agenda, political or otherwise. This *modus operandi* seemed necessary for three principal reasons. First, the keys I had been issued are arguably the most resonant symbol marking out the powerful from the powerless, the keepers from the kept, in this environment.[6] Secondly, because I relied on the officers' good will to let me use their offices and to select suitable participants for me to interview, and because I was interested to hear their views on a number of aspects of my research, I frequently found myself having to justify to inmates the many hours I spent in wing offices. This led to a third difficulty: while spending a great deal of time with staff, I none the less had to maintain an ideological distance from them, at least in the eyes of the prisoners. In many respects, I found the occupational culture of prison officers much more difficult to remain impartial towards than the inmate culture. I had gained some knowledge of the occupational practices and beliefs of officers at Gartree which afforded me direct experience of the structures and informal rules of the prison officers' 'canteen culture', including the residues of sexism, racism and lack of humanity towards convicted offenders that one might expect to encounter. On the other hand, during my many conversations and interactions with individual officers, I found that, far from being opposed to every aspect of their occupational culture, I identified with much of what they told me, including some of the contradictory feelings they expressed with regard to those in their custody. With both groups I found that the least troublesome strategy was discretely to concur with whatever was being said about the other.

In-cell television and 'Incentives and Earned Privileges'

Although the potential uses of the full range of media were of interest to me, one of the key factors in shaping my fieldwork was the concomitant introduction of personal television sets for individuals' use in cells (hereafter termed 'in-cell television' or TV). Consequently, at Gartree, Whitemoor and parts of Stocken, in-cell TV was being installed for the first time while I was there, and at Ashwell it had been present for only six weeks. At all the prisons, unsurprisingly, questions about entitlement, restrictions and cost of the new scheme were paramount. In-cell television had been a salient issue for at least five years prior to the start of my research, but it was of particular significance at the time of my fieldwork because the Home Office had just announced that the scheme – at that time restricted to 2,500 sets – would be extended across the prison estate. It was to be implemented as part of the 'Incentives and Earned Privileges' (IEP) scheme, an initiative introduced in 1995 following the publication in 1991 of the report of the inquiry into the disturbances at Strangeways by Lord Justice Woolf. One of Woolf's key recommendations was that prisoners' rights should be formally established in the form of 'contracts' or 'compacts' between governors and inmates, setting out the legitimate expectations to which an inmate is entitled. It was Woolf's intention that institutions would have to provide, in writing, the reasons for any decisions which would adversely affect any prisoner, such as being placed in an institution of significant distance from his home or being transferred to a new prison without warning or explanation, both of which are reasonably common occurrences. However, when it came to policy formulation, the prison service interpreted the findings of the Woolf report rather loosely, so that the basic entitlements which Woolf thought prisoners have a right to expect were, in the end, designated 'privileges' to be earned by compliance and good conduct, or withdrawn for bad behaviour or misconduct. There are essentially three categories which inmates may fall into, which determine the type and amount of privileges they can expect: Basic, Standard and Enhanced. In most of the prisons I visited, inmates enter the institution on Standard regime (although in some prisons inmates may start on either of the other two levels). After a period of time (which varies from prison to prison) Standard prisoners may advance to Enhanced status if they meet the pre-required criteria. If, however, they disobey the prison rules, they may be put on to Basic regime and, in some prisons, isolated in a specially segregated Basic Regime Unit (BRU), with consequent loss of status and privileges. One of the key intentions of IEP was to achieve some uniformity in the prison system as a whole (Liebling *et al* 1997). However, the anticipated coherence in policy has only been partly achieved because some acceptable earned privileges can be devised locally and some prison governors have interpreted privilege entitlement policy more liberally than others. In fact the scheme is frequently interpreted loosely enough for the staff of some institutions to talk of a 'Super-Enhanced' regime for the especially well behaved, and a 'Sub-Basic' regime for the especially troublesome. In the case of the former, accommodation is often separated from the main wings (in Stocken and Ashwell it is housed in mobile units originally built for oil workers in Scandinavia, and affords inmates the 'luxuries' of carpets, washing machines and 'real', i.e. metal cutlery). The latter usually refers either to the prison's segregation unit or 'punishment block', or to the threat of being moved to another wing or even being 'shipped out' to a more notorious prison.

Not part of the formal nationwide IEP policy at the time of my research, in-cell television was one of the privileges being implemented locally. For example, Stocken was one of two prisons which had had in-cell TV since 1992, when it was installed in one wing as part of a trial experiment, but during my research it was being extended to other wings accommodating Enhanced prisoners. In both Stocken and the other pioneer of the scheme (Garth in Lancashire), it was acknowledged by prisoners, staff and governors to be a success, yet between 1992 and 1997 rumours persisted that personal TV sets would be withdrawn at the demand of the Home Secretary.

Jupp (1989: 136) highlights the importance of timing in relation to research, noting that the nature of interplay between the key individuals – subjects, researcher, gatekeepers and sponsors – is largely dependent upon the political climate which is both reflected in, and framed by, the government of the day. The research on which this book is based was formally begun in October 1997, some five months after a 'New Labour' government had entered office with the biggest majority of any postwar government, following eighteen years of Conservative rule. A distinctive feature of the Conservative 'New Right' ideology had been that from the early 1980s there was a rapid drift towards a 'law and order society' (Hall 1980) which, among other things, resulted in tougher sentencing policies and more offenders being imprisoned (Dunbar and Langdon 1998). One of the key engineers of this hard-line policy in the latter years of the Conservative administration was Michael Howard, Home Secretary from 1993 to 1997. Following a brief period of optimism after the publication of the Woolf report in 1991 (in which the idea of in-cell television as a potential earnable privilege was first given formal recognition), prison reformers had to concede that despite all evidence to the contrary, Howard strongly defended the efficacy of imprisonment as a criminal justice strategy, and believed that the more humane prison regimes become, the less effective they are as a deterrent. The 'get tough' rhetoric of that political era – variously termed 'authoritarian populism' or 'populist punitiveness' – thus extended to conditions inside prisons. Although Woolf had brought an end to the practice of slopping-out and ensured that basic conditions in some of the worst prisons improved, the new Home Secretary did not want to appear to be 'soft' on any aspect of penal policy. So it was that, in April 1996, Michael Howard announced he was withdrawing television sets from prison cells.

Howard's decision did not come as a surprise for most prisoners and prison service personnel, as the availability of personal television sets for individual prisoners' viewing had always been a contentious subject. First discussed in 1981 by a working group set up to evaluate control in dispersal prisons, in-cell television has been the subject of fierce debate within the prison service and in political and public arenas. At the heart of the prison service's discussions about the scheme was that the potential advantages – that television 'normalises' the prison regime, that it provides a powerful incentive for good behaviour, that it links inmates to the outside world and so on – must be weighed up against the potential disadvantages, to both prisoners and prison staff. Among the drawbacks outlined by the original working committee were that in-cell television might result in a lack of interest in association and employment; that there was a risk of a decline in staff/inmate relations as a result of less face-to-face contact; that it might be seen as a way to make earlier lock-up times acceptable to prisoners; and that the numbers of inmates attending voluntary evening classes would drop (McClymont 1993). In addition, the scheme faced hostility from the Prison Officers' Association who feared that earlier lock-up times and reduced association activity would result in job losses for staff.

For the government, however, the main issue regarding in-cell television was almost certainly public (specifically, its own electoral constituency) opinion. In 1996 Howard publicly rejected the advice of Sir John Learmont who, in a report on the escape of three life-sentence prisoners from Parkhurst in 1995, recommended extending the installation of in-cell television across all prisons, and announced, to the contrary, that the twenty prisons which currently had the facility would be required to remove televisions from cells almost immediately. A tongue-in-cheek editorial in the *Guardian* announced the news on 22 April 1996:

> The *Sun* will be ecstatic. The hard-line, no-nonsense Michael
> Howard is withdrawing television sets from prison cells. Good old

71

Howard. British criminals have had it too soft for too long. It is time the nanny state stopped such namby-pambying. What thugs sent to prison need is an old-fashioned dose of austerity and hard discipline. That would make sure they didn't repeat their crimes on release. But would it? Indeed, will withdrawing TVs improve prison security? Ask Sir John Learmont, the tough army general invited by Michael Howard to review security after escapes from Parkhurst and Whitemoor. His 250-page report last year included a long list of ways in which security could be tightened. One involved extending the use of TVs in cells, currently restricted to 20 prisons. The reason was simple: TV reduces tensions, leaves prisoners with less time to dwell on grievances, frees prison staff for more constructive tasks than patrolling landings. Michael Howard knows this but prefers to maintain a tough image rather than pursue a realistic policy.

When a New Labour government was elected in 1997, many reformers and prison sociologists hoped that a more liberal approach would be taken to prison policy. Indeed, although it is arguable that the rhetoric, philosophy and policies of Blair's government are not strikingly dissimilar to those of their predecessors, their commitment to installing in-cell television across the prison estate is generally viewed as a humanitarian decision, even if its roots are economic. Furthermore, after a political era in which academic research was treated with suspicion, if not outright hostility (Jupp 1989), there can be little doubt that relations between the Home Office and the academic research community have improved in the last few years and, although psychological, quantitative research is still preferred, it has been noted that there has emerged in recent years a 'small number of more imaginative and sociologically informed pieces of prison research' (Matthews 1999: 92). Given this new relative openness, it was somewhat disappointing to discover in the course of my research that decisions concerning the availability and access to prisoners of media resources were still marked by a strong degree of sensitivity and official reticence.

Research strategy and methodology

Access is a continual process of negotiation and renegotiation in prisons which does not necessarily end when you are 'in'. In all prisons there exist a series of layers of people who have the power to grant or withhold access. The most obvious source of this power was the officers on wing duty on any given day. For much of my stay at Ashwell and Stocken I asked officers to suggest inmates to be interviewed, and they usually went to fetch them from their cells or rang the workshops to ask them to be released and returned to the wing. In general, they made their choices on the basis of those who were immediately visible or available, those who would be interested in the topic, those who were articulate and thoughtful or, occasionally, those who were serious offenders, or who would be aggressively opinionated. The latter were considered worthy of a 'wind up' and were brought to me amid much sniggering among the officers but, in the spirit of the sport that was being acted out, I went ahead and interviewed them and found them to be among my most informative respondents. This source of entertainment was taken only so far though, and was confined to those inmates who the staff found merely difficult or troublesome. On the whole, I trusted the officers to find suitable respondents for me to interview, and I was grateful for their knowledge and understanding of the people in their care.

Another important source of access was the inmates themselves. Such is the micro-politics of research that I knew that gaining formal, physical entry into the prison did not guarantee me informal, social access. On my first day at Ashwell, a life-sentence prisoner refused to speak to me, and predicted that none of the other lifers would agree to be interviewed either. His reason was that they had all talked to outsiders before and had not benefited in any way from the experience. It crossed my mind he may have influence among the other lifers, and might act as an unofficial gatekeeper, but happily this was not the case. All the other inmates I requested meetings with were only too happy to break the monotony of the day and tell their stories to an interested observer. After a day or two in each prison, the inmates got used to seeing me around, and word got out about what I was doing. Frequently people would stop me in the corridors and ask if they could talk to me, or those I had interviewed would suggest names of others who would be interested in my research. This proved a useful network, and gave me easy access to prisoners with strong views on my broad areas of concern, although it perhaps also had the effect of leading me to people with a particular axe to grind about in-cell television.

I interviewed seventy-two prisoners. Sixty-two were interviewed individually: twenty-eight at Ashwell and thirty-four at Stocken. Ten further inmates at Stocken took part in three focus groups: one of four participants and two of three participants. In line with other reception studies which have drawn participants from 'naturally' existing groups or communities that exist independently of the research, I did not restrict my sample to a particular set of variables. As mentioned previously, the main criterion for interviewing respondents was that they were prison inmates who had been 'selected' by an officer, recommended by another participant or who had volunteered to be interviewed. At the same time, however, the selection of respondents did have to be shaped by myself to some degree, so that they might highlight possible differences in perception caused by factors such as age, habitus, sentence type and length, IEP status, residence on a particular wing and so on. The particular benefit of being in Category C prisons was that my research participants ranged across the whole spectrum of ages, offending histories and prison sentences, from young petty offenders who were inside for just a few weeks, and who regarded their sentence as a mildly inconvenient interruption in their normal routine, to the older (in some cases, quite elderly) 'professional criminals' many of who had spent their lives in correctional institutions and had previously experienced several prisons at the 'heavy' (that is, Categories A and B) end of imprisonment. The sentence lengths of my subjects ranged from eleven weeks to life, with an inmate in his thirty-third year inside being the respondent serving the greatest continuous length of time. In both institutions, I interviewed more long-termers than short-termers, and there was a slight over-representation of lifers.

Most interviews were conducted on a one-to-one basis, although towards the end of the research period I experimented with changing the format to include some interviews with small focus groups of three or four people, anticipating that respondents might make sense of their experiences differently and in greater depth by talking them through in conversation with others (Hansen *et al* 1998). The vast majority of television audience studies have used focus group interviews as their primary means of investigation, in order to explore how viewers interact with a specified text and with each other so that meanings are *collectively* constructed through talk and exchange. This approach can, in part, be defended by the fact that for most of us, watching television is primarily a social activity, and interaction between people in a group situation is a normal feature of most people's viewing. In the prison context, however, media use arguably has more profound implications for the *self* than it does in general life, and the circumstances of most prisoners' viewing have altered with the introduction of in-cell television, so that media use is generally a solitary activity. Certainly, I found that group interviews simply encouraged consensus, and participants seemed rather more inhibited in volunteering their thoughts and experiences in front of each other than when they were simply talking to me.[7] As Hansen *et al* (1998) point out, part of the difficulty for the researcher in eliciting information about how people interpret, accommodate and negotiate media content is that most people do not consciously think about, let alone articulate, how they *use* media content in their daily lives. To encourage prisoners – who, by the very circumstances of their imprisonment are used to keeping their thoughts and feelings to themselves – to talk in depth about a subject usually discussed with a level of superficiality reserved for the weather (Höijer 1990; Hansen *et al* 1998) required careful handling. I therefore adopted some of the concerns and methodologies of oral history; a decision which was, to some extent, borne out of the interviews themselves. The result of the intentional interview bias towards lifers and long-termers was that I talked to some people (both inmates and staff) who had very long histories in the prison system, and several interviews took on structural-historical dimensions as life-histories were recounted and specific processes (for example, the introduction of radios into prisons) were described in terms of their particular historical-structural positioning. Although the current study cannot be said to constitute an oral history in so far as its interests are far broader than the relationship between present and past, it does share with oral history a commitment to exploring the 'felt texture of people's lives' (Deacon *et al* 1999: 291).

Like oral-historical accounts, its focus on talk, and in particular on the kinds of media talk generated in a discrete and bounded setting, required a level of mutual trust and respect that is most easily established in one-to-one encounters where interviews can be 'naturalistic', resembling unforced everyday conversation. Discussions which explored issues of identity and self in relation to both media preferences and to the lived experience of imprisonment frequently touched on topics that might be considered sensitive or taboo in a group setting. Moreover, the value of free-format, in-depth interviewing is that it can penetrate the defences people put up to prevent their hidden beliefs coming to light, uncovering hidden feelings, attitudes and beliefs of which they may be wholly or partially unaware (Giddens 1984; Berger 1998). This requires an atmosphere where information can be shared openly, and the interviews which yielded the richest and most detailed data were those in which a strong rapport was established early on between myself and the respondent.[8]

Because of this imperative, a further sampling bias should be noted; that is, that the majority of my respondents might be said to have demonstrated levels of articulation and intellectual depth beyond what might be expected from an 'average' sample of prison inmates. In keeping with other prison studies (Cohen and Taylor 1972; Lindlof 1987), I found that talking to more educated, articulate people eased the research process, both in terms of saving time in lengthy explanations regarding the nature and purpose of the research, and in the quality of information received. Additionally, it tended to be those inmates who were studying for academic qualifications and, in particular, university degrees, who were most interested in participating in the research project, and who volunteered most enthusiastically. However, in the interests of producing a maximum variation sample, and in order to avoid the elitism inherent in some of the prison studies of the past, I additionally sought out those who were less articulate or who had experienced only the most cursory level of education. But in the case of some of the most prisonised – indeed, institutionalised – of inmates, it was simply not possible for them to drop the public facade of cheerful stoicism and allow a stranger to penetrate their deepest thoughts about their experiences.

Among those who were most receptive, however, one of the key factors in establishing mutual trust and rapport was the structure of questioning, building from the general to the specific in a 'funnel-approach' (e.g. from the non-directive 'what do you think of x as a prison?' to the rather more focused 'to what extent do you feel like an individual in prison?' and the even more specific 'who is your favourite television presenter?'). The interviews were focused upon themes that had arisen from the literature review (although new themes emerged in the course of the fieldwork) and responses were written up under headings. All participants were asked about their attitudes to the prison they were in; about the effects of imprisonment on their lives, their social identities and their private sense of self; about the structure of their daily routines; and about the importance of media resources in prison. A list of pre-set questions gave a loose structure to the interviews, but I allowed the conversation to proceed in a fairly non-directive way to permit participants to describe their feelings and experiences at their own pace and in their own words. I obviously had to try to 'contain' the subject matter within the parameters of my research themes and I was keen to cover all the points on my list of questions with as many respondents as possible, so some prompting was inevitable. However, with most participants I was able to do this, while still allowing them to determine much of the pace and range of the conversation. Interviews varied in length between about twenty minutes to nearly four hours, although most lasted approximately $1\frac{1}{2}$ to 2 hours. When not interviewing inmates, I was either in the wing offices talking to staff, or on the landings chatting with inmates, often picking up on subjects we had previously discussed more formally in interviews.

As with all unstructured interviews there is a risk of personal reactivity; in other words, of the researcher altering the situation by her very presence. While this is unavoidably the case, I felt the vast majority of interviewees – while they may have slightly tempered their language and shown me a degree of what might be characterised as old-fashioned, 'gentlemanly' courtesy not usually found in general life – were unfailingly, candidly, honest in their responses to me. Indeed, many interviews yielded information, that was of a deeply personal nature, and breathtakingly frank. For several inmates, talking to me seemed to have a therapeutic effect (although I have no formal counselling skills, nor contrived to give that impression). Others were simply glad to have the opportunity to tell their stories in their own words and at their own speed, although in some cases this may have had a narcissistic edge as some respondents saw an opportunity to further their own causes. While some bargaining inevitably takes place between researcher and respondent (Lindlof 1995) I occasionally had to cut short interviews with those inmates who had very obvious personal agendas and who were keen to speak to me in an attempt to advance their particular political or personal interests. In some instances, ostensibly self-serving motivations for participation were also of interest to me (for example, in the case of the 'professional litigators' who are described below). But in other cases where it became clear the informant had an ulterior motive in speaking to me (such as the inmate who believed that I could influence the decisions of the Security Unit with regard to the early release of prisoners who had been electronically tagged) I discouraged their participation.

I decided not to use an audio or video recorder for fear of bringing an artificiality to the situation and disrupting the normal ongoing social process (Willis 1974: 13). My own 'presentation of self' was primarily that of a university researcher and, like others before me, I felt I would gain significantly more volunteers by explicitly stating I was conducting independent research than if I attempted any artifice of 'officialdom' (Grodin 1990, cited in Lindlof 1995). This independence from formal structures of power was reinforced by the informality I strove to create in interviews and which I felt was necessary for the generation of the kind of data I was interested in (Willis 1974: 13). I therefore rejected the idea of using a recording device because I felt it might lend an air of formality to proceedings and because of the concomitant possibility of reactivity, and especially the risk of respondents withholding information of a sensitive or personal nature or feeling that the tape recorder was a 'betrayal' of the informal and intimate nature of the relationship entered into (Hansen *et al*, 1998: 56). Confidentiality and the freedom to speak 'off the record' were of prime concern to almost everyone I spoke to, and a number of them reported they had confided in me information they had not told anyone else. For the same reason, although I made extensive notes as they talked, I wrote in full view of them. Much of my note-taking was in shorthand or illegible to anyone but myself, yet it seemed important to at least offer an impression of openness. In the three empirical chapters that follow, I have been careful to quote only what I know to have been recorded verbatim.

My identities

Finally in this section, I discuss aspects of my own identity on the grounds that, as Jennifer Hunt (1989: 42) eloquently puts it: 'fieldwork is, in part, the discovery of the self through the detour of the other' (see also Coffey 1999; Liebling 1999a). Of interest here are not only the identities that I sought to present, but also the various identities that were constructed of and for me by my respondents. At a superficial level my identities included those of doctoral researcher during the main interviewing stages at Ashwell and Stocken, tutor at Gartree and Stocken, conference speaker at Gartree, and dialogue group member at Whitemoor and Blakenhurst, all of which might be defined as 'outsider' identities. But at a more personal level, individual participants in my research assigned to me a number of different identities based on notions of my professional status, my social power and my gender. While not explicitly the identities of an 'insider', these constructed formulations certainly seem to indicate a transitional state somewhere between 'outsider' and 'insider', marking the passage between stranger and familiar acquaintance. Of course, these are not the only defining traits, and no doubt my age, social class, race, ethnicity and many other personal characteristics all shaped the research process (Warren 1988). But in terms of the identities that were constructed of and for me by inmates, it was my 'femaleness' in a predominantly male environment, my academic (and, by implication, non-prison service) credentials and my willingness to suspend moral judgements about respondents that appeared most salient in respondents' decisions about what, and how much, information to give me.

Professional Status

Many inmates positioned me as an 'expert' or 'intellectual' which was, on the whole, helpful in providing me with a non-threatening but responsive persona, and in allowing them to discard the more overt defensiveness with which they arm themselves during most encounters outside their own prison subgroups. This positioning generally placed me in a respected but somewhat distant position from respondents but was also used in support of their own views, as in one exchange at

Whitemoor where a participant in the dialogue group seized upon a minor disagreement between myself and one of the other Prison Dialogue representatives, Eric, concerning the safety of genetically modified crops and turned it into a full-blown verbal attack on him. The essence of the disagreement was that Eric, now in his seventies and retired, once worked in the chemicals industry and strongly believed that research into genetic modifications in the food chain should be allowed to progress unhindered. That I felt differently was hardly material when Dennis, a participant whose contributions to the group were frequently vociferous and confrontational, took over my position and started to ask Eric: 'Why should we believe *you*? *She's* the expert, *she's* the researcher, she hasn't got an axe to grind or a profit to make from it.' The noisy exchange continued for some time, and made both Eric and myself feel uncomfortable. Ironically, my argument had been hijacked by someone who was positioning me as the 'expert', yet was rendering me invisible and unheard.

At other times, their construction of me as an academic was far more inclusive, and on a number of occasions I felt that individuals were reaching out to me as a 'fellow scholar'. This first happened at Gartree where a prisoner introduced himself by that description on account of his status as a student undertaking an MA degree in music. Subsequently, several inmates related to me most strongly on the basis of someone with whom they could exchange information and ideas. Some took a paternalistic approach, seeing an opportunity to 'teach' me or pass on to me some of their own special interests. This occasionally happened with respect to television or radio programmes ('You must tune in to . . .'), but mostly occurred in relation to books, as with one inmate at Blakenhurst who was devoted to the work of Jane Austen, and an inmate at Ashwell who feigned profound disbelief that someone he had talked to happily for over three hours did not share his love of books by James A. Mitchener.

But it was again at Whitemoor that I encountered someone who emphatically and rather poignantly wished to relate to me as a like-minded and intellectual equal. On my first visit to the dialogue group, Robert told me that although he knew he would inevitably be regarded as 'one of them' (a 'con') he also felt himself to be like me. He said that if things had gone 'according to plan' he would have just finished university and be thinking about his career and marriage but, as things stood, he had to make do with reading for an Open University degree within prison. Over the next three months he always made a point of seeking me out and asking me about my research and teaching. He told me much about his family and his comfortable and happy childhood, all the while reinforcing his middle-class credentials and emphasising his 'otherness' compared to the group as a whole. His desire to be seen as someone other than a maximum-security life-sentence prisoner was profoundly affecting, and his 'otherness' was tolerated and even encouraged by the education staff who, on a later occasion, told me they had broken several prison regulations to allow him to continue studying for a science degree.

Social Power

A second dimension of my identity concerned the social power relations between my respondents and myself. As discussed earlier, I was attuned to the fact that, as in any encounters between strangers, signs of social, economic and cultural power can weigh heavily in setting the tone of the interaction (Lindlof 1995: 176) and I judged my dress and speech patterns accordingly. Given that social power relations between interviewer and respondent will inevitably affect how the event is perceived I was keen to establish a perception that we were equal partners in the interview process. This did not mean that we shared information equally, but that I was able to offer inmates the opportunity to express themselves and share their thoughts about their experiences of prison in ways not usually available to them. I came away from many interviews with the opinion that the quality of information I had gained from a respondent was matched by his own feelings of empowerment in participating. In many other research contexts, giving participants a sense of empowerment is a form of play-acting designed to give them the *impression* that they have a stake in the research project (Lindlof 1995). In the prison setting, however, a slightly different dynamic comes into play. As in other research locations, prisoners can assert their agency by resisting response to some questions, raising issues unforeseen by the interviewer, suggesting the relevance of some aspects over others and so on (Lindlof 1995). But unlike other research contexts, the prisoner exists in an environment where his opinion is rarely sought, and where he is seldom defined by anything other than his criminal history, the degree of respect he publicly shows for the prison's formal structures of power or his willingness to toe the institutional line. The fact I was someone who was not interested in their crimes, was outside the prison hierarchy and was giving them the time and space to tell those aspects of their stories which they wanted to divulge, combined substantially to reduce the power differences which characterise most of their interactions in prison.

Gender

The primary dimension of my identity, however, was almost certainly my gender. Relatively little has been written concerning gender issues in sociological fieldwork and, with the exception of explicitly feminist works, most studies of total institutions – Goffman's *Asylums* (1961b) being a prime example – are 'ungendered texts' (Warren 1988: 54) in which the gender of researcher and respondents remains unproblematised (although Gelsthorpe and Morris 1990; Sparks *et al* 1996; Rawlinson 2000; and Smith and Wincup 2000 are among those who do address issues of gender in prison fieldwork). Where gender is discussed at length, as in Genders and Player's (1995) study of Grendon Therapeutic Community, in which they elucidate on the experience of being female researchers in a man's prison, their account is marred by a vainglorious tone which does little to enhance their professional credibility.

Warren (1988) distinguishes four themes relating to gender in anthropological field research that have some bearing on the present discussion. First, she highlights the fieldworker's entrée and initial reception as being a reflection of her gendered characteristics, including marital status, age and physical appearance. Her conclusion is that women are generally more likely to be perceived as 'harmless' by males, to the extent they may be afforded access 'bordering on trespass' (ibid.: 18). Certainly I was surprised at the level of access I was permitted during my research, not only to areas of prisons usually kept hidden, but also to confidential files on individual prisoners. As it happened, I was uninterested in looking at documents detailing the criminal and prison histories of the men I was interviewing, as they were of little relevance to my research and potentially could have adversely affected my attempts to instigate relationships based on equality of power. But the very fact that several (male) officers offered me the opportunity to view private files to which prisoners themselves do not have access, despite very often having only a very limited understanding of my research, may support Warren's suggestion that my gender provided me with a harmless façade. Alternatively, it may simply indicate the disregard many prison officers have for prisoners, and their obstinate refusal to see them as human beings with rights to privacy and confidentiality.

Warren's second theme is that of 'finding a place' within a strange culture. Here the role of gender is problematised, for not only does the female researcher have to conform to assumptions about women being unchallenging and compliant (characteristics that are commonly associated with the private or domestic sphere), but she must also be seen to be operating successfully in the male-dominated public sphere. It was certainly clear to me that when interacting with prison officers, those characteristics traditionally associated with masculinity – participation in good-humoured banter, the ability to be seen as 'tough but fair' with inmates (or on occasions, just tough) and so on – were more highly prized than those traditionally associated with femininity – compassion, empathy and patience. This fact was brought home to me by Julie, an officer who was nearing the end of her probationary period, and who confided in me that she intended to leave the prison service because she felt alienated and victimised by her male colleagues. Of particular grievance was the fact that she was not allowed to display any signs of compassion or humanity to the inmates. If a prisoner asked for his cell door to be unlocked, the culture of the staff office dictated that you made him wait, even if you had nothing else to do. When Julie responded immediately her colleagues rebuked her.

The third issue Warren highlights as being an important consideration for women entering a predominantly male culture is that of sexuality and the body. As a novice to prison research, I went into the field with a set of expectations based on common assumptions about sexuality in prisons, augmented by knowledge of studies by researchers such as Sykes, who suggests that the deprivation of heterosexual relationships is one of the severest pains of imprisonment. It was something of a surprise, then, to discover that a number of female prison officers accentuated their sexuality through the use of make up, jewellery and perfume.[9] A number of my prison respondents talked about these women scornfully and the view that they might be 'asking for trouble' was widely expressed. For other inmates, the youthfulness and sexual attractiveness of some of the female staff only served to intensify their own experiences of ageing and fears of physical deterioration. For example, Herbie confessed he sometimes found himself 'running around after the girls as if I were still thirty years old'. Having spent several decades inside, the passage of time has stultified his awareness of his growing maturity: 'I haven't got a day older since being in prison. I'm still thirty. I forget that I'm really sixty-odd. I wonder why I'm not getting anywhere with the female screws and then I look in the mirror and of course get a shock.'

During my research I was not aware of any problems arising from my gender or my sexuality and, in general, female researchers probably exploit such factors to their advantage (Smith and Wincup 2000). However, Warren notes that in many cultural settings, the customs of gender restrict women partly or completely from some settings such as male-drinking locations. These 'men's huts' (Remy 1990) are where men traditionally spend time together in relaxation and 'play' and, in the prison setting, the closest approximation to such venues are the wing association rooms which often contain bar-style recreation facilities such as pool tables and table-football, as well as televisions. It was when these rooms were occupied that I most felt like an intruder, especially in the early evening when the formal structures and routines are relaxed. When surrounded by large groups of prisoners, constructing their 'own time' watching football on TV or playing pool, my presence seemed inappropriate and invasive. Warren (1988: 29) suggests that it is perceived wisdom that women who enter 'men's settings' transgress common and cross-cultural codes of behaviour and open themselves up to 'sexual overtures'. It was perhaps with this subconscious thought that I retreated to the staff offices when inmates were clearly at leisure.

In the one-to-one interviews, however (all of which took place during the 'working day'), my female 'otherness' – like my construction as an intellectual – served to place me in a respected but somewhat removed position in relation to the prisoners. Despite asking all my participants to call me by my first name, a small number insisted on calling me 'Miss' as they did the female officers and other staff. In her study of gang members, Horowitz (1986) notes she was constructed as 'a lady' which acknowledged her femininity and otherness, but also implied she was sexually unobtainable. It seems fair to suppose that the designation of the term 'Miss' served the same purpose. Horowitz goes on to suggest that the gang members' construction of her as a 'lady' was subsequently dropped because her persona did not fit in with the female social workers who were most frequently ascribed the label. She was much more personally and informally involved in their activities than were the social workers who remained emphatically 'outside' the cultural processes, alignments and codes of the group. In time, she was accordingly addressed by her first name and ascribed the role of 'reporter'; an identity that transcended gender (ibid.: 414–16).

For those prisoners who insisted on calling me 'Miss', however, there was no such chance of greater involvement, and interviews with these men tended to be of limited value. The ascription of a form of address more usually reserved for female officers, psychologists and teachers carried with it a range of obligations and expectations, which no doubt affected both my performance and that of the interviewee. In short, those inmates who constructed my identity as a 'Miss' – the equivalent of Horowitz's respondents' notions of what constitutes a 'lady' – were more restrained in their language and their manner than those who used the more personal form of address, and they were more likely to resist my attempts to build up a rapport with them. Likewise, those respondents who called me by my first name were, on the whole, more relaxed, and more inclined to accept and contribute to a sense of rapport[10]. They also more readily identified me as an independent 'researcher', an identity which – like Horowitz's status as 'reporter' – provided them with the necessary identity with which I could ask them questions and they could readily and openly respond (ibid.). Like Horowitz's informants, the majority of prisoners whom I spoke to were able to think of me as a 'researcher' in a way which transcended gender. For some, it even allowed them to befriend me and regard me as 'one of them' (or even as 'one of the lads' as one inmate said towards the end of my visits to Ashwell, as opposed to the more ambiguous 'one of *them*', referring to all those with officially sanctioned power over them). To this extent, and with a small number of inmates in each establishment, rapport was superseded by genuine, if very transitory, friendship.

It would, however, be a mistake to assume that the culturally ascribed identities that are commonly constructed around gender did not effect my research in any way. It would be naïve to ignore the possibility that some inmates were primarily motivated to speak to me because my gender and because my transience in the prison made me something of a novelty, and equally naïve to assume unproblematically that the intimate, 'confessional' interview – which itself is frequently characterised as a 'feminine' style – is guaranteed to uncover spontaneous yet 'authentic' material. Bourdieu (1996: 27) notes that the more confessional the interview, the greater the researcher's claim to have produced 'an extraordinary discourse' yet, as he further implies, and Murdock (1997) develops, interviews are never simple expressions of belief or experience waiting to be uncovered by a competent and skilled researcher. Rather, interviews are 'always performances in which respondents assume identities and manage impressions' (Murdock 1997: 188). Recalling Sykes' (1958) belief that the loss of opportunity for relations with the opposite sex is one of the most profound deprivations felt by inmates, it was perhaps of little surprise that some interviewees engaged in performance based on established cultural rituals of courtship. In most cases this amounted to mild flirtation or asking me personal questions about where I live, whether I am married and so on. Often such questions were asked in a knowing, ironic or tongue-in-cheek manner, although one amusing incident occurred with a respondent who had constructed his identity around the dual themes of 'romantic' and 'musician'. Following my interview with him, I looked up to see him with a guitar under each arm being herded back to his cell by two officers. He had apparently said he was going to serenade me! It is also worth remembering Sykes' suggestion that, as we partially define ourselves in relation to what we are not, it is women who, by their very polarity, give the male inmate a masculine sense of self. As has already been discussed, the prison society involves many permutations of the 'proof' of masculinity, made all the more necessary and extreme in its manifestations by the relative scarcity of women. It is perhaps of little surprise, then, that some inmates constructed my identity in relation to their own hegemonic masculine positions, either affording me a level of 'gentlemanly' courtesy rarely encountered in other spheres of life or, alternatively, asserting their masculine credentials by using language and behaviour that are characteristic of the prison culture.

Warren's fourth theme is sexual politics. The question of whether male and female researchers can enter the same field and produce the same findings is one that arguably should be more rigorously addressed within accounts of sociological research methods. As mentioned earlier, the characteristics usually felt to be most beneficial to the ethnographer – for example, the ability to communicate and gain 'confessional rapport' – are those most usually associated with femaleness (Warren 1988: 42). However, as Warren observes, there has been a tradition in sociological fieldwork of emphasising the advantages of using male fieldworkers to interview male subjects. Notwithstanding the androcentric history of most fields of academic inquiry, members of the early Chicago School, which did much to shape modern sociology, assumed unproblematically that men are more likely to achieve rapport with respondents (both male and female) than women (ibid.: 43). Such considerations are certainly pertinent in the prison context, and I have no real way of knowing whether my gender was a factor in the way my research was shaped, or whether a male researcher in the same circumstances would have obtained similar or very different information.[11] Sociological fieldwork is always partly autobiographical, reflecting the researcher's personality, as well as those of her subjects, and it is not uncommon for researchers to have different interpretations of similar settings (Hunt 1989: 41-42). Lindlof (1995: 139) goes as far as to suggest that it might have been much harder for a woman to have gained access to the (American) men's prison he studied. Thankfully, this was not the case with my study and I judge that being a woman did not hinder the research process in any perceptible way. In fact, although I had no common experiential grounding with my respondents, it is arguable that a greater level of insight is gained from the interaction of differences. As Lindlof (ibid.: 140) perceptively comments: 'A fascination with the border separating "us" and "them" is sometimes the impetus for inquiry.'

In conclusion to this chapter on research methodologies, it should be stated that what follows in the next three chapters is, of necessity, a distillation of my findings, although one which aims to capture the essence of the research experience in the prisons I visited. My primary concern is not just to report what respondents said, but to reconstruct how they *made sense* of what they were saying, and how their interpretations can *be made sense of* within the wider social and political context. To these ends, I have offered my own reflexive, theory-guided analysis of their accounts, so that far from simply attempting to present and synthesise the inmates' own descriptions and interpretations of their social practices, I have – in the tradition of critical sociology – attempted to 'relate action to that more inclusive constellation of facts in which it is set' (Burman 1988: 6). While my readings of their accounts may be markedly different from their own understandings of what they told me, and will almost certainly be expressed in very different language, my primary concern was to take a broader view of their first-hand experiences and the narration of their stories, and to contextualise them within the patterns and processes that inform the wider social structures, while at the same time taking account of the inner psychic realm which sometimes gives a significance to lived experience that is not transparent to the consciousness of the actor (Charlesworth 2000).[12] In short, a central tenet of the empirical accounts that follow is that neither the social practices of prison inmates, nor their descriptions thereof, are wholly the responses of individually orientated actors making rational decisions and statements with regard to the conditions of their existence (Giddens 1984). Actors' frames of reference are informed by a wide range of conscious and unconscious drives, and prisoners' actions will always derive from, and be a response to, the practices of others as they are ordered across space and time (ibid.).

As established throughout this book, the enveloping social structures that are internalised by individual prisoners (who subsequently act back on and shape those structures) represent the convergence of three separate spheres. First are the immediate spheres of personal history, family and friends that constitute the habitus of the individual inmate. Secondly are the intermediate spheres of the prison subcultures, informal networks of power, relations with prison officers and the everyday routines of life that constitute the unique habitus of the institution. Thirdly are the structures which shape, and which are shaped by, action in prisons, and which extend to the prison and probation authorities, to politicians, to the citizens who exercise political leverage on matters of penal policy, and to the symbolic and structural divisions brought about by capitalism and consumer culture. The fieldwork was thus conducted with three broad research questions in mind, each pertaining to the three respective realms: What meanings do specific media technologies and texts have for individual prisoners? To what extent and in what ways are media implicated in relationships between inmates and other inmates, and inmates and staff, within the prison culture? To what extent does prisoners' access to media address the requirements of the institution? My interpretations of my informants' responses to these questions are located within micro, meso and macro discourses of power, control, punishment, rehabilitation, normalisation, consumption, subcultural relations and identity formation.

Notes

[1] A term coined by Althusser, referring to the process by which ideology 'hails' individuals via familiar discursive, linguistic and symbolic representations and thus 'positions' them as an audience (O'Sullivan *et al* 1994).

[2] *Porridge, The Governor, Prisoner, Within These Walls, Jailbirds, Prison Weekly, Bad Girls, Maximum Security, Behind Bars* and *Oz* are some of the TV programmes about prisons and prisoners that have been aired on British television during the writing of this book.

[3] The number of non-uniformed staff in prisons is quite high and the university researcher does not particularly stand out from the prison psychologists, drugs counsellors, probation officers, tutors, administrative staff, management, outside contract workers and countless other anonymous personnel who are to be seen in prisons every day.

[4] It is perhaps worth reiterating that although a study of the impact of media in women's prisons would provide interesting comparisons, and allow for some of the feminist critiques of Radway, Morley, Gray, Livingstone *et al* to be developed, it was felt that such a comparative analysis was beyond the scope of this project. Feminist scholarship indicates that women use media very differently from men, and a study of media consumption in women's prisons would have thrown up a whole range of textual, social and interpersonal issues that could not be adequately explored here. Furthermore, the context of reception is very different: 'Even a cursory review of the subject reveals that there are major differences in the pace and processes of development of women's prisons . . . [as well as] noticeable differences in the organisation and functioning of women's prisons, and the types of offences for which women are incarcerated' (Matthews 1999: 13).

[5] Prison Dialogue – in brief – is a charitable trust working in prisons in the UK and USA that brings together inmates and staff and encourages them to talk openly and reflexively on any subject of interest to the group in an atmosphere of non-judgmental participation (see Chapter 5). See also Jewkes, (2001) for a fuller discussion of Prison Dialogue.

[6] Although aware of their potential symbolic significance (King 2000: 305), I encountered no resistance whatsoever as a result of having keys. Some officers expressed mild surprise that I had been entrusted with keys but inmates seemed completely unbothered; a finding that conflicts with Sparks *et al*'s (1996: 348) view that carrying keys is unprincipled and disadvantageous and that those researchers who do it should be 'taken to task for it by prisoners'. My experience was that having keys caused no problems at all, while *not* having them (at Gartree) presented numerous difficulties in getting around the prison, relying on officers to escort me, being 'stuck' in some areas of the prison for long periods of time with little to do, and even in reducing the legitimacy of my presence in the eyes of inmates and staff.

[7] The reticence of the focus groups to discuss their media habits with anything other than

the most superficial level of analysis may, in part, be due to the groups being so small. Hansen *et al* (1998) maintain that the ideal group size is between six and ten, although groups of twelve to twenty participants are not uncommon in audience studies. Certainly, in terms of stimulating richer and more sensitive data on viewing habits and the meanings constructed around them, the group discussions I had with the Debating Society at Gartree and the Lifer Discussion Group at Whitemoor – which numbered fourteen and twenty respectively – were much more informative and wide-ranging, and will be drawn upon in the empirical analysis which follows. In general, though, my experience mirrored that of Jacobs (1977: 221), who notes that 'skilled informants were able to provide far more information privately when less sophisticated inmates were not present to misinterpret what was being said.

[8] It is, in any case, much more common to find intensive interview techniques used in studies of prisons. The practical difficulties of gathering together a large number of prisoners, the security considerations which that scenario raises and the natural inclination of prison inmates to present a carefully controlled social identity when around other inmates make individual interviewing generally more accessible to the researcher than group interviewing.

[9] I always dressed comfortably and casually in clothes I would normally wear in everyday circumstances, neither consciously 'dressing up' nor 'dressing down'. Adams (2000: 391) provides an interesting account of her presentation of self through clothing while interviewing offenders, police and solicitors, concluding that 'dressing' for interviews (either 'up' or 'down') raised doubts in her own mind about her authenticity and integrity, amounting to the presentation of an 'unreal' or 'false' self. Jacobs notes that part of his presentation of self as a student researcher, independent of any formal structures of power, was to sport a beard – a strategy which is clearly only available to male researchers!

[10] For the sake of clarity, I am using the term 'rapport' here in the sense that others (e.g. Spradley 1979; Patton 1990; Lindlof 1995) use it, to denote a quality of communication that dispenses with the fear of being misunderstood, and signals to both parties that, on *this* occasion, conditions are right for disclosing thoughts and feelings (Lindlof 1995: 180). The existence of rapport does not imply any sort of bond between people; it usually involves respect for a person and for what they are saying, but it does not necessarily imply any degree of fondness or affection (Spradley 1979: 78). Rapport is thus a quality of a communication event, not of a relationship (Lindlof 1995: 181).

[11] One of the few obvious restrictions that my gender placed on my fieldwork was the reticence with which interviewees discussed matters of a sexual nature. Occasionally, participants would talk only in the most general terms about other prisoners' sexuality, but none spoke to me of their own sexual experiences in prison. Sparks *et al* (1996: 348) note that this is a common problem for female researchers carrying out fieldwork in predominantly male prisons.

[12] Charlesworth (ibid.: 84) puts it thus: 'sociology has to operate somewhere between ontology and poetry...find[ing] a mode of writing that can articulate being-in-the-world and yet which has the sensitivity of a poet's sense of the deeper meanings locked away in [speech].'

Chapter 4

The microsocial contexts of media use

As Chapter 1 demonstrated, the cumulative importance of emergent approaches to the study of media audiences is that they represent a significant shift in emphasis and methodology from what has gone before. Challenging the dominance of those who studied television and other media as fundamentally textual phenomena, these theoretical and methodological perspectives turned their attention to the social contexts and wider dynamics of cultural consumption (O'Sullivan 1991). Yet the contribution of media in shaping the cultural fabric of the twentieth century, and the ways in which specific media resources and texts have been employed by 'ordinary' people as sources of individual identification, empowerment and resistance, remain important but under-researched areas. In particular, there is still little understanding of how personal and subcultural identities are shaped by primary, secondary and tertiary uses of media resources.[1] The aim of this chapter is to address these issues and, specifically, to examine the media's role in relation to prisoners' adaptations to confinement and their constructions of a healthy, private, interior sense of self.

As the sociological prison literature reviewed in Chapter 1 illustrates, the exclusion of individuals from the social order is, ultimately, an injury to the self; 'it is the self which absorbs the lessons of rejection, which feels the syntax of practices shifting out of its control' (Burman 1988: 187). Agency is thus not simply the ability to 'do', or to 'make a difference', but perhaps should more accurately be conceptualised in the way that DeNora (2000: 20) defines it, as 'feeling, perception, cognition and consciousness, identity, energy, perceived situation and scene, embodied conduct and comportment'. This chapter will explore further the suggestion that the primary resource required to survive a prison sentence relatively intact, and to be able to revert to one's pre-prison identity on re-entering the community, is a deep backstage area where one can 'be oneself', 'let off steam' and restore one's ontological reserves. Media resources can help in this respect:

> I get angry and lonely, but not bitter. I know I can only blame myself. Thank God we're allowed CD players in here. I get rid of frustration by listening to Black Sabbath or Led Zeppelin very, very loud. It gets rid of the frustration but the anger is still there (Dave).

> I'm in my element now with five weeks of cricket on the telly. I find it very calming. It takes me back to who I really am (Bill).

These two quotations illustrate how individuals use media in highly reflexive ways to move through moods and reconfigure themselves in terms of who they really are. Using media as a virtual means of expressing or constructing emotion ('anger', 'frustration', 'calm' and so forth) is simultaneously to 'define the temporal and qualitative structure of that emotion, to play it out in real time and then move on' (DeNora 2000: 58). Furthermore, although media content changes its meaning according to the context of its reception, it can transport its audience out of their immediate confines, enabling them to transcend the mundanities of everyday life.

This notion of individuals using media temporally and spatially intersects with sociological accounts that note the special characteristics and organisation of time and space in prisons. This chapter will argue that time and space are dramatically reconceptualised in the light of their particular meanings and applications in the context of imprisonment and, moreover, in the context of the introduction into prisons of electronic and print media. The seemingly paradoxical relationship between media as a means of regulation and control, and as a source of identification and personal agency, will be explored in its microsocial context through place, time and space in an attempt to uncover some of the ways in which media culture (as well as specific media texts) produce material for identities, pleasures, resistance and empowerment, and how the introduction of media into the prison society 'fits' alongside other domestic priorities and (re)constitutes everyday life (O'Shea 1989; O'Sullivan 1991).

Identity and place

> They could lock you up twenty-four hours a day, I wouldn't care. Everything's superficial compared to the loss of liberty (Ray).

Loss of liberty and sequestration from the rest of society are t¹
features of imprisonment and for many observers these 'pain⸀
aggravated by the deprivation of material goods and services anᴜ
lack of recreational opportunities in prisons. It therefore seems reasonable
to suggest that media resources – and, in particular, television, being both
a material symbol of consumer consumption and the primary means of
electronic communication in the developed world – are a rare pleasure
that take on a level of importance which few of us in the outside world
can fully appreciate. Yet it is arguable that a limited and regulated level
of exposure to the outside world via the media of mass communications
paradoxically serves to intensify feelings of being removed from normal
life. There is a story – perhaps apocryphal – that in the famous prison at
Alcatraz, the punishment cell every prisoner most feared being placed in
was the one that had a barred window facing San Francisco Bay, where
people could be seen enjoying themselves on the beach and in restaurants
on the seafront. To be exposed constantly to a place they could not go
and witness scenes of enjoyment in which they could not participate
served only to heighten the inmates' sense of separation, and was seen
as the severest kind of punishment. And so it is with many long-term
and life-sentence prisoners in the UK, who reported they watch little
television simply because it is too painful to be reminded of a world they
are no longer part of:

> When the news comes on I flick over, I don't want to hear about it.
> It reminds me of what I'm missing . . . the outside world no longer
> exists. I don't dwell on what I could be doing. It's an utter sheer
> waste of time, the futility of being in here. Seeing it all on TV would
> only make it even worse (Neil).

For some, the sense of being segregated from the rest of society is
reinforced by exposure to visual media images to the extent they resist
opportunities to rent personal television sets. For others, it is audio media
that causes distress, reminding them of happier times in the past: 'it
sometimes gives me a real downer listening to music – it's the one thing
that makes me feel really separated from the world.' Others still seek
comfort in broadcast and print media, but feel frustrated that their sense
of isolation cannot be mitigated by their mediated access to the wider
environment. Pat, a life-sentence inmate at Gartree, told me how he had
had a life-long interest in Britain's industrial history, and was particularly
fascinated by the transport systems of the industrial age. He avidly tuned
into anything on television and radio that met this interest, and was
studying for qualifications in history and English in a further attempt to

develop his understanding of early industrial Britain. It was therefore with a degree of irony that he told me about Foxton Locks, the longest flight of working canal locks in the country, which is approximately half a mile from HMP Gartree. He said he had read about their importance and had intended to visit from his home in the north of England for years. Now the locks (and associated pub, shop and museum) were a short distance away, and he was reduced to asking friends to go there and pick up leaflets about them, on their way to visit him in the prison.

However, despite evidence of ambivalent or even hostile feelings towards the media, for most inmates any disadvantages associated with having wider access to media resources are generally offset by the fact that such means of communication may be the only way of keeping in touch with events beyond the prison, a feature that is more important to some inmates than others. On the whole, young and short-term prisoners were most likely to appreciate the media and were especially keen on in-cell television. Regarding their sentence as an unfortunate interruption (or in some cases a welcome respite) in their lives and offending careers, they tended to watch the most TV, relative to the prison population as a whole, and particularly appreciated the role of media in keeping them in touch with local events in their home regions, and with the story lines of their favourite television serials. Indicative of the general feeling was Nick, a young first-time prisoner serving three years, who said: 'it would be enough to drive people crazy if you didn't have media . . . you need to keep in touch.' John, serving ten months, took a more practical approach: 'it's important to keep in touch with outside. People in here have relatives serving in Bosnia, and they need to know . . . '. Older and long-term inmates were more conservative in their viewing preferences, tending to watch mainly the national news and perhaps one or two carefully selected programmes each day. Many older inmates said they would much rather have radio than television, a preference that may support Alasuutari's (1999b) contention that radio is a stimulant and that people often listen to radio as a way to stay awake or to raise their activity level. Consistent with Cohen and Taylor's (1972) research, many long-term and life-sentence prisoners equated television viewing with possible mental and physical deterioration, and feared being reduced to a vegetative state, almost literally a 'couch potato', although one respondent who was more than halfway through a twelve-year sentence said he watched more television in prison than he had outside: 'I like 15 To 1, 100%, all the quizzes. I like answering the questions just to make sure I'm not losing my mind.[2]

Another interesting difference between short-term and long-term prisoners (although one that I can only quantify in the most general terms because it was not a subject that arose in every discussion) was that while most inmates go to great lengths to 'colonise' their environment (Goffman 1961a, 1961b) by personalising their cells, a number of very long-termers and lifers said they had never done so. The finding that most inmates try to make their cells as individual as possible is hardly surprising; it is, after all, one of the few ways in which prisoners can publicly display their identities. But more extraordinary was that some inmates who were in their second, third or fourth decade inside reported they had never personalised or decorated their cells in any way, although their primary reason – 'it would institutionalise you to make it like home' – is rational and understandable. In most cells, however, it was customary to see family photographs and other personal artefacts and, while rules governing the use of prisoners' own duvets, curtains, carpets and other furnishings vary from prison to prison (an inconsistency in the regulations that most inmates consider grossly unfair), it is of some comfort to those who are eligible that personal television sets can give their cells the ambience of home: 'It's really nice to get in your pad in the evening with your tea and biscuits and watch TV in bed . . . it's like a little bed-sit' (Lloyd). In addition, cells often contain numerous symbolic indications of personality and self, many of which are assertions of masculinity and male (hetero)sexuality taken from the world of media and popular culture. 'Page three' style pictures of semi-clad women, pin-ups of young female celebrities, photographs and posters of racing cars or high-performance sports cars, and pictures of masculine role models from the worlds of acting, popular music and sport, are all common, as they are for the young adult white male population from which the prison population is predominantly drawn. By way of comparison, I saw some indications that African Caribbean inmates may have sought more political affirmations of their identities. In some of the cells occupied by black inmates, I saw posters of Malcolm X, Martin Luther King and Muhammad Ali. The conspicuous display of pictures of black heroes supports the view that images from media and popular culture can provide private reassurance to prisoners seeking to come to terms with their identities in an environment where those identities do not have majority public support (Gauntlett and Hill 1999).

In Morley's (1986) *Family Television* and Gray's (1992) *Video Playtime*, private consumption is most commonly associated with women, many of whom take 'guilty pleasure' from watching a sentimental video or romantic television series on their own. The pleasure gained from indulging in a 'nice weepie' was little diminished by the fact they were unable to watch this kind of material in the family context, because the male 'head of the household' had defined a hierarchy of material in which this kind of show came at the bottom. Many examples pertaining to the prison audience could be used as similar illustrations of this point, and are referred to elsewhere, but one example concerns the gay man who said his sexual preference was known only to one other inmate. Since in-cell television had privatised his leisure time, he had been able to view programmes that may have provoked derision or intimidation (or worse) had he attempted to watch them on communal, association room television sets. He cited the Channel 4 programme *Queer as Folk* (a drama series about the lives and relationships of three homosexual young men) as being among his favourite shows. Not only did this programme provide support for a personal identity he kept largely hidden, but it challenged conventional media representations of masculine hegemony, as well as the 'reality' of masculine heterosexuality in prison.

Styles of personal media use emerge as a product of both the inmates' normative consumption patterns in the outside world and the prison-adaptive modes they adopt inside. For some inmates access to media resources can remind them of their pre-prison identities. Lindlof (1987: 186) describes this need as a 'ratification of the continuity of self':

> Many inmates have a need to remind themselves of the primacy of their original, pre-institutional personal selves. This is, in a sense, a ratification of self that usually remains concealed in an environment of extraordinary distrust of others. This may be especially important during the early stages of incarceration, as new inmates decide their social personas . . . For most inmates, personal media represent a natural dimension of their lives. The media qua artefacts, with their familiarity and locus of control, become highlighted in the prison context.

Two important points are raised here. First, the familiarity of media content is highlighted as being important in relation to the ratification of self. Lloyd, a young man with three small children, commented: 'I still watch kids TV because I know my own kids will be watching at home, and I want to see what they're seeing', a sentiment that was reiterated by several other respondents. Secondly, personal media as a locus of control is emphasised. In an environment in which the most innocuous of negotiations can be fraught with possible misunderstandings and conflicts, and where personal agency is virtually non-existent, any element of control is likely to be treated as sacred. As a consequence, the opportunity in-cell television affords inmates to control their information flows by determining programme selection, viewing schedules and even when the on/off switch is used, represents a rare kind of freedom for many respondents:

> If you have a TV, it's as if there's a person in the cell with you, it's company . . . for some people television is important because it gives them a feeling of being in control. Even just being able to switch it on yourself and knowing that someone sitting in their house in Oakham is watching the same programme as you gives you a good feeling. With some of them though you could say it's because they have no sense of self. Without their television they don't feel like a whole person (Mr B).

In addition to helping prisoners maintain a sense of control of their environment, and an appreciation of their pre-institutional selves, access to media can result in the adoption of different consumption habits and in new identities being created in prison. Usually, this new persona is constructed around interest in, or loyalty to, a particular medium or text. For example, Sam, who had embarked on several educational courses since being in prison, spoke about how – on the advice of one of his tutors – he had 'discovered' the *Guardian*. He had since read it every day, and his strong allegiance to its style and political ethos had changed his view of his own identity and positioning in society, making him in his eyes 'literally a better person'. Similarly, Scott had started to read the *Daily Mail* regularly, which he also took as an indication he was changing for the better: 'I'd only ever read the *Sun* before I came in here. Well, not even read it really, just looked at the pictures. Now I read a proper paper and take much more of an interest in world events.' Another notable example was Dave, who claimed he had literally 'reinvented' himself since being convicted:

> I tried to reinvent myself when I got sent down. I wasn't happy with my identity before I came in, I felt a failure. Now I need to prove I can do what I'm doing. I'm doing an Open University degree . . . I read newspapers and watch TV, but select things that are a lot more intellectual than I would have before. It's all part of the reinvention of myself. I've matured more in the past five years than in the thirty-four years before. I'm studying Ancient Greek and I read proper newspapers. If I'd been put inside when I was sixteen I might have turned out a better person. I was a wimp when I came in; now I'm much more assertive.

Even among readers of the tabloids (who, according to prison librarians and officers, constitute the biggest reading public in prisons), strategies of resistance and empowerment are evident. Of relevance in this context is Fiske's (1992) analysis of why the tabloid press are so popular among the working classes. Arguing that the 'quality' press share the dominant ideology of the power bloc and are geared to producing belief rather than scepticism in their middle-class readers, Fiske suggests that the tabloids are more likely to take an oppositional stance to official sources of information, subversively blurring the distinction between facts and fiction, and thus actively engaging readers in the production of meaning. The polysemy of the popular press invites 'sceptical laughter', offering the 'pleasures of disbelief, the pleasures of not being taken in . . . of "seeing through" them (whoever constitutes the powerful *them* of the moment)' (ibid.: 49). Thus, while excluded from direct involvement in the power-sharing processes of democracy, the tabloids' generally lower-class readership can none the less be engaged in more micro forms of involvement in a 'semiotic democracy' (Stevenson 1995: 93).[3] This view was illustrated by Michael:

> I read everything in the *Sun* and the *Mirror* – the gossip, the politics, you name it. I enjoy reading about the latest cock-ups the police have made, and when NATO messes up, that's good to see. You shouldn't get taken in by what the politicians say and do. Most of them are clueless. I never used to read the papers, but now I try to read them every day. That was the first thing I was told when I got to prison. Try and read a paper every single day.

All these men might be said to fall into Irwin's (1970) classification of 'gleaners'; individuals who have rejected some of their previous subcultural values and undergone something of a 'conversion' (Goffman 1959; Cohen and Taylor 1972). To find that their access to media has augmented this process is interesting, for viewed in this way, mass media can be characterised as an effective leveller of inequalities between people of different social and cultural origins, providing them with a facility for stepping outside their normal habitus. Many of the claims that media use was related to changing attitudes and behaviour were accompanied by assertions that the individual in question had seen the error of his ways and would not be re-offending when released from prison.[4]

So, media can be used not only to reinforce their identities as prisoners or 'professional' criminals (as will be discussed in the next chapter), or to help them to keep a sense of their pre-prison selves, but it can also aid them in creating an entirely new identity independent of their past or present circumstances. In all these senses, media are providing an ontological narrative. Structuring experience in narrative terms creates order out of chaos and gives meaning to what otherwise would be experienced as fragmented (Mackay 1997: 76). Specific media texts help to create and support the stories that people tell about themselves within a physical environment that sustains frequent attacks on the fragile self, and also have an important performative role. But, in addition, media texts, and the discourses they provide, also supply a temporal continuity, a 'dailiness' that fosters routine. And as has been established earlier in this book, routines, both spatial and temporal are, crucial to the reproduction of social life, and to the warding off of personal anxiety.

Identity and time

Time is experienced differently in prison. As Chapter 1 suggested, although imprisonment is in essence about time, it is experienced as a form of 'timelessness', a state of suspended animation that led one of my interviewees to comment: 'it's as if someone has pressed the "pause" button on my life for five years.' Numerous commentators have made distinctions between different 'types' or conceptualisations of time, but one of the simplest and most pertinent distinctions in the current context is that made by Weigert (1981: 198), who suggests that all of us can conceive time in terms of its two major facets: when we make time – either for personal uses or to connect our time with other people's – we are involved in 'temporal construction'. Yet we must also cope with external demands on our time, that is, 'temporal imposition' (ibid.). In prison the overlapping processes of temporal construction and temporal imposition are arguably felt more acutely than in other spheres of life. Every aspect of prisoners' lives is governed by the institutional routine, from the moment that a klaxon rings out around the prison to signal the start of the day, to the demand for lights out in the evening. Yet within the externally imposed, rigidly structured time schedule, there may be an immense amount of unstructured time that has to be filled by the individual. A number of sociological studies have found that a surfeit of unstructured time can take its toll on people, resulting in disorientation and stress:[5] of 'being caged in a boring, regressive present' (Burman 1988: 139).

Research into whether length of imprisonment is correlated with a reduction in intellectual faculties is contradictory and inconclusive. Psychological research using methods such as structured questionnaires and psychometric tests has, on the whole, concluded that there is no causal relationship between length of time spent in prison and deterioration of mental faculties (Banister *et al* 1973). This, of course, is in direct contrast to the findings of Cohen and Taylor who were concerned with prisoners' deterioration in a much wider sense than could be measured by statistical tests of intellectual and cognitive ability (Jupp 1989). The key point is perhaps less to do with whether deterioration actually occurs or whether long-termers are more at risk than short-termers, and more to do with how prisoners *feel* about the possibility of their mental and physical health eroding. I found that the tedium of everyday life in prison was palpable, among both inmates and staff. But the distinct regressive quality of a life of confinement was expressed eloquently by prisoners, both in terms of feeling in a permanent state of arrested development or adolescence: 'I sometimes look in the mirror and don't recognise myself . . . your body changes, grows older, but emotionally you stay the same . . . you stay an adolescent', and also in fears of growing old and, in some cases, of dying in prison: 'that's my greatest fear – being carted out of this place in a box.' One inmate said he felt old before his time: 'I'm thirty-four but I feel fifty.'

Confinement, then, presents the inmate with great difficulties in using time and conceiving of future plans (Lindlof 1987). Many long-term prisoners deal with the 'uninterruptible stream of time' (Burman 1988: 140) by viewing parts of the day, week or year as distinct segments of time which are then judged to be either 'good' or 'bad' time. Most respondents, when asked to name the worst time in prison, answered 'night-time'. When in bed at night, introspection became a 'psychic quicksand' (ibid.: 189) that could no longer be avoided.[6] At one of the prisons I studied, there was a curious anomaly whereby lights had to be switched off by 11 pm, but TVs could remain on. Many respondents would thus watch television until late into the night, for reasons Burman (ibid.) illuminates:

> One can see the attraction of TV in this context. While television brought in the images and voices of the outer world, its 'competitor', introspection, gave a view of the inner world. The inner 'screening' (to continue the analogy) replayed past hurts and rejections . . . It unearthed suppressed longings, and images of roads not taken. The worst time . . . was lying in bed at night.

For some, the weekend represents 'bad' time. With little structure and few purposeful activities in which to engage, time can seem to drag interminably. For others, the desire to normalise life as far as possible encourages them to see weekends as they would on the outside, as special or 'self' time when the usual restrictions of imposed time are relaxed somewhat, and they can construct their own activities.[7] In between these polarised positions, several respondents isolated weekends as being periods of conflicting emotions, containing both good times and bad. Like many people in general life, one of the most salient features that determined whether specific periods of the weekend were enjoyable or not was the mass media, and stories about how weekends are spent in prison demonstrate the extent to which media are integrated into prisoners' lives and routines. If inmates subscribe to just one newspaper a week, it is overwhelmingly a weekend title. The predominant reason for this is that Saturday and Sunday newspapers contain TV listings for the whole week. The most popular title in this respect was the *Mirror* on Saturday, which includes a glossy TV listings magazine containing 'behind-the scenes' stories, celebrity photographs and soap updates, in addition to the actual schedules. For most respondents, though, it is the schedules alone which determine their decisions to buy the paper, and several described how studying the listings and circling the programmes they most wanted to watch was an important routine that helped to structure not only the day on which they carried out this task, but also the rest of the week, which was mapped out in advance around 'must-see' TV viewing. A secondary reason for buying a weekend newspaper is that most contain several supplements, including colour magazines, cartoon pages, crosswords and in-depth sports coverage. It often takes a great deal of time to read a weekend paper ('it can take me the whole week to get through it') and it therefore represents good value for money, in addition to being a useful and absorbing way of passing time.

Saturday mornings are typically relaxation times, and many of those who have in-cell television reported it provides them with an excuse for staying in bed longer which, in common with many people in the wider society, was seen as another private pleasure. In particular, the cartoons and music/celebrity shows aimed at children and teenagers that fill the Saturday morning schedules can be seen as escapist fantasy, and may support Lindlof's (1987: 187) assertion that inmates' psychological orientation to television content is determined by those aspects of their selves requiring nurture. Furthermore, although there is evidence that these kinds of programmes are enjoyed by adult viewers across the country (Gauntlett and Hill 1999), it is arguable that without the obligations of family or domestic chores to fulfil, people in prison can watch these shows with a great deal less guilt than the 'average' adult viewer. Indeed, as indicated above, many prisoners said they made a point of watching programmes aimed at children in order to keep abreast of the media influences their own children were being exposed to.

A further 'weekend time' that is the subject of mixed emotions is Friday evening, which, in line with the work ethic of post-industrial societies, is often designated as a time for socialising with friends or relaxing after a week's labour. In Ashwell and Stocken, there is apparently little to distinguish Friday evenings from any other nights of the week, although several long-term prisoners looked back nostalgically to when they were in Category B or Dispersal prisons and had their own kitchen facilities. Fridays were then special occasions when several inmates would get together and prepare a meal:

> Once Lifers come to terms with the fact that they've got a hefty sentence to do, they set about enjoying it as much as possible. At Wakefield we had cooking clubs . . . every Friday night, four of us got together and cooked a meal, usually a curry or something like that. We'd sometimes make an apple pie and have a teapot – not tea bags – and a tea strainer . . . We'd put the radio on – something classical – it was really civilised. It's a link with the outside as well, we'd try and make it as homely as possible, put a proper table cloth on the table. We were trying to replicate something from outside, and time passed because you were always looking forward to Friday and then gearing up for the next one, planning it . . . Then on the last Friday of the month we'd have a monthly survival party to celebrate another month gone. We'd have a meal and some hooch. I suppose it was the equivalent to a midnight feast in a girl's dormitory! (Ray).

But despite the loss of this 'small extension of personal autonomy' (Sparks *et al*, 1996: 164), not everyone felt Fridays had been deprived of their special significance although, like many people in the wider society, Friday evening was a high point which was followed all too rapidly by Sunday evening:

> I always listen to *Radio 1* on a Friday night, always have. Judge Jules, Pete Tong . . . it's part of the Friday night ritual. Believe it or not, I've come across guys in here who, on a Friday night, go through all the motions – shave, wash, dress up – it's like they're going out for a big night out. Then on Sunday night, it's early lock-up and they come back down to earth. Nothing on telly except *Songs of Praise* and *The Antiques Roadshow* and they get the Sunday night blues. Ridiculous really, innit? (George).

In general, 'good time' – whether interacting with others or engaged in self-time – is that which is filled with activity. Good interaction time is thus usually spent in the company of others who share similar interests, while good self-time is frequently spent in absorbing work, study or creative pursuits. A number of prisoners spend a great deal of their spare time pursuing hobbies, and one of the most fascinating features of prison life is the skills to be found in a variety of arts, crafts and other creative pursuits, both legitimate and non-legitimate.[8] For many, absorption in an artistic project is not only a primary means of killing time but it also restores a sense of self-worth and may enhance one's social standing among the rest of the prisoners. Some of my respondents had learned new skills or uncovered previously hidden talents while inside. Some of these – like the brewing of hooch or the manipulation of telephone cards so they permit more calls than their face value – are valuable skills in prison and can create commodities to be traded freely in the prison economy. Others are more legitimate pastimes which, although they may also involve the manufacture of goods which can be sold or exchanged, are not always primarily undertaken for that purpose. Most notable in this respect was the construction of models and artefacts out of matchsticks, a hobby which is frequently regarded as the archetypal prisoner (or prisoner-of-war) pastime. Lloyd, a life-sentence prisoner in his late fifties, showed me a carriage clock he had made out of matches, and described some of the numerous other models and artefacts he had constructed over the years. He said he had been taught by an 'old lag' during a previous prison sentence in the 1960s and, although he used to sell some of his models, more recently he has made them solely to pass time in an absorbing and self-fulfilling activity. He was now, in turn, passing on his skills to a new generation, and one inmate in his mid-twenties took great pride in showing me a matchstick jewellery box he had constructed under the tutelage of Lloyd. The passing on of such skills gives prison culture a certain sense of timelessness and nostalgia, which some fear will be diminished by the introduction of in-cell TV. In addition to crafts which might be said to be virtually unique to (or at least epitomise) the prison world, some inmates are keen to continue hobbies which were an important feature of their lives on the outside. Again, the primary gain of importing into prison one's favourite pastimes from outside may be ontological: as Burman (1988: 153) puts it, hobbies may give those who are marginalised 'small experiences of mastery in a familiar terrain'.

A different, although increasingly common, response to the weight of unstructured time with which inmates are faced is the use of drugs. The essence of their appeal – hallucinogenics, in particular – is that they do more than simply tranquillise or anaesthetise the prisoner (Matthews 1999: 41). They 'remove' him from his physical environment and they 'readjust' the temporal flow, releasing the user from the seemingly endless mass of formless time. For Matthews, these benefits can be weighed up in terms of more than just fantasy or mental escape. The tangible, physical attractions of drug use are summarised as follows:

> For those who were regular drug users before entering prison, drugs normalise time, in that its passing corresponds to those forms of social time which were previously experienced on the outside. By the same token, the drug subculture that has been found to be prevalent in many prisons also provides a way of organising daily life and giving meaning to the prison routine that for some approximates to the normal routines of life outside the confines of the prison. Thus by engaging in an activity whose objective is to create what we might call 'fantasy time', prisoners can spend their days involved in activities – buying, trading, hustling, scoring – which correspond to familiar 'real time' activities conducted on the outside (ibid.).

Media consumption is often equated to drugs use and, in the context of the prison, the comparison may appear particularly apposite for, like drugs, the presence of television can normalise or readjust time so that the temporal rhythm experienced in prison is akin to that which was experienced prior to confinement. This sense of temporal continuity, together with the familiar, sequential or ongoing form of much television content, brings comfort to the prisoner who, in the early stages of confinement at least, is likely to experience some degree of disorientation. Like drugs, then, television can provide a refuge from the harsh realities of life, filling large amounts of self-time which otherwise might be given over to introspection. But like any habit-forming substance, it is the object of complex and frequently conflicting emotions. Of those respondents who had in-cell television, most said they watched more television inside prison than they did on the outside and many clearly felt they were 'hooked'. Some resented what they saw as the 'intrusion' of television and were trying to resist it for as long as possible, so that the relationship between respondents and the medium had frequently become a struggle of wills, akin to going 'cold turkey'. At Ashwell, where in-cell TV was mandatory for those inmates on 'Enhanced' or 'Super-Enhanced' status, several inmates had extremely ambivalent feelings about it. One, Andrew, was a life-sentence prisoner who had constructed his identity around his status as an Open University degree student. Fearful that television would interfere with his studies, he had resisted the offer to have a set installed in his cell for some eight months. However, under increasing pressure from the governor, he had relented and had had his TV for three weeks when we met. In his case the battle of wills was being lost, and he talked about his waning commitment to his university coursework with self-deprecating honesty. For him, succumbing to the lures of television – like those who give in to the temptation of drugs – was evidence of his all too human frailty.

Other long-termers and lifers, meanwhile, placed a great deal of emphasis on selectivity of viewing. Those who watched little television or who were extremely discriminating in their choice of viewing saw this as a matter of pride, a clear indication of their self-restraint in the face of overwhelming pressure to conform to subcultural norms. Of course, as uses and gratifications research has emphasised, the characterisation of television consumption as a non-purposeful activity may be a problematic assumption. But most prisoners in my study adhered to this view; hence their unease at it cutting into time previously spent reading, studying, pursuing hobbies or writing letters ('I've had in-cell TV for seven or eight months now, but it's stopped me reading. I have to fight to read now which really annoys me. It's a vampire that draws you in'). When questioned, however, most were able to identify specific important meanings and motivations associated with TV viewing beyond simply 'killing time' (see below). A final, related point is that many respondents, while resenting television for distracting them from other activities, none the less expressed relief it could also fill time usually spent sleeping or doing nothing at all, both of which might otherwise be spent in painful self-contemplation. This would appear to demonstrate that for many inmates, time spent watching in-cell TV has replaced both action and *in*action, and that, paradoxically, good 'self-time' can be both time which is spent on a journey into the self, and time which prevents or distracts them from making that journey.

The common features of good time, both self and interaction, and the main criteria by which time is judged to be 'good', are that it passes quickly, or that the slowness of its passing is minimised or transcended. In general, seasonal changes are barely noticed by prisoners, although inmates at Ashwell, the most 'open' of the prisons I visited, commented that they enjoy the summer months because they are permitted to go outside during evening association time. The worst time to spend in prison is almost universally felt to be Christmas and New Year. It is during these traditional holiday periods that the reality of losing one's liberty and the distinction between prison life and 'normal' life is most sharply felt by the greatest number of inmates. As with many people in general life, television is rapidly becoming a prominent feature of the prisoners' enjoyment of Christmas, and the introduction of in-cell television has augmented the centrality of the medium in the festive season. This development was most noticeable at Gartree where the implementation of in-cell TV was accelerated so that it was installed just in time for Christmas. Several inmates commented that having their own TV sets in their cells had made the festive period more bearable in helping to take their minds off what their friends and families were doing outside, or in uniting them in a common experience, and television undoubtedly helped to normalise the prison during this notoriously difficult time. With no restrictions imposed on how long they could watch television in their cells, some inmates admitted to having viewed over fifty hours of programmes in the first week. In part, this high viewing quota can be understood in terms of the novelty of having their own television set, but it can also be explained by reference to the traditional content of the Christmas TV schedules which incorporate higher-than-average numbers of blockbuster movies, specially commissioned dramas and light entertainment shows, but also rely on repeating Christmas 'specials' of the past. Several prisoners mentioned the particular pleasure of watching repeats of favourite TV shows from long ago (*The Morecambe and Wise Christmas Show* being one example) which reminded them of happier times and places, while some appreciated being able to watch repeated episodes of more recent programmes (such as the special Christmas episodes of *One Foot in the Grave* and *Only Fools and Horses*) that they had missed before in-cell television was implemented in prisons.

New Year is a similarly painful period for many prison inmates which, like Christmas, makes them feel especially isolated. The approach of the end of the millennium served to intensify the emotions felt by some inmates who would see in the new millennium from behind prison walls, especially the young and those serving relatively short sentences:

> New Year is definitely the worst time, knowing all your mates are out there, having a good time. The millennium's going to be even worse. I've already started psyching myself up for that little gutting feeling I know I'm going to have. I can feel the little knot forming in the pit of my stomach already, just thinking about it (Neil).

Several mentioned that prison riots are common around Christmas and New Year, and I heard many rumours (unfounded, as it turned out) that disturbances would accompany the dawning of the new millennium. Others, however, were more philosophical, seeing the millennium as no different from any other New Year's Eve; a night where a degree of relaxation of the prison rules allows them to 'celebrate' the occasion, thus making it significantly better than most evenings inside. A group of prisoners at Gartree described how most prison officers on duty would 'let their hair down' on New Year's Eve, not only tolerating the consumption of hooch, but also frequently joining inmates in a drink. The prisoners I spoke to greatly appreciated this abatement of the formal prison rules and did not have a problem with officers returning to 'type' the following day. In an evocation of the story of the First World War encounter between British and German soldiers who played football in No Man's Land on Christmas Day before resuming normal hostilities the following day, the stories told about New Year's Eve in prison illustrate that it is regarded as a unique point in the year when boundaries on both sides can be transgressed in the spirit of the occasion and then reverted to without repercussions the following day.[9]

Christmas and New Year, then, are times when prisoners – like most of us – are perhaps most likely to reflect on the past, often indulging in nostalgic fantasies about previous years' celebrations with family and friends. Of course, like many lapses into nostalgia, the past is doctored to meet the requirements of the present (Brittan 1977: 89) so that such memories are frequently tinged with sentimentality or regret. But with an uncertain future ahead of them, and a barely tolerable present, many inmates hold on to a sense of their pre-prison selves by remembering the past. Of particular interest in this regard was the potential of various media to evoke memories, which was a common theme in interviews. Bill, a middle-aged inmate serving five years, described the particular joys of watching repeats of old TV programmes such as *Dad's Army* and *Steptoe and Son*, which allow him to reminisce about times gone by:

> I love those old programmes because you get transported back in time. Radio is important too. I listen to Radio 2 for all the old tracks from the sixties and seventies. I haven't got anything to go back to when I get out of here, so I need my roots. Watching and listening to things from the past helps me remember.

In a similar vein, Del, who is nearing the end of a life sentence, commented:

> Dad's Army brings back a lot of memories. They're showing all the old black and white ones at the moment – that really takes you back. I'd love to see Quatermass and Z Cars shown again. I suppose that's what was on when I was on the out. Blimey, I am in a time warp, aren't I!

105

Lowenthal (1985: 197) explains that 'remembering the past is crucial for our sense of identity', a sentiment echoed by George, serving twenty years, who said: 'you've got nothing in prison without memory . . . without memory you'd become institutionalised, an automaton.' David, although rather younger, appreciated the continuity that having media in prisons provides: 'I do get nostalgic watching TV or listening to the radio . . . but at least I've got the luxury of enjoying the same things in here.'

For Lowenthal, recalling past experiences links us with our earlier selves, however different we may since have become. However, as Del indicated above, and as has been described elsewhere in this study, there is among prisoners a common tendency to feel caught in a moment in time, so that differences in their identities over time are much less marked than they would be in other populations. This state, described by Del as a 'time warp', was graphically illustrated by Ray, a lifer who had spent much of his life in prison:

> Music takes you back . . . silly dances you used to do, half-cut at parties. I'd hate to lose my radio, that would be far worse than losing the TV. I used to go to the *Proms* when I lived in London, out for dinner and then to the *Proms*. I never miss the *Proms* on the radio now. And I used to go to Victorian Music Hall nights. We'd toast Queen Victoria, that kind of thing. I used to go to the *Old Time Music Hall Show* with Leonard Sachs and to *Sunday Night at the London Palladium*. I went a couple of times. My mother got tickets through the *Reader's Digest*. I even saw the Beatles once. It was horrendous!

For Spigel and Jenkins (1991) one of the most interesting aspects of their research on memories of *Batman* was the ways in which people constructed past events to meet the requirements of the present which caused the researchers to doubt that what they are being told are photographic records of the events described. Past events were remembered in such a way as to conform to conventionalised cultural understandings of them, and made into narratives which were familiar to people in the present. To recall a previous example from British television by way of illustration; it is common for people to 'remember' watching the science fiction series *Doctor Who*, as children, from behind their parents' settee. In most cases, such descriptions are likely to be myths; memories recast to conform to a set of shared cultural conventions, rather than actual recollections of a real individual experience. In this way, memory is used as a mechanism for binding together the individual with a larger community of ideas. As Spigel and Jenkins (ibid.) note, media texts – especially those which, over time, take on a cult status – serve to evoke a collective past, remembered according to shared, cultural narrative codes, rather than simply individuated codes of story-telling.

Recalling memories in daydreams and everyday contexts can also be a useful means not only of escaping or transcending everyday realities, but also of understanding them. As one inmate poignantly said: 'I listen to a lot of Celine Dion . . . it reminds me of the time I spent with my ex-missus, and I think about what went wrong, what *I* did wrong, and that.' Memory is thus a function of context although, in Freudian terms, it may be limited by defence mechanisms which distort and frequently repress the past: 'memory can be upsetting. Thinking can be your worst enemy in prison. I prefer not to do it, to be honest with you.'

Place-time-space

Not only do time and place take on different dimensions in prison, but the relationship *between* time and place does too. In modern, post-industrial society, our personal horizons have expanded to the degree where terms such as 'global village' are commonly evoked to describe the international distribution of media technologies and cultural images. The prison has, until very recently, remained relatively impervious to the new communication technologies of the outside world and has prevailed as one of the most bounded of locales (Goffman 1961a). Indeed, one of the characteristics that marks out a total institution as being 'total' is the compression of spatial experience. In other words, while people in ordinary life act, and are acted upon, through a variety of social dimensions including home, neighbourhood, suburb, city, region, nation-state and world (Burman 1988: 123), the prison inmate has traditionally found his world reduced to his immediate physical environs. But with the introduction of mass media, the world has to some extent opened up again, and prison walls are no longer impenetrable barriers that wholly isolate the inmate from the community and society at large. For some prisoners these developments are best conceptualised as a process of illumination. Echoing Scannell's (1996) comment that early radio opened up a world that was 'truly magical', one respondent recounting the introduction into prisons of radio remarked that 'it was marvellous – like someone opening up a window on the world', while another said it was like a 'light bulb being switched on – better than Christmas'.

In his analysis of the impact of electronic media on social behaviour,

Joshua Meyrowitz (1985) has provided an authoritative and wide-ranging theoretical analysis of the ways in which electronic media have altered conventional notions of place, time and space. In the Preface to *No Sense of Place*, he sums up the declining significance of physically bounded spaces thus:

> [W]*here* one is has less and less to do with what one knows and experiences. Electronic media have altered the significance of time and space for social interaction. Certainly physical presence and direct sensory contact remain primary forms of experience. But the social spheres defined by walls and gates are now only one type of interactional environment. The walls of the mightiest fortress no longer define a truly segregated social setting if a camera, a microphone, or even a telephone is present (ibid.: viii).

It is common to regard media technologies simply as material products introduced into a pre-existing environment, which rapidly become part of the fabric and furniture of their surroundings. But for critics like Meyrowitz, once widely used, electronic media can transform their surroundings into new social environments with different patterns of social action, feeling and belief, and these may in turn lead to modified or radically altered social conceptions of traditional identities such as 'childhood', 'adulthood', 'masculinity' and 'femininity' (ibid.: 15). Furthermore, television, computers, telephones and radio 'democratise and homogenise places by allowing people to experience and interact with others in spite of physical isolation' (ibid.: 143).

But while electronic media undoubtedly weaken the relationship between physical space and social place, it would be a mistake to follow Meyrowitz's argument entirely that being in prison affords the same kinds of communications experiences that most of us in the broader community enjoy. For example, while it is theoretically possible to blur previously distinct group identities (for example, that of 'prisoners'), and allow inmates to 'escape' the immediate confines of their imprisonment via the media of mass communications, in practice it is not yet happening in prisons to anything like the extent experienced by the rest of the developed world. Communication in this context almost always flows in one direction, inmates being forbidden to transmit information back to the world outside. Consequently there is a palpable sense of frustration that the outside world can, and does, impact upon them, but that they can do little to impact upon it. One way in which this was manifested was in the responses of those inmates who enjoy 'phone-in' broadcasts which invite viewers and listeners to telephone presenters with their opinions. Many inmates told me they were devoted listeners of Talk Radio and Radio 5, both of which are interactive channels which rely heavily on audience participation via electronic mail, fax and phone-ins. Forbidden from partaking in their favourite programmes in these ways, many prisoners felt that they were experiencing a pale imitation of these shows, and were being denied something of the authenticity of the common experience. Dave commented: 'I like listening to *Talk*, but I get frustrated because I like to have my say', while Brian voiced a similar sentiment: 'I get mad because I can't ring in.'

A second but related point is that broadcast media can act as a form of large-scale communication allowing people in different parts of the country and even different areas of the world to 'participate' in a single event. In a recent study by the British Film Institute, in which five hundred participants wrote about their TV habits over a period of five years, one respondent summed up this facility in a reflection on how he would feel if he could no longer watch television news:

> I would feel cut off from the world . . . I feel part of humanity by sharing a television experience with people all over the world. I remember watching the first moon landing and reflecting on the fact that people all over the world were sharing that moment with me. I feel a tingle of excitement that I was at one with humanity at a momentous event in human history. Similar events since then include Live Aid and the Royal Wedding (!). If I could not share these pivotal events with the rest of humanity, I feel that my humanity would be diminished (46-year-old unemployed man, cited in Gauntlett and Hill 1999: 57).

Yet despite apparently now being able to experience these global television events, prisoners may again feel at a disadvantage. It is well documented that, for many of us, events seem more 'real' if they are reported in the media than if we witness them with our own eyes (Meyrowitz 1985; Giddens 1991a; Scannell 1996).[10] In this way, representation becomes a kind of reality which, in turn, frequently serves to give individuals a sense of keeping in touch with other people as well as with what is 'happening' (Meyrowitz 1985: 91). But for prisoners, such events may act further to enhance their feelings of isolation from 'normal' life. Far from experiencing homogeneity or 'humanity' with the wider society, several inmates reported their incarceration in a total institution caused them to feel decidedly removed from the public forum that unites people in a common experience. One event that occurred during my fieldwork, which crystallised this feeling of being sequestered from normality, was the murder of the well-known television presenter, Jill Dando, in April 1999. The unexpectedness and violence with which this story was marked stunned many people in the UK and was felt strongly by a number of prisoners who raised the subject with me and talked about their shock and grief on hearing or reading about the event for the first time. The disbelief with which many people received the news was seemingly intensified by the circumstances of imprisonment:

> Seeing something like that is different somehow when you're in here. It's unreal. You feel completely helpless. You just can't bring yourself to believe it. It's almost as though you're always looking out on life through a thick pane of glass. Everything seems a bit fuzzy, you know? (Bill).

In the course of the same conversation, Bill said that when he had first heard the news of Dando's murder on the radio, he found himself flicking through all the other channels, partly in a quest for more detailed information, but partly also as if to authenticate the original story: 'it was almost as if – if I found another channel, it would be alright, it wouldn't have happened.' Another respondent, Sam, found that the event took him back to the death of another media icon – Diana, Princess of Wales – two years earlier. He talked with great clarity and insight about the tendency of many people to see such high-profile public figures as little more than soap-opera characters whose lives are stage-managed to the degree where unforeseen events – like the violent and premature nature of her demise – are beyond the public's comprehension: 'her death, well, it wasn't part of the script, was it?' These examples are prime illustrations of the phenomenon known as 'para-social interaction' (Horton and Wohl 1956). Put simply, it is suggested that even when the communication is unidirectional, broadcast media allow a special relationship to develop between media personalities, or characters, and their audiences. Unlike print media, new electronic media offer the illusion of face-to-face interaction so that, paradoxically the para-social performer is able to establish 'intimacy' with millions (Meyrowitz 1985: 119). Not confined to television, several respondents commented they get annoyed when their favourite radio presenters are dropped unceremoniously by stations. This was a particular source of frustration to fans of the interactive talk-based station, Talk Radio, which had experienced major changes of direction and personnel in the months preceding the period of my research. Listeners can build up unusually close relations with presenters of talk shows, so that when they disappear without warning, their loss can be taken very personally, almost as if it were a bereavement. As one respondent put it: 'I was gutted when they got rid of Tommy Boyd, and "Caesar the Geezer" before him. It was like losing a friend. If they axe James Whale I'll be done for.' This phenomenon is well known to audience researchers and has been used as partial explanation for the deeply personal sense of grief felt by some individuals when confronted with news of the deaths of public figures who they have never actually met. It is difficult to be precise about the particular nature of para-social interaction experienced within a total institution; after all, the extent and form of public and private mourning following the deaths of both the Princess of Wales and Jill Dando surprised many in this country and elsewhere. But Horton and Wohl (1956: 223) may well be right when they suggest that the para-social relationship has its greatest impact on the 'socially isolated, the socially inept, the aged and invalid, the timid and rejected'.

A third difference between experiencing communicative interaction inside prison and in the wider context, which Meyrowitz overlooks, is the 'mobility rate' at which we move through space and time (Burman 1988: 123). Prisoners today might enjoy unprecedented access to technologies of the mass media, but the rate at which they are permitted to move through space and time is limited by their spatial horizons and by their restricted means of mobility. A number of prisoners spoke of the claustrophobic atmosphere of their surroundings and talked of feeling 'trapped' or being 'like a caged animal'. For many, the primary coping strategy was to 'take themselves out' of their immediate surroundings, and absorbing hobbies, education and the gym were all used to this end. But all these activities, while they may provide some degree of 'escape' from the immediate, pressing confines, are still wholly structured by the demands of the prison regime and take place according to the institutional timetable. In other words, spatial experience, however it is individually constructed, will always be tempered by the institutional imposition of time and, as numerous respondents pointed out, time passes very slowly in prison.

This perception of time moving at different speeds inside prison and outside it was a common theme in my conversations with inmates. Interestingly, Matthews (1999) extends von Hirsch's (1992) argument that there is a problem with uncritically linking imprisonment to the principle of proportionality. For Matthews, the fact that the mobility rates at which we physically move through the world have speeded up means that time taken from a person can appear to be slowed down (hence the metaphors of imprisonment being akin to experiencing a state of 'cold storage' or 'deep freeze'). That a five-year sentence given in 1950 might be experienced as a significantly longer sentence in 2000 means that the overall increase in the average length of sentence in recent years may have an even greater significance than might at first be apparent (Matthews 1999: 40). For most of us, the primary means of expanding spatial experience through time is via the mass media while, equally, it is new forms of electronic communication that have had the effect of accelerating time in physical space. This time-space compression is a central feature of late modernity, but as has been established earlier and throughout this book, time and space are experienced differently in prison. These differences are especially germane in the context of how media reorganises the time–space relation. First, although prisoners may have experience of the time-space compression facilitated by established technologies such as television and radio, they are largely immune from the further transformations of time and space that have arisen from new communications technologies. While most of us are aculturised to a world where time is speeded up, slowed down, suspended, repackaged, re-ordered and re-experienced through the mediums of film, video, television and, most dramatically, computer technologies (ibid.: 256) – a set of processes known collectively as 'timeshifting' – most prison inmates (certainly those who are serving long sentences) experience time in a more traditional, chronological sense. Thus, time becomes conceived in spatial terms, with prisoners existing through time in a much more linear fashion, as if in a pre-media age (ibid.; see also Adam 1995).

This sense of linearity of time may further enhance the impression of isolation of physical place. Detachment from the outside world is particularly keenly felt by long-serving prisoners, and many reported that no amount of watching television or reading newspapers can fully prepare the long-term inmate for release back into an ever-changing social environment. One respondent said that after serving eleven years of a previous sentence in prison, it took him four months to pluck up courage to catch a bus, because he simply no longer knew how to: 'I knew they didn't have conductors any more, because I've seen it on telly, but I didn't know what to do, how you were supposed to pay. I felt like a Martian.' He added: 'the world moves at a million miles an hour. It's terrifying and anyone who tells you different is lying.' Numerous respondents commented on the vast difference in the pace of life in prison compared to the world beyond, but perhaps the most striking observations were those of Herbie who was sentenced to life imprisonment in 1966. His descriptions of leaving court in a Black Maria, with police motorcycle escorts in tin helmets and garters, making a slow procession through crowds of football fans leisurely walking to the local ground, evoked impressions of a gentler and less hurried time, and contrasted strongly with his perceptions of a frenetic and impersonal society thirty-three years later, which have been partly informed by images from the mass media, and only very recently by experiencing it for himself on escorted day visits to nearby towns.

A fourth point worth noting in relation to how media may be experienced differently in prison as a consequence of the physical, structural conditions of the environment concerns the ability of new media to make people feel disempowered as well as empowered. Although usually thought of as a source of liberation, media resources can in fact include *and* exclude participants (Meyrowitz 1985: 7). One way in which media reinforce a feeling of exclusion and isolation is in their ability to create a notion of 'them *vs.* us' (ibid.), a sentiment that is played out in a number of different ways in the prison setting. The characterisation of prisoners as an 'undeserving' underclass is prevalent in our culture, and is a judgement regularly articulated in relation to inmates' viewing of in-cell television by some prison officers ('Why should *they* get TVs when my auntie can't even afford one?' is how one officer at Gartree put it). But the implication behind Meyrowitz's argument is that new media blur traditional distinctions between authorities and those who are marginalised, isolated or disenfranchised. While this may be true for those who have unhindered access to emerging media, it is not the case for the majority of prison inmates who still face limited access to telephones and televisions, and who are rarely permitted to use computer technologies. Indeed, some inmates believe the restricted access they have to new communication technologies and, in particular, the ban that has been imposed on them using the Internet, is a form of censure that renders them second-class citizens in the information age. Far from sharing with the wider society the privileges of the advancing communications networks as Meyrowitz suggests, prisoners are impoverished by both their lack of technological hardware and by their concomitant inability to exchange information in ways that are becoming increasingly commonplace. Furthermore, many feel they are being placed at an additional disadvantage when they come to re-enter the community and seek employment because they do not have the information technology skills many jobs now require.

In short, while Meyrowitz has provided an admirable (indeed, award-winning) treatise on the power of electronic media radically to alter notions of 'here' and 'there', and dismantle traditional concepts such as gender, power and authority, his theories are valuable only in so far as they are *hypothetically* valid. At this point in time, many of his observations on the impact of electronic media in everyday life are simply not applicable to prisons and prisoners. For example, he states that those aspects of identity, socialisation and hierarchy that were once dependent upon their physical location have been altered by electronic media, so that previously disparate environments now share a strong sense of group identity, and a prison cell is now essentially no different from any other media context (Meyrowitz 1985: 125, 143*ff*). I would argue, however, that the prisoner's cell is fundamentally and symbolically the same as it has always been. Although cosmetically different now that posters and photographs are allowed on the walls, in-cell television has been installed (in some institutions) and integral sanitation has been introduced to replace the previously unhygienic and degrading practice of 'slopping out', it still bears little relation to other environments in 'normal' life.

Perhaps, then, it would be wise to address these issues according to notions of 'relative' rather than 'absolute' deprivation, and to that extent I believe that Meyrowitz's thesis has to be refined. The underlying assumption of his work is that structure is now an illusion; prisoners may be incarcerated behind walls and bars, but electronic media can blur or dissolve the structural shackles and barriers that hold them. Inmates can reconstruct their identities at will, and physical confinement is no longer a key component of punishment because electronic media can move people informationally to a different place (ibid.: 145). While there is certainly some validity in this argument (it is undeniable that prisons are more normalised than they once were), it is not the case that the benefits of new media are experienced uniformly in contemporary society. Prisoners are arguably prime candidates for the label 'underclass' because they are exiled from the new information era. But more fundamental than that, and a factor which Meyrowitz again underplays, is how *physically* isolated from the rest of society prisons actually *feel*.[11]

Relationship between different media

The introduction of in-cell sets at the time of my research resulted in an inevitable focus on television: it is arguably the most significant medium to be introduced into prisons in terms of both the prolonged debate which preceded its instalment and the impact it has had on the normalisation, and day-to-day experience, of imprisonment. Quite simply, it was the medium that most people I spoke to – inmates *and* staff – wanted to share their views on. Other media had become relatively taken for granted since the advent of personal television sets, with the result (as highlighted earlier) that some individuals resented what they viewed as the intrusive or soporific qualities of the medium. Many inmates who had in-cell television felt it had usurped other media and were now more inclined to switch on their TV when they returned to their cell than listen to the radio or read:

> It's just there, I suppose. I'm paying for it, as well – I don't know whether that's a factor. But, yeah, I always switch the telly on as soon as I get back. It's just automatic (Craig).

> I used to listen to the radio all the time, it was my lifeline. Now I'm much more likely to put the TV on. God knows why, but I do. I wish I didn't to be honest with you. I used to listen to all the plays on Radio 4, but I haven't done that for months now. Television doesn't transport you the way that radio does, but it's just more immediate, more *there*. It's habit, I suppose (Ron).

Other media evidently took precedence over television for some inmates (especially those who had been in prison for many years), as described elsewhere in this book. But for many individuals – especially those who were young and/or who were serving short sentences – other media simply served a supporting role, with magazines and newspapers sometimes only being consulted in order to check out the TV viewing schedule, and personal radios being rendered more or less redundant. Music was of great importance to most of my respondents, with some keen to use it as a means of connecting them with their past, and others more concerned that they should keep up to date with current trends and not lose touch with the vagaries of the music and culture industries. But many respondents in their late teens or twenties still felt that experiencing music via television was a more complete experience than listening to it via non-visual media:

> They've started showing concerts late night on BBC 1, and I really like music shows like that one that Jools Holland presents. I even watch *Top of the Pops* and all them kids shows. I love my music. Don't listen to it much though. We're only allowed twelve CDs in here and my radio's bust. Besides which, it's better with pictures isn't it? (Carl).

> I like listening to music, but I prefer television now. I only wish we could get MTV installed in here (Richard).

Meanings and motivations sought in specific media content

Researching the exact nature of the relationship between television and identity formation is not at all straightforward. Consistent with other media studies (Silverstone 1994; Hermes 1995; Gauntlett and Hill 1999), I found that empirical support for the theoretical premise that prisoners use specific media content to shape their identities in everyday life was difficult to trace. As Chapter 3 highlighted, there are inherent methodological difficulties in eliciting *any* information in conversation about how people interpret, accommodate and negotiate media content, let alone how they might consciously or subconsciously structure their identities around it. Most people do not consciously think about, far less articulate, how they *use* media content in their daily lives. Television viewing, more than any other media-based activity, is most frequently regarded as a trivial or mindless pursuit, and whatever effects it might have on an individual's identity are, of course, but one strand within a much wider nexus of influences. However, throughout this study, a case has been constructed for the merits of a developed and refined version of the uses and gratifications approach, the central theoretical premise of which – that audiences actively choose, use, resist or ignore media influences – and revised empirical methodology – which involves talking at length with respondents about the mediation and formation of their attitudes, behaviour and identities – provided me with a constructive means of exploring the 'internal' gratifications that media fulfil. It was therefore satisfying to find that a number of inmates *were* able to articulate the ways in which they use specific media texts as frames of reference in everyday life. This reflexive awareness was most evident in those people who were cognisant of the ways in which media had shaped their political views, their language and their understanding of current affairs. But more strikingly, several inmates described how strong allegiances to particular media genres helped to structure their worldview. At issue here is not the belief that media creates people's identities in a crude, deterministic fashion. In casual conversation many people make conscious references to popular culture, repeating jokes, stories or script lines they have heard, or mimicking TV personalities or advertising jingles. But more interesting to explore are the ways that representations from media and popular culture provide the signifying practices and symbolic systems which position us as subjects and through which we produce meanings (Woodward 1997: 14).

As already indicated, the primary concern of this research is not to compile a list of prisoners' favourite media. But the specific texts mentioned by individuals as being of particular importance to them yielded some surprising and potentially illuminating findings with which to analyse the impact of media on the lived experience of imprisonment and the identities of prisoners. Of particular interest were respondents who reflected on how they had been exposed to media texts in prison that were previously not only outside their normal consumption patterns, but were beyond – even at odds with – their usual habitus. The social psychologist, Sonia Livingstone (1990: 21), notes that: 'there is now ample evidence . . . that people construct various and often unexpected interpretations of programmes, reading with or against the grain, depending on their own contribution and the knowledge resources available to them.' It would be extremely speculative to suggest what kinds of media content might constitute the normal habitus of inmates, or to make generalisations about their tastes and preferences. However, given that surveys of what men in the general population of Britain watch yield few surprises (for example, of the top-twenty TV programmes watched by men in 1996, nine were football matches, unlike the women's top twenty which featured no sport at all[12]), the general observation that televised football matches were regarded with an almost ritualistic reverence in prisons was not unexpected. Similarly, the fact that prison officers in every establishment reported that the most popular daily newspaper was the *Sun* in part reflects its status as the best-selling title among the wider reading public.

But as Livingstone (1990) intimates, it is those tastes that would be widely interpreted as going 'against the grain' which are potentially of most interest and, in general, the examples which most graphically illustrate this are those tastes and preferences that appear to be outside the boundaries of popular culture. As Bourdieu's (1984) work indicates, hierarchies of taste are largely to do with the length of histories of the art form, which operate independently of subjective factors, although it must be said that those cultural forms that are deemed to be 'high' culture are invariably of élitist and therefore minority appeal. In most societies, greater value is placed on 'culture' (which is deemed of high artistic merit) than entertainment (which is popular, and sometimes populist), even though these may themselves be largely subjective judgements. Consequently, while it is arguable that critical, subversive and emancipatory moments can be found equally in high culture and low culture (Kellner 1995), most people in our society would none the less concur that reading Shakespeare is more worth while than reading Stephen King, and that classical music is higher up the music hierarchy than reggae, 'whatever their personal tastes, or indeed their opinions about this ranking' (Brunsdon 1990: 75). These deeply entrenched cultural hierarchies result in some taste formations appearing more eccentric than others, as when a working-class prisoner articulates patterns of media consumption more typically associated with the upper or upper-middle classes. The unusualness of tastes which go against the grain was graphically illustrated by Bill who said he would love to listen to Radio 3 or Classic FM in his cell, but 'would get lynched by the other residents of D-Wing' if he were to do so. Other inmates were less worried by what their peers would make of their media habits, although tastes which confound stereotypical expectations frequently involved elaborate self-justification: 'I know it's rubbish but . . . ' and 'you might not think it to look at me but I'm a big fan of . . . ' were typical prefaces to statements of taste.

One of the most interesting findings of this research was that several inmates had created new identities and whole new outlooks on life as a result of being exposed to previously unknown media texts while in prison. Examples have been offered in relation to inmates' relations to the press, and in general it was broadsheet newspapers with what might be described as a mission to educate, like the *Guardian*, that were most frequently mentioned in relation to 'improving' respondents' sense of themselves and developing a 'broader frame of reference within which to evaluate life choices' (Gaes *et al*, 1999: 163). However, television and radio material could also fulfil this role. Denzel put it as follows: 'I watch news, *Panorama*, documentaries. I never used to on the outside. In-cell TV's made me more aware of news, and everyone in here talks about stuff.' Another striking example involved Paul, an inmate at Whitemoor, who talked about his radio listening. It is tempting to make assumptions about the media preferences of a young, black, maximum-security prisoner in one of the country's most notorious dispersal jails. But that this would expose this study to accusations of perpetuating stereotypes was illustrated when Paul revealed he was a devoted fan of Radio 4 and particularly enjoyed *The Moral Maze*, a 'talking heads' style of programme that involves academics and other prominent intellectuals attempting to unravel and resolve some of the most complex ethical dilemmas facing modern society. The characterisation of *The Moral Maze* as a programme that challenges some of the greatest minds in the country is not to make a judgement that it is intrinsically more worthy than, say, *EastEnders*, or that Paul was in some way 'odd' for listening to it. Indeed, the fact he demonstrated a high level of critical engagement in the discussions of the most recent broadcast illustrates that the divide between 'high culture' and 'low/popular culture' is gradually becoming obsolete. Yet at the same time, peer-related notions of what is 'highbrow' or 'élitist' and what is 'mainstream' or 'cool' still persist, and I was impressed that Paul told his story – albeit somewhat self-consciously – in the public forum of

Whitemoor's Lifer Discussion Group.

Another case of tastes that go against the grain, and a striking example of how media have, to a great extent, supplemented or even replaced the 'significant others' who mediate to the individual the cultural values and meanings of the world he or she inhabits was Tim, who described himself as a 'Christian heavy metal biker'. Dressed in a leather jacket over his prison uniform, and sporting numerous facial and body tattoos and piercings, I was somewhat surprised when he described his enjoyment of the BBC1 programme, *Changing Rooms*:

> I love that *Changing Rooms*. I get loads of ideas from it – I can't wait to get out of here and decorate my own place. I definitely want deep red, textured walls. I've learnt a lot, like how to mix coarse building sand in with paint. Gives it a fantastic texture. I like Laurence Llewellyn-Bowen. I'd like to *be* Laurence Llewellyn-Bowen. I know he's a bit camp, but I'd model myself on him. He's cultured, he's stylish. Classy without being boring. That's how I want to be.

Through a process of symbolic interactionism Tim was projecting himself into another person's cultural identity and, at the same time, internalising the meanings and values which are culturally available, and making them part of his own aspirational identity. Any sense of irony in his choice of role model – a clean-cut, foppish interior designer known for wearing velvet suits, brocade waistcoats and frilled shirt cuffs – was not apparent in Tim's account.

Of all television genres, two emerged as most popular among my sample. The first, news and current affairs, is consistent with the findings of research analysing the viewing preferences of 'gendered individuals': while women are more likely to prefer fictional programmes with a high comic or romantic content, men are more likely to express preferences for news, current affairs, documentaries and programmes with a high factual or 'action' content (Morley 1986; Fiske 1987). These findings are in themselves problematic (Philo 1990; Gauntlett and Hill 1999), but that male prisoners watch television programmes (and for that matter, listen to radio and read newspapers) in order to keep abreast of national and international events is not especially remarkable, whether it is gender related or not. For individuals who have been stripped of many rights it is, as Hermes (1999: 83) notes, 'a safe bet that watching the news has to do with strengthening one's sense of citizenship'. What is arguably more interesting is the degree of knowledge that some inmates demonstrated about national and world events that they could play no part in, a phenomenon that was particularly evident among some of the inmates who attended the dialogue group at Whitemoor. With very limited opportunities to watch television (in-cell television had not been installed at the time of my research), prisoners at Whitemoor relied greatly upon newspapers and radio broadcasts, both of which may contain a greater degree of editorials, opinion and in-depth analysis than television. Consequently they had a breadth and depth of knowledge about current affairs which, I reflected at the time, was probably greater than that of most university students.

Local news was of extreme importance to the few prisoners who originated from the local area, and of little or no importance at all to the majority, who were drawn from other parts of the country. Some inmates had newspapers from their own locality sent in by members of their families. The familiarity of layout and content of regional titles not only helped to soften the blow of being removed from normal life, but was also perceived to aid reintegration into the community on release. Apart from news, the other genre that was identified as being almost universally popular, and one that cut across all demographic distinctions, was nature/wildlife programmes on television. Reasons given for love of such material were varied, although for most respondents there was a suggestion of their educational value. Mr B observed that nature programmes present educational material in a way that is palatable to the prison audience. Aware of the poor literacy and numeracy levels of many inmates, he said that many of his fellow prisoners would never take up the education facilities in prisons: 'education is often not seen as "for me"' (Mr B). Television content therefore provides an accessible alternative which, as Carl put it, 'keeps the brain ticking over'. Mr B's own reason for watching wildlife programmes betrayed something of his own feelings about his current situation: 'I watch them because animals don't make judgements.' Others expressed different reasons: 'It's freedom isn't it. It's soothing'; 'When you're behind bars, it's wonderful to see animals roaming free'; and 'I love to see the colours of tropical birds and beautiful flowers; all you see round here is varying shades of grey, so it really wakes up your senses to see a fantastic kingfisher or amazingly coloured fish', were typical comments, suggesting these viewers find space for contemplation or revitalisation in depictions of nature. The inmates' idealised vision of the natural world echoed the often-romanticised representation mediated to television viewers. The comments quoted above recall Simpson's (1984: 16–17) description of the appeal of the now defunct BBC 2 programme, *One Man and his Dog*:

> Against the assault by the manufactured noises of work or play, which is constant in most lives, the sounds of the programme are

beautifully definite and assertively 'natural': wind and water, abrupt commands, occasional thunder, all captured and relayed to us with a transparent simplicity and directness made possible by advanced technology and sophisticated production skills . . . Actual sheepdog trials are often carried out over terrain which can be rugged and dull, but here . . . the camera can sweep in the classic elements of rural imagery – nearby fields, distant hills, a patterned sky and reflecting water.

However, Mal, a senior officer at Gartree, had a more pragmatic explanation for the popularity of wildlife shows: 'It's about power, and killing, and hierarchies, isn't it. Law of the jungle, survival of the toughest, the natural pecking order where the ones at the bottom perish . . . That's why I've always assumed they all watch them'.[13] In a similar vein, another very popular programme type was gardening shows. Rarely a reflection of an actual hobby, gardening programmes seemed generally liked because of their depiction of natural surroundings; an important feature to residents of what was frequently described as a 'sensory-deprivation' environment. For some, an interest in nature and wildlife programmes extended to real life. At Stocken, there was a small aviary attached to G-Wing, and many inmates described how they spent hours watching the budgerigars and other small birds in there. Bill, meanwhile, who spoke of nature shows waking up the senses, described the pleasure gained from having a small pot of lemon thyme on his cell window sill: 'the smell when you rub the leaves is unbelievable, I tell you. Out of this world.' Paul talked about the birds which migrate to a nearby reservoir: 'From my cell window I can sometimes see herons and cormorants . . . I love watching the birds . . . I watch all the wildlife shows.'

In its capacity to act as an immediate, democratic and visual 'springboard for the imagination' (Gauntlett and Hill 1999: 131), television consumption is of particular interest in relation to the forming of subject positions and, in line with other media studies, I found that 'cult' TV shows opened up distinct possibilities of understanding the relationship between television and identity. Most notable in this respect was science fiction; the genre most explicitly related to by prisoners for the construction of personal identities. Of all the science fiction texts mentioned, the various *Star Trek* series stood out as being those that most commonly facilitated the playing out of those identities.[14] For example, Mr B's appreciation of the *Star Trek* series was far more than mere superficial enjoyment; it was an integral part of his identity formation from an early age: 'As an adolescent, you use TV shows when you are trying to find your identity. Something resonates.' Like *Batman*, *Star Trek* is a text open to multiple interpretations, and appeals to both adults and children on different levels. But Mr B's comment about something resonating in adolescence is telling. *Star Trek* is typically characterised as a programme that appeals to adolescent males, but the fact that many older men (and women) continue to follow both the most recent series and its previous incarnations may, as Spigel and Jenkins (1991) suggest, be evidence of a desire to celebrate youthful fantasy and turn the present into the past. It also purports to be a show that is aimed at an intelligent and discriminating audience. Although keen to deny that the programme formed any kind of fixation, Mr B nevertheless admitted that aspects of it were an integral part of his fantasy life and provided relief from depression, anxiety and feelings of inadequacy, even joking that his allegiance to the show must be proof of his 'arrested development'. But he also used the show to explore the relationship between emotion and intellect in his own life, to the extent where *Star Trek* formed a major part of his correspondence with his wife who, as his co-accused, was serving a prison sentence in a women's prison in another part of the country. Spigel and Jenkins (1991) and Tulloch and Jenkins (1995) suggest that memories of popular culture can assume a Utopian quality, offering a fantasy that denies the reality of present circumstances and allows us to reinvent our present selves as we evoke powerful and poignant moments from the past. And so it seemed with Mr B and his wife, whose personal histories were intertwined with the many series of the show spanning over thirty years. In their correspondence to each other, they used *Star Trek* to ward off the difficult realities of their current lives, and to construct a romantic vision of a better past when they had been together. Additionally, although a self-confessed loner who had little time for other inmates, Mr B admitted that those prisoners who he *did* socialise with were a community with mixed class, nationality and ethnic alignments who were loosely organised around their shared fanship of *Star Trek*. This in itself was interesting in so far as most of the staff who knew that I had interviewed Mr B described him as pompous, aloof and 'full of himself'. I found him to be someone who had a very strong public identity; he presented himself as a cultured, sensitive, highly educated and erudite man, well aware – and keen to emphasise – his differences from the rest of the prison population (as a black American, his nationality and ethnicity were obvious aspects of his difference). He knew that some of the staff and other inmates felt him to be snobbish and condescending, and with some justification. Yet when it came to sharing information and views about *Star Trek* with other inmates, social and cultural differences appeared to be transcended.

Another science fiction programme that inspired a particularly potent form of fandom was *Doctor Who*. Like *Star Trek* it might be said to constitute a somewhat extreme form of escapist fantasy, but its appeal is also potentially grounded in more mundane interests. Gauntlett and Hill (1999: 137) quote a writer of *Doctor Who* novels who claims that the core appeal of the eponymous hero is that he 'doesn't take up guns or weapons . . . [but] defeats the bad guys by being more intelligent and wittier and wilier than they are',[15] a sentiment that was expressed by a number of respondents who likened the Time Lord to a criminal mastermind. Dunn (1979: 351–52) surmises that the appeal of sci-fi programmes is they represent a 'religious/magical belief in technical mastery over evil forces'; again an attractive element in a context where religious and superstitious beliefs exist in roughly equal measure. Moreover, in the prison environment, where time is so fundamentally linked to relations of power, there may even be some attraction in the idea that time can be possessed, travelled through and re-ordered.

There certainly seemed to be evidence of enjoyment in being part of a discrete fan culture associated with all these shows, and in the cases of *Doctor Who* and the early *Star Trek* series, part of their attraction was being able to decode the subtle – and sometimes rather camp – humour. But for other respondents, there was a more serious purpose to viewing them. Joe, a life-sentence prisoner, viewed *Star Trek* in relation to his own position as someone whose sense of agency has been diminished since going to prison. His statement that: 'you have no control over anything in prison . . . I'm a Trekkie and I believe that there's got to be something bigger and better than us out there – I believe that governments are holding out on us', led to a lengthy discussion about conspiracy theories, and was an indication of his own feelings of paranoia in the face of overwhelming authoritarian, and frequently faceless, bureaucratic structures. In addition, the idealistic social vision offered by science fiction shows, and their special emphasis on values such as community, morality and equality, are themes that have been described as 'an ideal prescription for viewers routinely suffering from feelings of alienation, powerlessness and confusion' (Dunn, 1979: 352). Any form of fandom offers a place of acceptance and tolerance, but the particular enthusiasm and loyalty generated by science fiction texts indicate that many viewers use them as a major point of reference in their lives. In particular, there is evidence that viewers who might be classed as minorities (of racial or ethnic origin, sexual orientation and so on) or who simply have a sense of dislocation from the 'real world' and who desire, but perhaps also fear, change, are attracted to the representation of a future not yet formed.

Texts like *Star Trek* and *Doctor Who* may interpellate prisoners because they frequently highlight injustice or discrimination and open up new possibilities for the formation of a Utopian future.

Apart from responses identifying science fiction programmes, which might be said to promote an extreme version of fandom and – at the other extreme – news, current affairs, documentaries and wildlife or nature-orientated shows, which had a very broad appeal, the question, 'what is your favourite television programme?' yielded disappointingly vague or bland replies. Most respondents had difficulty singling out one specific show and, even if they could, their reasons for identifying it as their favourite programme proved intangible. I therefore experimented with the format of the question and found that 'who is your favourite television presenter?' provoked much more explicit and discursive responses, while still providing me with the information I sought. The most common responses to my inquiry about favourite presenters involved naming young women who are as famous for posing as glamour models as they are for their broadcasting skills. In this context, Gail Porter, Denise van Outen, Melinda Messenger and Kelly Brook were all mentioned several times, although it was not necessarily their more obvious attributes that were dwelt upon: in fact many inmates offered quite detailed critiques of the shows with which these women are associated. The search for an acceptable masculinity was none the less strongly evident in the number of responses that explicitly mentioned female nudity or female sexuality as a primary requirement of film, TV and magazine content. This imperative ranged from the mild (the infamously bra-less TV gardener, Charlie Dimmock, a presenter on several BBC shows, was named by no less than fourteen respondents in answer to the question, 'Who is your favourite TV presenter?') to the extreme, with several respondents complaining about the restrictions on hard-core pornography in prisons. Rules governing the importation into prison of soft-core pornography vary from institution to institution, although in most establishments it is tolerated in the interests of normalising the prison environment. Interestingly, an inmate at Gartree who was blind complained vociferously about the unfairness of the governor's decision not to allow him to have pornography on audiocassette. His argument was that sighted inmates are permitted to subscribe to 'top-shelf' magazines, so why should he not enjoy the same kind of benefit?

Other common responses to the request to name a favourite presenter were Angus Deayton and Nick Hancock, specifically in relation to their roles presenting the BBC2 news quiz *Have I Got News For You* and the BBC1 sports quiz *They Think It's All Over*, respectively. A number of respondents talked at length about their enjoyment of these programmes and about their appreciation of other, regular guests on each show (Paul Merton and Jonathan Ross in particular). In the case of *Have I Got News For You*, two respondents mentioned they used it as an alternative to watching the news, believing it kept them up to date with all the week's important events – or at least those that were likely to be of most interest to them. In the case of both programmes, the inmates who highlighted them seemed particularly to like the anarchic, satirical and irreverent style of them, and they used these elements as ways of reflecting the differences between their own attitudes and values and those proposed to them by the dominant social norms. Both shows are characterised by a candid disrespect for figures of authority (politicians, celebrities and members of the royal family in the case of *Have I Got News For You* and well-known and loved sports personalities on *They Think It's All Over*). Indeed good-humoured banter can quickly degenerate into something much crueller and many guests are invited on to the programmes only to face humiliation at the hands of the presenters and panel regulars. Not only is the mocking repartee of these shows reminiscent of much social interaction in prison, but the offensiveness of much of the humour, and the fact that it is largely directed at those with authority or high cultural status, marks it out as something which is not 'officially' approved of. In other words, in their derisive, devil-may-care attitude, these programmes challenge conventional top-down power relations and provide prisoners with support for those social identities they make for themselves which are based on resistance and their disdain for officialdom. The mostly male domination of the programmes, combined with what might be termed their 'laddish' humour, is also of appeal to many respondents who reinforce the relaxed, rebellious and macho tone of the programmes in their choice of viewing mode ('feet up on the bed', 'bit of puff', some hooch, etc).[16]

For others, the search for identity reinforcement is not so fruitful. Three respondents who originated from London reported they had tuned in to the soap *EastEnders* only to be disappointed by its inaccuracies and failure to represent 'their' East End: 'I miss London, London accents. *EastEnders* is hopeless – it's nothing like the East End.' Soap operas generally provoked mixed reactions. Widely accorded relatively low status, few inmates confessed to watching soaps, although several commented that 'everyone else in here watches them all the time'. Ray, a lifer, mocked: 'some of them in here watch all the soaps and then they watch all the repeats of all the soaps as well. I sometimes wonder if they're expecting the plots to change in the omnibus!' Giddens (1991a: 199) suggests that their repetitive, formulaic nature is precisely what makes soaps so attractive:

Soap operas mix predictability and contingency by means of formulae which, because they are well known to the audience, are slightly disturbing but at the same time reassuring. They offer mixtures of contingency, reflexivity and fate. The form is what matters rather than the content; in these stories one gains a sense of reflexive control over life circumstances, a feeling of coherent narrative which is a reassuring balance to difficulties in sustaining the narrative of the self in actual social situations.

That soaps give a sense of reflexive control over, and coherence and continuity in, otherwise fragmented lives would suggest they are potentially of profound importance to those who live in unpredictable and disrupted circumstances, so the unwillingness of my prisoner respondents to admit to watching them is puzzling. However, the scornful attitude towards soaps, voiced by many of my respondents, is held to be typical of men (Morley 1986; Gray 1987; Livingstone 1990), and often seems to constitute what they regard as expected behaviour. But with a little probing some respondents who began by mocking 'soap addicts' eventually admitted to being regular viewers themselves, although usually with a proviso such as 'my cellmate watches them, so I have to' or 'I only watch them if there's nothing else on'. This reluctance to acknowledge their enjoyment of what are usually thought of as 'women's programmes' may be a reflection of the requirements of the environment publicly to maintain an overtly masculine facade. However, given the capacity of soap opera to allow escapism (in its positive sense as a rational and purposeful strategy for removal from an oppressive present reality) men in prison may find themselves using media in ways more commonly found among women. For those inmates who are vulnerable to unwanted attention from other prisoners (sexual advances, physical assault, bullying or whatever), and who might thus be said to represent the feminised 'other', media may provide a sanctuary in which to escape from a routine consisting largely of domestic drudgery and mundane, repetitive work. Like the women who read romantic novels (Radway 1984) and the female devotees of soap operas (Hobson 1982), those male prisoners who are deemed weak or subordinate in the eyes of other inmates may use media texts in conventionally 'feminine' ways in order to subvert, opt out of, or simply take a break from the conventional site of hegemonic, masculine power.[17]

There were two notable exceptions to the general public disdain for soaps. The first, *The Bill*, was generally classed by respondents as a drama rather than a soap, thus avoiding the characterisation of it as a 'women's programme'. It also contains a relatively high level of violence for a pre-watershed series, which was noted as an attraction to some respondents, and which again could be interpreted as evidence of masculine hegemony. Also pertinent in the context of this study is the fact that *The Bill* is a dramatic portrayal of the police, in which the story lines inevitably and invariably revolve around their dealings with criminals. Several respondents said that *The Bill* was better viewed in association with other prisoners, where common decoding strategies could be employed: 'We like taking the piss out of it' and 'we enjoy seeing the police being portrayed as the idiots they are . . . we can have a good laugh when they cock things up' were typical comments.

The other show that seemingly transcends the generally patronising views towards soap opera was *Emmerdale*, which was popular with inmates right across the spectrum of age, class and sentence length. So widespread is its popularity that it seems to constitute something of an institution in prisons and, together with *The Bill* and sports fixtures, was the only programme explicitly mentioned as being more enjoyable watched with other inmates. Few, however, were able to articulate what it is about the programme that they like so much, and comments along the lines of 'It's just the best, isn't it? I don't know why, but it is' were frequently made. It may be popular for similar reasons to those Tulloch and Moran (1986) uncovered in their study of the Australian serial, *A Country Practice*, a soap which succeeded in attracting audiences from teenagers to over-sixty-fives by using age-focused subplots and characterisation. Equally likely, given the reasons stated for the widespread popularity of nature and wildlife programmes, *Emmerdale* may appeal to the desire for freedom and escapism. Tulloch and Moran's (ibid.) comment that *A Country Practice* incorporated a pastoral myth of Australian space, and appealed to a subconscious yearning for the country, may be mirrored among the prisoners I met, many of whom hailed from urban spaces and had spent a significant proportion of their lives behind bars. Most of *Emmerdale*'s devotees had only started to watch it when they first entered prison, which may indicate that the soap – set in a rural location and contextualised by farming and countryside issues – is popular because it evokes that same myth. The fact that many respondents mentioned *Emmerdale*'s title sequence which is a sweeping camera shot over verdant, rolling countryside, may support this theory.

In conclusion to this chapter, I hope that the exploration of the micro-context of prison societies has demonstrated how the many assaults that are inflicted on one's identity by the experience of imprisonment are mitigated by private, localised media consumption. The discussion of the meanings and motivations sought from specific media texts has revealed some particularly interesting findings relating to media consumption and personal identity. As indicated, it was the unusual, idiosyncratic and genuinely perception-changing examples of media content that proved most enlightening. Some commentators have criticised ethnographic accounts for failing to provide quantification of their findings (Schroder 1999), and concomitantly losing sight of any *patterns* of media reception Murdock 1997; Mackay 1997). However, the limiting of context to a particular environment, and the concentration on one particular social grouping, in part avoids allegations of diversity over consistency. The fact that I did not set out to quantify respondents' individual media preferences, or to seek their interpretations of pre-identified texts, was a significant feature of this study and an important departure from recent audience studies. In rejecting the assumption that there are as many meanings or gratifications available in a text as there are viewers (Morley 1980), this study is less concerned with how audiences relate to, make sense of and use a preselected media text, and more interested in how viewing activities are organised by individuals within specific and unique private settings that are arguably more subject to material and structural forms of power than most. Furthermore, those examples that *were* discussed were mentioned more or less spontaneously by interviewees, and can therefore be presumed to be genuinely important. Other researchers have reflected with hindsight that participants 'produced' responses to a programme which they otherwise would not have watched (Morley 1992), sometimes simply to have something to say, or to please the researcher.

In any case, the quantification of data could not have shed any light on the ways in which media use nurtures the self or facilitates social affiliation within the highly structured and regulated world of the prison. It perhaps goes without saying that hobby or special interest magazines can help to maintain sense of self inside; or that among a population where many individuals have reading difficulties and short attention spans, *the Sun* is the most widely read newspaper. Given the extreme displays of masculinity and physical toughness that one finds in prisons, it was also of little surprise that the film genre most favoured by young prisoners was the masculinist hero movie in which actors like Arnold Schwarzenneger and Jean-Claude Van Damme use excessive, if often cartoon-like, violence to resolve conflicts. But the advantage of conducting lengthy and intensive interviews was that it was possible to explore beyond the expected or taken for granted, and investigate the complex ways in which media resources – and specific media texts – are consumed, enjoyed and used as a primary site of meaning and identity-construction in the reflexive project of the self. The chapter has highlighted some of the ways in which media are used as material for presenting oneself *to* oneself in order to hold on to a coherent image of "who one knows one is" (DeNora 2000: 62). But introjection is not the only basis for the construction of self-identity. Also significant is the media's role in providing the material for 'projecting' identities; devices for 'spinning the apparently continuous tale of who one is' to others who inhabit the same social milieu (ibid.). It is to the social milieu of the prison – where structural demands from 'above' merge with social and 'self' imperatives from 'below' – that we now turn.

[1] These distinctions denote the different levels of engagement with media texts. Primary involvement occurs when the medium is the exclusive and focused activity. Secondary involvement occurs when media consumption is accompanied by other activities; for instance, listening to the radio while driving the car or listening to music while working. Tertiary involvement is the least intensive, where one might glance briefly at a newspaper, perhaps opening it at the TV schedule or the sports page, or have the television switched on but with the sound turned down while awaiting the next programme (Tunstall 1983; O'Sullivan *et al* 1994).

[2] Alasuutari (1999b: 100) states that, while radio could be equated to coffee – a stimulant – television is more like an alcoholic drink or narcotic, used as a means of relaxation and escapism. These metaphors seem apt in the prison context where many older and long-term inmates favoured radio to keep up to date with news and cultural events, and felt compelled to offer elaborate justifications to explain or justify their television viewing choices, yet most younger or short-term inmates praised the soporific qualities of television, and admitted their TV viewing was sometimes accompanied by hooch or drugs use.

[3] Hermes (1995: 142) describes a similar process among the lower-class female readers of gossip magazines who describe the 'game' of 'ferreting out a truth' from between the lines of salacious text as making them 'feel more alive'. In relation to the reading strategies of the tabloid audience, Pursehouse's (1991) study is also of interest.

[4] Any connection between media use and recidivism is beyond the scope of this project, although evidence suggests a link between education opportunities in prison (with which media resources are often associated) and a decreased proclivity to reoffend (Gaes *et al* 1999).

[5] In addition to the many prison sociologists who have found this, and whose work was reviewed in Chapter 1, there are, once again, striking similarities to be found in studies of unemployment.

[6] The terms 'introjection' and 'introspection' have been used interchangeably in this book, although their meaning is slightly different. The former is a psychoanalytic term referring to the 'unconscious incorporation of external ideas into one's own mind', while the latter is a more general description of the 'examination of one's thoughts and feelings' (OED).

[7] Sparks *et al* (1996: 233) report that recorded disciplinary offences reach their lowest point on Saturday, and that prisoners (like most of us) view the weekend as being qualitatively different from the remainder of the week, with greater opportunities for leisure pursuits. Staff, too, are likely to adopt a more relaxed approach at weekends, imposing sanctions only as a last resort.

[8] The collections of home-made weapons, communications devices and other assorted artefacts that many prison security offices house bear testimony to the resourcefulness of people who have time to develop and hone their already considerable skills of

invention. Some of the most interesting items I saw included a home-made tattooing machine and a television constructed inside a car wing mirror.

9   Arguably, it is only in those prisons where there is a strong sense of legitimacy that such boundaries can be broken down, albeit temporarily. For Goffman and other situationists, the roles of prisoner and prison officer would have to be both clearly defined and inherently stable (independently and in relation to each other) for such inconsistent behaviour to be reversed and previous definitions reasserted the following day.

10 For example, Scannell (1996: 95ff) notes that if by chance we witness an accident or disaster – for example, a car crash – many of us will later check it out on the television or radio simply to confirm that it was the disaster we thought it to be and to validate our personal assessment of the experience.

11 Prisons provide only a peripheral example in Meyrowitz's work and there is no evidence his discussions of the impact of electronic media in prisons have any basis in empirical investigation. In my view, while his observations concerning the *potential* of new media are perceptive, his estimation of their current application is speculative and overstated. He does at one point, however, acknowledge that the freedom provided by information access *alone* is a limited one (Meyrowitz 1985: 180).

12 Figures taken from ratings organisation, BARB, survey of 1996 (in Gauntlett and Hill 1999: 218).

13 Interestingly, though, the walls of the senior officers' room in which I interviewed Mal were bedecked with pictures of wild animals, which, we reflected humorously, might be an indication that prisoners and officers are more alike than either party would like to think.

14 Gauntlett and Hill (1999) also note the special significance of *Star Trek* in their study of the viewing habits of five hundred British TV viewers. There have been several different versions of *Star Trek* over the years, with various changes in cast, production teams and so on. Several prisoners engaged in lengthy discussions about the relative merits of each, although most comments concerned the version of the show being transmitted on BBC2 at the time of the study: *Star Trek: The Next Generation*.

15 Cornell, P. (1998) We are time's champions. Interview with Dave Owen. *Doctor Who Magazine* 267 (July): 46–51.

16 Fiske (1994) notes something similar in his analysis of the cultural practices of American teenagers and young adults watching the show *Married . . . With Children*, although in this case resistance is to the top-down power relationship between the youngsters and their most immediate figures of authority – their parents.

17 Interestingly, although numerous respondents readily admitted to reading tabloids, and especially liked the magazines that come with the weekend versions, none mentioned the high content of celebrity gossip that dominates these publications. Given the reasons that women read 'gossip magazines' – to feel connected to a wider community, to feel involved in an 'extended family' of celebrities, to experience the *frisson* of melodrama when something shocking occurs to a well-known personality and 'enjoy it when things go badly for rich and famous people', to validate their own personal knowledge or experience etc. (Hermes 1995; 1999) – it seems strange that none of my interviewees mentioned this feature of the magazines they routinely read, especially as gossip is an integral feature of the prison community. The only reason I can suggest for the omission is that, like soaps, 'gossip' is considered a feminine activity, to be engaged in, but not admitted to, by men.

Chapter 5

The meso-sphere of culture, interaction and hyper-masculinity

In adopting the term 'meso' to describe the sphere of culture and social interaction where inmates suspend their pre-prison identities and construct social identities that will conform to the expectations and demands of the fratriarchal, hegemonic prison culture, the aim is to avoid some of the tensions found in studies which privilege either the micro or the macro in their analyses of power, identity and accountability in prisons.[1] In general, these studies have developed largely independently of one another, the former resulting in mostly small-scale qualitative studies which have neglected to give sufficient weight to the structural constraints placed on action, and the latter failing to explain differential responses at the level of the individual (Jupp 1989: 123). Within these polarised positions, little attention has been paid to the relationship between private troubles, impersonal and inaccessible structures, and the 'middle ground' of community experience or common struggle. Even Sykes' classic prison sociology *The Society of Captives* (1958), which might be described as a 'meso' study in that it establishes the importance of the inmate culture as compensation for the pains of imprisonment, fails adequately to account for the interface between prisons and society, and also – much like Foucault – neglects to recognise diversity among the inmate population, assuming that all prisoners are fundamentally alike. Furthermore, most of the studies that refer to inmate subcultures resort to reductive typologies of inmate and many assume unproblematically that all a prisoner has to do to adapt successfully to a life of confinement is to obey the unwritten rules of the inmate culture, which are usually broadly characterised as 'never back down from a fight, do not grass on other inmates and never rat to the authorities'. While we should recognise the importance of these values, it should be apparent by now that the prison society is more complex than this rather negative code of conduct suggests, and that the mass media and wider sphere of popular culture have an intrinsic role to play in shaping both positive and negative constituents of the inmate community. In essence, this returns us to the view that the prison world is a microcosm of the wider society and that media consumption is profoundly implicated in social relations and the unfolding of everyday life. In this respect, much of what mainstream audience research has to say about media use has as much bearing on the prison culture as on any other environment. Cultural meanings are produced in the 'discursive layer between individuals and their surroundings' (Hermes 1999: 70) and in the interpersonal relations of communities and subcultures.

As before, however, it will be argued that the prison is an unusually insular and inward-looking environment and that the social uses associated with media in the wider community are likely to be magnified in this setting. As Lindlof (1987: 175) argues, in circumstances where personal autonomy is continually constrained and normal relations with the world become tenuous, access to media may take on unusual importance. Three specific aspects of the role of media in the prison culture will be examined accordingly: how media help with the initial entrance into prison and the demands of socialisation; the impact of media on the general inmate culture and its various subcultures; and how media aid the management of social networks and, in particular, the forming of friendships and partnerships.

Reception and socialisation

As the review of the prison literature revealed, for the majority of inmates there is no more stressful time than the point at which they first enter prison. Unlike most spheres of life, where socialisation is a relatively slow process, the transition that occurs during the processes of reception and induction to a prison is sudden and often marked by a brutal lack of preparation. But once the 'entry-shock' of reception has been endured, three features of life dominate in total institutions: uniformity, conformity and contingency. Stripped of individuality, their uniqueness disregarded and living a life that is marked by a level of fear not found in most other areas of existence, inmates must strive to conform to the prison service's rules and regulations and to adapt to the pains and deprivations inherent in the experience of incarceration. These structural imperatives combine to give prisoners a feeling of being dehumanised, and many of my research participants said they had little sense of individuality or autonomy. They claimed that most aspects of prison life function to render them indistinguishable from their fellow inmates so that, to the prison staff, governors and to most of the world beyond, they are a faceless body of men only discernible by the degrees of negative traits that can be assigned to them:

> The prison officers see us as numbers. We're just a wage packet to them. They've lost sight of us as people. As for the public, I guess we're just all a bunch of animals as far as they're concerned (Herbie).

> You haven't got an identity in prison – I'm a number. I think when I get home I won't be able to answer to my first name, I'll just answer to my surname and number. When I've had to go out to a funeral or to the hospital, you're handcuffed all the time. They treat you like scum – you don't have any dignity (Del).

The immediate and dramatic loss of personal identity that imprisonment afflicts on inmates can inhibit their ability to become aculturised to their new environment and can make them wary of social interaction:

> I don't take anyone at face value. I'm distant with everyone, even my own family. I've built a wall that wasn't there before. There are no light moments in prison . . . they take away your personality. They've killed me. Crippled me (Jim).

> I fight to keep my individuality. I put forward my personality but I don't draw people in. It's a fragile form of reality in here, it's not reality at all. Prison destroys part of your soul (Tom).

It is of little surprise, then, that many inmates report that the mass media substantially ameliorate the passage from the outside world to the world of confinement. In particular, the provision of in-cell television allows inmates to continue past routines, and provides them with a familiar temporal structure: 'You might be stuck in here and missing your family like mad and feeling really desperate, but *Eastenders* is still on at seven thirty and that's some kind of comfort' (Bill). Routines, both spatial and temporal, are crucial to the reproduction of social life, and to the deflection of personal anxiety and insecurity (Giddens 1984; Bottoms *et al* 1990). However, routines are also borne out of patterns of interaction, and media in prisons can therefore both aid ontological security (by providing a familiar temporal rhythm) and undermine it (by replacing face-to-face contact). In other words, although carefully controlled stages of socialisation are perhaps the best means of facilitating a slow and gradual acclimatisation to the prison environment, for poor copers in-cell television has provided an excuse for avoiding socialisation, and withdrawing almost entirely from the social sphere. This point was not lost on inmates or staff, several of whom observed that vulnerable, fragile or 'anti-social' inmates had become invisible as they stayed behind their cell doors watching television. At one of the Gartree Debating Society meetings, a prolonged discussion took place on this subject, with many participants reflecting that criminal activity itself is often the result of poor socialisation skills, and that it was often those inmates who were least able to engage in social intercourse who were most likely to turn on their TV sets and 'tune out' of the prison culture. An important, and related, point that was evident in this discussion and borne out in later interviews, is that not all prisoners feel able to cope with prison life, or even see why they *should* cope. Anne Worrall (2000) has criticised what she sees as the 'outward bound mentality' of the prisoner coping literature, arguing that, in women's prisons, the over-riding expectation that prisoners should find ways of coping is incompatible with inmates' own expectations: some simply do not want to cope. And so it was for some of the men I interviewed who talked movingly of their suffering and losses, and who had experienced periods of deep depression that were only exacerbated by the demands of the performative masculine culture. The facility of in-cell television to provide an excuse for disengaging from prison routine, as well as facilitating inmate conviviality, thus makes it central to patterns of both pro-social and anti-social adaptive strategies.

But for other inmates, the desire for self-insulation from the stark realities of incarceration is superseded by the need for human communication. While the majority of prisoners might feel ambivalent towards their fellow inmates (expressions of differentiation from others were common among my research participants) they spend too much time in the presence of others to avoid all interaction (Schmid and Jones 1991). Furthermore, for newly admitted inmates, there is a need to learn from others the rules of the prison (both formal and informal) and assimilate the culture as quickly as possible. According to Schmid and Jones (ibid.: 415), who conducted a study of identity transformation in an American maximum security prison, this assimilation primarily involves the suspension of pre-institution identities and the temporary construction of 'inauthentic prison identities' to mask the true self. The presentation of a public persona enables inmates to thwart more radical identity change and to maintain a more or less consistent sense of identity throughout most of their prison careers (ibid.) Like Cohen and Taylor, they refute Irwin's assertion that prisoners enter prison with a common 'criminal' identity and are therefore all essentially alike, but claim that the degradations and deprivations that confront them inside constitute a common experience and provoke collective responses. Broadly speaking, these amount to the internalisation of feelings of vulnerability and emotional fragility.

It is arguable, however, that prisoners are not quite as adept at role-playing and impression management as is sometimes assumed, particularly when they enter prison for the first time. For some, the projection of a 'false' identity will be beyond their impression management skills, and they will be forced to withdraw – literally and emotionally – into their private self. For others, far from being a 'false' identity as Schmid and Jones suggest, the presentation of self will be a familiar, if exaggerated, version of the social identity developed prior to entering prison. Indeed, for one of my respondents who, by his own admission was 'living a cosy life' at Ashwell, the real mask was worn outside prison:

> People in here aren't as hard as they make out. It's on the outside that you have to be a hard man. I'm in here for dealing, right. On the outside you have to put up a front, defend yourself. You're on the front line. But in here you don't have to be like that. I'm not nearly as aggressive as I used to be. To be honest it's a relief to be in here and to be able to let the mask drop (T).

T's experience was relatively unusual, however, and most of my respondents were aware of the need to be able to interchange between private and public personas:

> I hate prison because I have to pretend to be someone I'm not. In my cell I can be myself but as soon as I come out I have to stand differently, present myself differently. When I'm on the phone I have to remember to swap over to myself . . . People can't spend enough time being their private selves in Ashwell. I did an HND at Stafford in Business Studies. It gave me confidence and self-esteem. I achieved something. But generally in prison I have a sense of not having my responsibilities, not being a man. I feel less of a father, less of a man while I'm in here. I can't let them know that though. I feel like I've got a split personality, I have real mood swings (Craig).

Some inmates feel compelled to present a 'front' even with their loved ones:

You have to put on a mask to your family. Sometimes it would be easier not to have visits. You have to get in a right good mood, whether you feel like it or not (Dave).

People wear a mask when they're with their family, but it's false. Everyone needs their own time. We all shed a tear inside, but only behind our doors. You can't offload on to your family – I mean it's not their fault you're in here, is it? (Joe).

One of the few spheres of prison life where inmates *were* apparently able to 'drop the mask' was at the (semi-)informal meetings of Prison Dialogue where approximately twenty prisoners (and sometimes invited staff or outside guests) gathered to discuss subjects of interest, often prompted by an issue from the week's news (see Jewkes 2001). On the occasions when these forums worked well, the breadth and depth of discussions permitted participants to present aspects of their self publicly which were normally kept private, and this seemed to be the factor that ensured that most participants returned. Not only did this allow for a temporary denial of the primary identity 'prisoner', but it also served to diminish the stigma of their convictions and convict-status (although on the rare occasions when someone alluded to their violent past or said something like 'I know I've killed someone but. . .' it caused the kind of *frisson* that Cohen and Taylor (1972) describe when one of their informants on Durham's E-wing casually said 'of course, I'm a murderer'). The long-term benefit of Prison Dialogue is hard to measure, although I had no doubt that it has the capacity – at least in the short term – to restore the beleaguered self and provide a rare opportunity in prison for individuals to reclaim a sense of their personal identity and stand out as 'figure' against 'ground' (Burman 1988). It also has a slightly paradoxical social benefit in that, while addressing the needs of the self, it precludes indulgent self-interest. Although personal reflectiveness is encouraged, the opportunity to identify with and learn from the experiences of other inmates prohibits over-introspection and self-regard, both of which can afflict the self under 'normal' prison conditions. In Burman's account of unemployment, he describes the social effects of the 'Unemployment Working Centre', a loose coalition of various interested parties which provides a range of services to unemployed people, including an opportunity for them to get together and share their experiences. His assessment of the success of this group in bridging the gap between self and social world exactly mirrors the experiences of many of those who attended Prison Dialogue:

In these forums for the telling and handling of personal accounts, one's experiences were seen to occur on a more general plane, where they were elements and outcomes of complex practices and discriminations. The social findings learned so vividly with experienced others became conceptual tools of escape from self-blame. No longer a solitary sufferer, one was taking part in a slow, collective awakening to the social conditions from which many suffer. Out of these gatherings . . . was born a basis for new solidarities and understandings . . . In these groups, practices changed from pure self-interest to the synergistic combining of self and others (ibid.: 105–106).

The dialogue group also gave participants the opportunity to exhibit quite separate and multifarious identities (for example, at various times Simon constructed his identity around his roles as a black man, a 'Brummie', a musician, a father, a son and an Open University student), or quite subtle and inseparable identities, as in the many discussions that took place concerning aspects of black people's histories, cultures and ethnicities. As Westwood (1990: 570) observes: 'one can be, at one and the same time Afro-Caribbean *and* Jamaican *and* various religious identities *and* a "black man" and many other things.' Nowhere was this potential more evident in the constrained and limiting world of the prison than in the relatively democratic and mentally stimulating space which constituted the meetings organised by Prison Dialogue.

Schmid and Jones (1991) argue that the typical inmate sees the prison world as an artificial construction, and that he believes he will revert completely 'back to his old self' upon release. This was not, however, borne out by everyone in my study, especially those inmates serving very long sentences: 'prison changes you for ever, there's no doubt about that.' Others, however, supported Schmid and Jones' finding that the authentic self can be recovered upon release: 'I left my identity at reception and I'll pick it up on my way out.' But whatever degree of authenticity one pre-supposes in the presentation of self or in the prison world, there is little doubting Schmid and Jones' view that the new inmate arrives at prison with a fairly consistent image of what prison is like (often informed by media-generated images of violence and intimidation) and then proceeds to adjust his perceptions as he observes and interacts with other prisoners:

Through watching others, through eavesdropping, through cautious conversation and selective interaction, a new inmate refines his understanding of what . . . prisoners look like, how they move, how they act. Despite his belief that he is different from these other prisoners, he knows that he cannot appear to be too different from them, if he is to hide his vulnerability. His initial image of other prisoners, his early observations, and his concern over how he appears to others thus provide a foundation for the identity he gradually creates through impression management (ibid.: 422).

You definitely have to wear a mask in prison – if you don't you're going to get eaten away. When I came in I was green. I thought I was quite streetwise on the outside, but no. You have to act tough, there's always the threat of violence. I remember for the first six months I was here, standing in the queue for meals, trying not to make eye contact with anyone in case they took it the wrong way. I'm a bit more relaxed now, but you still have to be on your guard the whole time (Simon).

Simon's comment illustrates how, in addition to adapting to a life of confinement, the new inmate starts to absorb, and then acts back on and shapes, the informal culture of the prison. To be accepted by other inmates as 'one of them', the new prisoner must pay close attention to rules of presentation concerning such details as eye contact and posture, and it is through such observations that acceptable social behaviours are replicated and masculine hegemony is preserved.

Culture and subculture

Having mastered how he should present himself in the company of others, the new inmate must then learn to recognise and respect the complex patterns of group networks and hierarchies that characterise inmate societies. Variously based on age, communities of origin, gangs, drug trafficking or previous criminal and prison experiences, these hierarchies form the basis for a whole style of conduct and, in many respects, resemble an 'occupational culture' which is cemented by jokes, gestures, the exchange of favours and the recurrence of certain topics of conversation (Tolson 1977). They may be pro-social or anti-social in attitude, and the primary task of the new inmate is to decide whether he is going to adopt a prison-adaptive strategy of integration into, or avoidance of, one or more of these subgroups.

Underpinning many features of the prison culture is the illegal socioeconomic system that allows inmates to buy drugs or other commodities, but frequently leads to them becoming victims of debt, bullying and protection rackets. Those who are involved in contraband economies are arguably deflecting attempts to socialise them through formal channels and instead constructing their identities around notions of resistance and counterculture, demonstrating that there may be an inverse correlation between prisonisation and socialisation.[2] The conclusion that has to be drawn is that, in spite of the prison service's own attempts to shape social-isation processes, prison inmates assert a strong degree of agency in deciding exactly how far they are prepared to be socialised. Many partic-ipants in my research were almost continuously involved in the business of making plans, trading goods with other inmates, devising ways of 'getting one over' on a fellow prisoner or member of staff, or keeping abreast of new legislation which might affect them. Defying the conven-tional, formal codes of socialisation, they were none the less engaged in constant thought and interaction, once more suggesting that the assump-tion that prisoners' behaviour – both pro-social and anti-social – can be controlled by administrators as long as they have control over the reward system of the prison is highly questionable.

Mathiesen (1965) suggests that one of the most striking features of all inmate cultures is the frequency with which prisoners compare their own fate with that of others, both inside prison and outside it. Some inmates may feel themselves to be outcasts from the wider community and, indeed, most research participants spoke about 'society' in a rather detached way, as if they were not part of it. For these individuals, the feeling of stigmatisation and of being part of an underclass, with all its connotations of subhumanness and subterranean invisibility, is the foremost aspect of their identity. They might feel themselves to be a husband, partner, father, son, builder, Londoner or any number of other identities, but it is their physical location that inevitably bestows upon them their primary identity:

> I am a professional prisoner I suppose – after sixteen years in here, what else could I be? The judge said I was ruthless, but I'm not ruthless. They say we're hamsters, not gangsters in here – that's how ruthless we are. But yes, I am a prisoner, nothing more (Dave).

According to Mathiesen, a common response for such an individual is to perceive his lot as deplorably deprived in relation to the pleasures of the outside, although – in an anomic twist to this view – I encountered several inmates who blamed the media for instilling in them needs and desires which, they claimed, are not gratifiable by means other than criminal. As a means of protection against the damaging self-image that such reference points can instil, the prisoner may turn to the institution, using other inmates for self-comparison. He may also devote himself to making the prison a home, a strategy of colonisation which is perhaps most evident in those prisoners who feel a particular degree of attachment to their wing or accommodation unit: 'I'm fussy about hygiene, cleanliness, personal space . . . I'm lucky to be here [in the "Super-Enhanced" unit] because I've got my own TV and toilet . . . it's got to be better than over there' (T).

Of all the prisons in which I conducted fieldwork, Stocken was the one in which different accommodation units had the most distinct identities. The individual histories and characteristics of each unit create a unique habitus and result in many of them feeling like a prison within a prison (or what Sparks *et al* 1996 term 'micro-climates'). One resident of G-Wing, the Scandinavian mobile unit, talked about 'that jail' in reference to the other wings, as if it were an entirely separate establishment. In addition to G-Wing, there are two wings at Stocken that have waiting-lists: F-Wing, which was one of the first prison units in the country to have in-cell television (including satellite channels, although there were plans for their withdrawal in April 2000; a move which no inmate mentioned to me, leading me to believe they did not know about it), and H-Wing, which had been open for less than two years, a fact that accounted for its popularity:

> 'It's new. That's the only reason I'm on here . . . at least I know my cell's not been contaminated . . . it's had nobody die in it. In fact nobody had even slept in the bed before me' (Ralph).

A-Wing, the 'lifer wing', also had a distinctive feel about it, although one of its residents expressed mixed feelings:

> Lifers and staff come to a nice understanding. If someone gets a pasting they wouldn't grass, but in all probability the staff would probably turn a blind eye anyway. I like being on an all-lifer wing because it's more peaceful and because the staff understand that we want to be left alone. But I suppose on balance I'd prefer a mixed wing because it stops it getting stale, you get to see fresh faces and they bring in news from the outside (Ray).

Unpopular among some inmates on other wings because of the perceived perks that lifers are afforded, one of D-Wing's inhabitants, serving five years, was scornful of the preferential treatment given to lifers: 'Lifers always get more. In some prisons I've been in, only the lifers can wear their own clothes. Here they can go and sit out on the grass in the summer. It's like you have to kill someone to get privileges' (Bill).

Some inmates extend their life-sphere beyond their accommodation unit to the prison as a whole, and adopt a strategy of adaptation that involves making themselves seen or heard as much as possible. In some cases, such noisiness and visibility can appear to be a deliberately aggressive stance, although Tolson's (1977: 43) interpretation of aggression as 'the basis of "style", of feeling physical, of showing feelings and protecting oneself' seems relevant here. As one respondent put it to me: 'You have to shout to get anyone to take any notice of you in here. Besides which, it's about the only way you can feel alive' (Billy). Virtually any act of communication can be regarded as a kind of performance, and performance in prison is often intrinsically bound with concepts of masculinity and challenges to power. Among the most 'staged' performances I witnessed were the interactions between inmates and prison officers where the management of a masculine 'presence' was paramount for both parties. On occasions tempers were lost, but there is an implicit consensus that masculinity is, as Tolson (1977: 43) says, 'more impressive played cool', and 'point-scoring' on both sides was achieved by choice gestures and witty put-downs rather than by resorting to violence. The apparent arbitrariness of prison officers' decision-making is a constant source of frustration for inmates and has been described as the 'hallmark of the English prison experience' (Vagg 1994: 85), but one of the most common provocations I observed was when prisoners had made a request, either directly to an officer or in writing to the prison governor, and a reply was not forthcoming. In some cases a 'stand-off' would emerge, whereby an inmate relentlessly pursued a particular officer in search of an answer to his inquiry and the officer would use various tactics to avoid addressing his complaint. Often, an inmate's frustration at being denied information on a previous occasion was used by officers as an excuse for later avoidance tactics, a chain of reactions that Goffman (1961b) refers to as 'looping'. Such 'mind games' are a common element of everyday relations between inmates and staff and recall de Certeau's (1984: 18) conceptualisation of everyday life as a conflict between the powerful and the powerless, where there is a 'certain art in placing one's blows, a pleasure in getting around the rules': 'You're always playing a game – with the staff, with the other prisoners, the governor, solicitors . . . you have to try and stay one step ahead all the time. Every week a new rule is introduced here. They're just going round and round in circles' (Brian). One research participant described it as being like a ritualised dance in which the inmate is locked with his tormentor, taking one step forward, but then condemned to taking several steps back. This dramatised motif seems appropriate for there were several occasions when staff members appeared to be 'performing' and the prisoners' interpretations of these performances were that they were directed at me, an interested audience. With some notable exceptions, inmates' presentation of self in front of staff was usually one of quiet acquiescence or exchanging non-threatening banter, although many respondents pointed out this too was just an act. In particular, some of the older inmates had trouble maintaining the veneer of mutual respect with officers who were significantly younger than them. As one long-termer put it: 'I've got kids older than him.' The inevitable violations of privacy that come from having one's criminal and prison histories (together with personal details of family relations, illnesses and so on) on file and accessible to anyone with authorisation to look at them was also a problem made especially sharp by differences in age between offender and officer, although one inmate reported he took great pride in amassing details about individual officers' lives in an attempt to redress the balance.

That public presentation was of paramount importance to prisoners was demonstrated in many different ways, although perhaps most incontrovertibly at the meetings of Prison Dialogue where participants attached a great deal of kudos to winning the argument and not losing face. Dominance of the group was based on different factors: at Blakenhurst, the local prison containing a wide range of offenders awaiting classification, discussions were led by a small number of individuals who had clearly developed a repertoire of stories, jokes, routines and gestures, which had the primary purpose of entertaining the audience. One individual in particular, Mikey, had constructed his identity around his skills as a performer, a persona that was itself reinforced by the fact that his brother is a well-known musician and actor. In an extreme version of the tendency noted by Tolson (1977) in his analysis of working-class masculinity, this individual's every action and utterance was aimed at reproducing the expectations of his public. Even his clothing, which was expensive, yet flashily so, constituted an integral part of his performance which almost literally involved 'putting on a show'. His interpretation of the requisite masculinity demanded by the prison culture was to act the clown, and he created an atmosphere of jovial camaraderie and bonhomie. A further point of interest in relation to Mikey was that he assigned nicknames based on television characters ('Dirty Den', 'Betty Boo', 'Homer Simpson', 'Mr Bean', etc.) to all the participants at the dialogue meeting. This use of media content in defining individuals paralleled the experiences of Lindlof (1987: 194), who tells of the inmate named 'Benny Hill' by his fellow prisoners because of his resemblance to the comedian, and the inseparable duo known as the 'Smurfs' after the animated characters of the 1970s.

Similarly, prison researchers Richard Sparks and Will Hay recount how they became known by their respondents as 'Pinky and Perky', 'Bill and Ben' or 'The Dynamic Duo' after Batman and Robin (in Sparks *et al*, 1996: 350), while Roy King and Kathleen McDermott became 'Dempsey and Makepeace' during their prison research (in King 2000). Like these examples, Mikey's nicknames were meant – and taken – good-humouredly but, as Lindlof (1987: 194) suggests, such ascriptions that are at once familiar and amusing to an audience may be primarily designed to deflect seriousness from what are, in fact, serious circumstances. Mikey also sought to gain maximum credibility from his relation to his high-profile brother and, indeed, throughout my fieldwork, many respondents emphasised their knowledge of, or friendships with, stars of the media who had spent time in prison. Prisoners who had *become* media figures as a result of their notoriety, or the infamy of their crimes, were also evoked in this way.

At Whitemoor, by contrast, the demands of a 'tough jail', together with the serious or violent criminal histories of many of the inmates, meant that the dialogue group was an altogether more unpredictable affair, and the Prison Dialogue facilitators frequently had skilfully to prevent dialogue from degenerating into monologue. Here, the forum was dominated by those who could assert themselves most forcefully. Often, it was the strength of an individual's intellect or the breadth of his knowledge that gave him a platform, but it could also be a person's ability to shout louder than anyone else that determined his precedence! Examples of such performance styles have been given elsewhere in this book, but suffice to say here that among a few participants, their outward presentation of aggression and physical strength had become, as Tolson (1877: 8) predicts, part of their internal self-image. Indeed, the conventional characteristics associated with masculinity – authority, competitiveness, physical presence, aggression and so on – were always conspicuously displayed at these meetings.

Across all the prisons I studied, it was noticeable that mass media texts were exploited to enhance individuals' identities as aggressive criminals, 'hard men', prisoners or 'experts' in law and the criminal justice system. Many respondents counted among their favourite television shows such as *Crimewatch UK* and other programmes that use either covert filming techniques or dramatic reconstructions to demonstrate types of criminal activity. Neil, serving three years, admitted: 'I watch programmes like *Police, Camera, Action!* and *Crimewatch* to see if there's anyone on I know . . . it makes me feel a sense of reality[3]. For Jon, serving life, media texts served to legitimate his persona as a violent criminal:

Reading is better than TV. You read a book and it takes you somewhere else and then you see it on TV and they've ruined it. Take *Misery*. The book is so much better because it's more violent. In the film she only cripples him, but in the book she actually cuts his legs right off.

Earlier media researchers may have interpreted this as cathartic, suggesting that media act as a harmless vehicle for the relieving of one's own feelings of aggression. But as stated previously, whatever gratifications we seek from media content are not divorced from our environment, and mediated identity construction should be understood as a process of meaning-making borne out of social interactions and available cultural resources (Hermes 1999). The creation of identities has to be meaningful not only to the individual concerned, but also to his peer group. In this case, the individual's cultural repertoire is dominated by the imperatives of an enforced and somewhat extreme masculine code. It is therefore unsurprising that it is very often violent or criminal media figures that provide identification for prisoners.

Consistent with uses and gratifications research, many others exploited the democratising nature of media, using it as a means of surveillance of any new developments in the prison service or in law which might affect their sentences. Gary said: 'when you watch something, you identify with it emotionally. I watched *Scum* the other night . . . I do watch things about prison because I relate to them.' Most notable in this respect, though, were the two inmates at HMP Stocken who were known by staff as the 'professional litigators'. Like Cohen and Taylor's (1972: 140) 'professional complainers' who pursue their grievances with such dedication and persistence that it 'virtually becomes a style of doing one's time,' these two men had constructed their identities and formed a bond with each other largely on the basis of their mutual interest in the political and social rights of prisoners. Although they had refused in-cell television, they read a wide range of specialist publications, including law books, criminological journals and newspapers such as *Inside Time*,[4] as well as gleaning information from television (in association rooms) and radio. They then used this information to try to hold the prison service accountable for any perceived wrongdoing. The growth in access to channels of communication and information exchange may partially explain why the law is increasingly becoming involved in many institutions that once handled their own internal problems privately, and certainly during the course of my research I heard several stories concerning the prison service being sued by prisoners who were unhappy with their treatment (see also Jacobs 1977 on the role of law in shaping prisons).

The use of media in these ways undoubtedly helped individuals to construct an appropriately tough facade to present to their peers. Masculinity was also a key factor in the comparative reference points of those inmates who – rather than measuring their status against other specific individuals – chose to gauge their status in relation to other *types* of offenders. It is common to find in prison literature expressions of prisons being the 'garbage cans' of society or 'human zoos' but it seems that a key feature of the prison hierarchy is the need for convicted criminals to feel morally superior to *someone*, a judgement most clearly shaped by the codes of the informal masculine hegemony (hence the position of 'feminised' sex offenders near the bottom of the pile, and child sex offenders even lower than them). Aside from these judgements, which are common to most prisons, hierarchies may be constructed around more mundane crimes. For example, many respondents expressed disdain for burglars, while commercial burglars made a distinction between their own crimes and those of domestic or 'house' burglars. Several respondents, when asked who were at the bottom of the informal hierarchy of power, replied 'bag-heads', the heroin addicts who were widely felt to have no scruples and to be responsible for the lack of solidarity among prisoners today. Yet somewhat ironically, the inmates most frequently held to be at the top of the pecking order were the drugs dealers, who – with startling self-delusion – were themselves quick to justify their own activities compared to those of other inmates: 'nobody died from what I did and that can't be said of everyone in here.'

The distinction between these low-status and high-status crimes was illustrated by two respondents, who echoed Sykes (1958) classification of 'real men':

> At the top of the pile you've got the drugs dealers, the real men. If you've got drugs in prison you've got friends. I'd say burglars are the most despised here (Simon).

> I came in with a view of prison from American movies . . . thought I was going to be raped and everything. But much of the violence is just bravado, skirmishes. There is a hierarchy . . . those at the top are the quieter people, they have something about themselves, 'old school', you might say. At the bottom are the dumbos. I'd say it's the intelligence factor [that separates high-status from low-status inmates]. A lot of people in here can barely write their own names. It used to be heroin users that were at the bottom, but not anymore. When it was a dirty drug outside it was in here too, but now it's

considered chic, or something. Drug dealing is hip. They'll emphasise that. Violence too. House burglary is looked down on with the media pumping it out all the time. I'm not bad though. I'm commercial (Tom).

What both these quotations reiterate is the link between 'high-status' crimes and machismo. Drugs dealers were frequently characterised as 'real men' (one said he liked the fact he was considered a 'Mister Big' both inside and outside prison) and, in this respect, dealers ranked alongside 'gangsters' and armed robbers in the hegemonic masculine structure. Deserving little respect and near the bottom of the informal power structure are the 'wannabes' or 'plastic gangsters' who contrive to be like the 'real thing', but are, in truth, 'bag-heads', 'phoneys' or petty thieves. Masculine credentials may be further enhanced by the brutality that one has survived:

> I was proud entering Wormwood Scrubs at fifteen. Before that, I was in a remand home at the age of twelve. It gave me status going to the Scrubs . . . we'd gone thieving and had look-outs and everything. We thought we were the real thing, we felt like big men. Once inside you had to go through 'recepo-bashing' – a kind of initiation where you were beaten by your 'friends' to within an inch of your life. I won the fight . . . beat up three out of the four [assailants]. That made me 'The Chap' (Jim).

As Sykes (1958: 98) reminds us, the definition of masculine behaviour in a society composed exclusively of men is 'apt to move to an extreme position' and such initiation rites are a common feature of men's prisons. Such brutality seems to confirm Bowker's (1977: xi) assertion that what prisoners do to each other is often far worse than anything staff have ever done to them but, as Jim's quotation indicates, it is often only those who pass such barbaric tests of manliness that gain the advantage of solidarity. Male bonding in prison, as in other predominately male spheres, reaffirms masculine hegemony not only by excluding women, but also by preying on weaker men (Newton 1994).

Jim's pride at being sent to Wormwood Scrubs also indicates that masculine credentials extend to entire prisons, and of those inmates who compare their fate to that of prisoners in other establishments, the 'hardness' of a prison regime (in terms of both the weight of deprivations encountered, and the extent of tough, masculine qualities needed to survive them) can be a primary reference point. At both Ashwell and Stocken, comparisons with local, dispersal and Category B establishments were frequently made. Gartree was generally held to be a 'proper man's jail' although that status seemed to be largely based on its past reputation as a dispersal prison where riots and daring escapes occurred. At Gartree comparisons were made with Whitemoor, which was usually described as a 'dumping ground'; an assessment that, again, is likely to be based on the prison's history. At Ashwell and Stocken reactions to being in a 'Cat C' jail varied greatly. The following comments all concern Stocken:

Stocken's brilliant . . . I'm a reformed character [since coming here]. I used to be difficult . . . I just don't like being treated as a number. But it's ok here. Treat them [the staff] with respect and you get loads back. I hate to say it but I've enjoyed my stay here. It's pleasant compared to other jails I've been to (George).

I've been here before so I'm used to it – I just see it as a break . . . I was in Glen Parva first and I turned twenty-one so I had to come to an adult jail. I had all the usual fears of violence and rape, and so on, but then I got here and found I knew half the people in here, so I was alright (Michael).

I hate it here. This prison is a dumping ground for lifers. If someone messes up in another Category C prison they get shipped here. It's useless . . . no facilities . . . no work. We're down to one association room because they're using the other one as a storeroom for TVs. It's crap, I tell you (Billy).

Ashwell generally compared favourably with local prisons Leicester and Nottingham, and 'hard' prisons such as Albany and Wormwood Scrubs, or Frankland, which was disliked because it contains a high proportion of sex offenders. Yet Ashwell was viewed less favourably by some because of the high numbers of young inmates, which mitigate against it being a 'man's jail': 'it's like a children's home' and 'it's a Mickey Mouse jail – full of young scallies and inadequates' were typical comments. One long-term inmate commented: 'Ashwell could be the best prison in the country for long-termers to finish off their sentences, but it's spoilt by the short-termers on heroin.' The same man was one of many inmates who complained they had come from 'B' jails where they had been allowed to wear their own clothes and cook their own meals, and where other perks, such as family visiting days, had been introduced. Indeed for just over half the inmates I interviewed at Ashwell, the relative freedom which the prison offered was either a problem, because of the long periods of unstructured time that has to be filled, or it was illusory, because the relatively relaxed level of security offered more opportunities for drug-taking, debt-collecting and bullying. In comparatively 'open' prisons such as Ashwell, a great deal of emphasis is placed on dynamic security. However, in-cell television has resulted in many inmates who would previously have been involved in communal work or association activities under the watchful eyes of staff now confining themselves to their cells to watch television:

> You only see some people at meal times now . . . those who lack social skills are going to lose out . . . if they're not out on the corridors, they're not socialising. There's also a danger that they think that what they're seeing on TV is real life, and they lose their grip on reality. Staff–prisoner relations are fragile now and they'll only get worse. Interaction is minimal (Ray).

The invisibility of many inmates has increased levels of drugs use and bullying to the extent where many interviewees said they preferred the twenty-three hour lock-up regimes of local jails to the relaxed and relatively open conditions of Ashwell. Indeed, for some inmates, the freedom of Ashwell paradoxically induced feelings of paranoia. Andy said: 'you have to develop a sixth sense for trouble because it's more hidden in a jail like this' while Paul summed up the suspicions of many when he said: 'this prison seems lax, but there's a lot of mental psychology being used in the background.'

Another interesting point in relation to different categories and regimes of prisons is that the worse the circumstances of confinement are, the less may be required to be considered important (Mathiesen 1965). Put simply, I came across many inmates who told stories of being in solitary confinement or in hospital and who, after a period with no media, were given a radio or a newspaper. Assertions that it stopped them from going mad or that it even staved off thoughts of suicide were not uncommon. Similarly, I found that although in-cell TV was generally eagerly anticipated, several inmates at Gartree and Whitemoor favoured a radio or stereo system over television while, at the other end of the spectrum, many inmates on Stocken's F-wing, not content with having satellite television available in their cells, complained about having only four satellite channels. However, it may be that the inmate's frames of reference are built around what is *present* rather than what is *absent* (Goffman 1961b; Cohen and Taylor 1972). Prisoners at Gartree and Whitemoor may feel they can afford to be blasé about television before it is installed in their own cell, but had I returned some months later and asked which they would be most prepared to relinquish – their radio or television – many may find themselves more reluctant to part with their TV.

Among those who *do* want television, there is – aside from the obvious attractions of its programmes – a desire for in-cell TV as 'goods' (Liebling *et al* 1997); a motivation that may be understood as a further indication of masculine worth. Symbols of conspicuous consumption are intrinsic to rituals of display, courtship and manliness: 'they reflect the proper order of things and are clung to' (Fineman 1987: 238). Although prisoners earn an average of £7 a week it is none the less important to be visibly consuming if their adequacy as a man is to be upheld (Bostyn and Wight 1987), and in many prisons the influences of commodification can be seen in a variety of prisoners' possessions, from the media 'hardware' he owns to the brand of trainers he wears on his feet. 'Lifestyle' thus has a place in the prison culture; indeed, material aspirations arguably become increasingly salient under conditions of severe material constraint. The notion that lifestyle patterns can indicate both conformity to the dominant group or, conversely, deliberate rejection of more widely diffused forms of consumption was illustrated in a number of ways by my research participants. One notable indicator of both lifestyle aspirations and the need to signal to the group something of one's pre-prison identity, was footwear. At the Whitemoor dialogue group, most participants were young and street-wise, and they literally wore their masculine credentials on their feet. Their new and expensive designer-label trainers indicated a desire to fit in with the dominant norms, and yet also suggested a degree of competitiveness; for some inmates it seemed important not to get left behind in the rapidly moving worlds of fashion and footwear technology. By contrast, a Dutch prisoner whom I met at Stocken, while resigned to wearing his shabby and threadbare prison uniform, had on his feet a pair of elegant, highly polished, brown leather brogues. Not only aesthetic, but clearly expensive, this man admitted it was important for him to be allowed to wear his shoes, not only to maintain a sense of himself as a man of taste and culture, but also to signal to the other inmates and, importantly, to the prison officers, that he was 'different, more refined, than they are'.

Managing social networks

One of the most common coping strategies among those who are incarcerated is to be found in the choice of reference group commitments, and a typical response by prisoners to the institutional requirements of uniformity, conformity and compliance is to draw strong distinctions between 'likeness' and 'otherness'. Any common experience, information or role that separates two or more people from others will give them a sense of common identity (Meyrowitz 1985: 54). Consequently, while there is little evidence of the universal inmate solidarity that Sykes (1958) describes, there now exist social networks consisting of many and varied subcultures, whose affiliations may be based upon shared nationality or regional identity; religion or faith; the culture of the gymnasium; drugs use; gambling; contraband trading; shared music or education interests; or any number of other common concerns. My research also uncovered evidence of bonds being formed between some of the younger, short-term prisoners on the basis of shared constructed identities of deviance and delinquency. A great deal of macho posturing was evident in these groups, and boasts about violent histories and deviant activities were common, although given that it was these men who were the 'plastic gangsters' according to the older inmates, the incidents they presented as daring and dangerous might in fact be rather spasmodic and tame (Little 1990). Little's view is that the justice system can be counter productive in that it not only brings together young people with similar criminal pasts, but it does little to discourage them from constructing their disappointing and limited life experiences as positive, necessary components for their chosen 'career' (ibid.).[5] It is arguable (and it *was* argued by several prison officers and inmates) that the implementation of in-cell television reinforces deviant self-images, leading to statements of the sort that Little (ibid.:7) describes in his study of criminal identities among young offenders: 'Oh it [prison] was easy, you just do your bird and get on with it; no problem really.' Such sentiments were common at Ashwell and Stocken, and frequently expressed in relation to the impact that in-cell TV has made to the quality of prison life.

But for a group to be an 'us', there must also be a 'them' and antagonisms between different factions are common. Moreover, because inmate experience and roles are situation-bound, and the patterns of stratification (of power, influence, access to scarce resources) are complex and unstable, any significant change in the structure of the situation will affect group identities and may change people's sense of who are 'us' and who are 'them' (Sparks *et al*, 1996). This not only results in shifting dynamics of power, but it may also be a partial explanation for the fact that very few prisoners claim to have friends in jail; it is simply rarely possible to put your trust in another individual in a society as unpredictable and volatile as the prison:

There's no solidarity any more. No 'fellow feeling'. Especially in a prison like this, full of kids and short-termers (Jim).

I relate to one person I knew on the outside. I know his company is safe to keep. My co-accused was in here – I'd have taken any problem to him. We all need someone to lean on but you have to watch out. This is a very dangerous place and if you've got any sense, you won't get too close to anyone. They've blagged their way through life, and they do exactly the same in here. You can't trust no one (Tim).

The exception to the general rule of 'no friends' is the groups of two or, more rarely, three inmates who form an especially close bond. Cohen and Taylor (1972: 75) note the importance for long-term inmates of seeking a companion or intimate, and the difficulties posed by such endeavours, but they fail to elaborate on the particular significance of close dyadic friendships, other than to note they develop as a result of not having a wide network of potential friends available, each of whom might serve a different need. In such circumstances a single personal relationship may be required to sustain the various functions which would be distributed across several individuals in normal life. In the course of my research I encountered many inmates who were 'paired off' in partnerships which may have been, although by no means necessarily were, of a sexual nature.

Most interesting from my point of view were the inmates who had chosen to share a cell with a fellow prisoner:

I share a cell, yes. Would I describe us as friends? Well, I'm hoping with this geezer I'm with, yes, but before now what I've thought were friends have let me down. But it's important to have somebody to talk to. I have quite deep conversations with my cellmate. He's a Muslim, and he's travelled a lot, so we talk about religion and where we've been and that (Simon).

My only real friends are my co-defendants, but you can't make friends in prison. My only friend is my cellmate, Mark. I used to get on really well with an older guy at my last prison – we did weights training together. I suppose you could say he was a bit of a father figure, looked after me and that. But now I'm very self-sufficient. I don't borrow and I do everything for myself. I'm self-contained I suppose (Ralph).

I share a cell – that's my choice. It's someone I met in prison. We both enjoy being twoed-up. I enjoy his company, it's company that I choose. I don't like crowds, I never go in the television room. But he's a friend . . . You do get large numbers of pairs in prison. If you have anything to do with one, you know you've got to deal with the other one as well. You can't survive in prison at either of the two extremes – making friends with everyone or keeping yourself entirely to yourself . . . The main attraction of twoing-up is having someone to talk to. It's like therapy. I'd done a year on my own but to share with someone was quite attractive. I'd not really spoken to anyone for a year, only very shallow conversations. Same with Theo, the Dutch guy. Another Dutch man came in and it really opened up his world. He used to be in his cell all the time before (David).

Negotiations over in-cell television created friction, however:

I watch more television than I would naturally wish because my cellmate watches more than me. He relies on the TV more for his stimulation – to be honest, he'd struggle without television. He's spent a lot of time in prison. Although we get on, I think I'll be glad when he's gone. Our cell's no bigger despite being doubled-up, and it's a bit cramped especially now the weather's getting warmer. . . We used to have two TVs on sometimes! But now we've got just one, so we have to agree on what to watch. There's no point in falling out. I used to watch *Newsnight*, but my friend, he likes soaps because it fills the time. He'll watch them twice sometimes. He's not a reader and he doesn't like radio, both of which I enjoy . . . On my previous sentence I read twenty years worth of books in eighteen months. I'm doing this English 'A' Level now, but it's much harder to read in this environment with the TV on (David).

My cellmate and me get on well but he's moving out and I'm quite glad because it's starting to do my head in. I fancy a change. We're always arguing about what to watch on television. [How do you resolve these conflicts?] We turn it off and play Monopoly or Scrabble (Michael).

Ralph's comment about doing everything for himself was somewhat contradicted when his cellmate, Mark, brought in a cup of coffee for him (at which point Ralph said cheerily, 'Here he is – my other half!'), but his mention of an older inmate being a father figure was one of several references to partnerships that were constructed as mentor–student or father–son relationships. David, the drugs-dealer who enjoyed his 'Big Man' reputation, said that he had always sought out role models who were older than him, and enjoyed talking and listening to some of the lifers. His mentor was an older prisoner, a boxer who had encouraged him to use the gym and build up his physical strength. It was with some pride that he described his special friend as the 'hardest man in the prison' and someone who everyone respected and feared. Other prisoners described their role as the senior figure in the partnership:

> I've got one friend here who I met in my last prison. I can be myself with him. He's got a few problems though at the moment, he's being bullied and that. I call him 'Calamity'! I try and look after him though, give him a shoulder to lean on (Matt).

For some prisoners, the role of paternalistic mentor is passed down through a chain of relationships. For example, it was important to Harry both to *have* and to *be* a father figure. He described his role model who, in teaching him to play the guitar, had opened up new possibilities for him in terms of how he viewed himself, how he adapted to prison and how he saw his future. In turn, Harry was trying to help the young man in the cell next door to his, whom he described as a poor coper. He related how he had 'pushed' this man into doing a City & Guilds course, and how he would spend many hours talking to him and trying to make him view his life more positively. So attentive was he towards his friend that he had turned down the opportunity to move to the Super-Enhanced 'Rutland Unit' because he believed this young man could not cope without him. Others, however, are not so lucky in their choice of friends. Cohen and Taylor (1972: 76) observe that even the closest relationship can be perilous in so far as it is inevitably cut short when one individual is moved on to another prison or comes to the end of his sentence, and that it is pointless to try to maintain contact. This sentiment was borne out by several inmates:

> I thought I had a good friend in my last jail, thought we were really close. We used to spend Friday nights together having a drink and a smoke. I thought we had a bond to tell you the truth. He was released, and he said 'send me a visiting order, I'll come and see you', so I did, but he never came. So, I think it's impossible to have real friends in prison (T).

> You get a lot of prison talk – 'Oh we'll come and see you, send a VO and we'll be over'. You never see them again. You can't blame them though. The last thing you want when you get out of this dump is to come back on a visit (Del).

You have what I call 'prisoner friends', people you've come up the ranks with, if that's the right way of putting it . . . On the outside, though, we'll go our separate ways – well, I certainly don't intend to keep in touch! Friendship is fake because it's forged through the system, it's part of the survival game . . . I have one real friend. We share the same religion. He's going to Kirkham for his Cat D and I'm hoping to follow him there, but that's it. It'll be the third prison we've been in together. We play badminton and use the gym together, but I wouldn't seek him out on the outside. He's from the North and I'm from the South and we're from different circles. Besides which, on a life licence you can't associate with known criminals (Ron).

In an environment where so much effort goes into the construction of social identities, these kinds of experiences can be potentially damaging to the self, only serving to demonstrate the artifice of prison relationships. But for those who succeed in finding a 'partner' in prison, such relationships – even though they are constrained in time and place – can to some extent replicate or replace more conventional relationships with loved ones on the outside, which can prove too difficult to sustain during a prison sentence. For those who work hard to maintain relationships with partners and spouses, however, their efforts can be double-edged. In some instances visits from family and close friends not only reassure them they have their love and support, but can also provide them with a touchstone for their previous lives. Several respondents mentioned the importance of media in this context: one father spoke of how important it was for him to follow the fortunes of his favourite football team while inside, and to be able to discuss their progress with his young son on visits, while many other respondents talked of how specific media texts gave them something to talk about with their visitors, frequently acting as an 'ice-breaker' in tense situations. Conversely, visits from loved ones can cause tremendous strain. Telephone interaction with family can also be highly stressful, and the pent-up frustrations felt by both parties are frequently exacerbated by the particular characteristics and properties of the medium and by the often-public context in which inmates have to negotiate their most private relationships.

In my interviews, talk about family and relationships was marked by profound contrasts. Some respondents described the immutable strength of their relationships with partners, children and parents, and saw them as the main support without which they could not endure the pains of imprisonment ('She's my rock. I wouldn't be able to get through it without her to be honest'). Moreover, for some inmates, relationships with wives and girlfriends appeared to have intensified as a result of the enforced separation. This was most obviously the case among those prisoners who wrote detailed letters or diaries for their partners:

I write letters between 9.30 and 10 every night. People know not to disturb me then. I write two sides of A4 every evening. I keep two diaries as well, one for my missus and one for me. That's good – an outlet. I'm terrified of losing Sharon. I'm lucky, I shouldn't be in here but she's stood by me. She's my wife, my lover, my best friend, everything to me really. But I get this little . . . 'belly feeling', I call it. Anxiety I suppose. That's why it's so important for me to keep writing to her, to let her know how much she means to me (Craig).

Letter writing is very important. My wife and I have gone right back to our earliest memories in our letters, right back before we knew each other to when we were very young children. We know things about each other now that we never did when we were with each other every day (John).

I write to my wife who is my co-defendant, at Foston Hall [women's prison]. I write to her every day and she writes to me every day. We write very romantic letters – proper old-fashioned love letters, you could say. I have got to know her so much more intimately through her letters (Mr B).

Other respondents, however, spoke of once close relationships solely in terms of their frustrations and difficulties. The fragility and fragmentation of contact with loved ones on the outside are one of the most profound sources of stress, particularly to long-termers (Cohen and Taylor 1972; Flanagan 1982) and the fear these relationships will be irrevocably lost or immutably altered engenders a unique and harrowing set of concerns. One interviewee, Don, spoke movingly about how, after sixteen years apart, he and his partner were more like brother and sister than husband and wife. So physically and emotionally disconnected were they that he viewed his application for early release with extreme ambivalence, saying he feared returning home to a stranger. This sentiment was all the more poignant because his wife had been diagnosed with a terminal illness and had a predicted life expectancy of six weeks. Yet more pathos was added when, on the day before I interviewed him, Don's application for parole was turned down.

For some prison sociologists it is the patterns of social interaction that are established among inmates that most effectively mitigate against the pain of situations like Don's (Sykes, 1958). Unfortunately, however, the reduction in association time that has accompanied the introduction of in-cell television in most prisons has diminished opportunities for social interaction and although small groups of inmates sometimes congregate in one individual's cell to watch TV together during association time, one of the primary means of group interaction – watching television on the communal TV sets in wing association rooms – has now been lost in many establishments. For some prisoners, this loss is a source of regret, particularly when it comes to watching major sports events which, many agreed, were most satisfying when viewed as part of a group. For general viewing, however, most respondents greatly preferred the privacy and safety that in-cell TV affords them, and held communal viewing in very low regard. When in-cell television was first introduced at Stocken, prisoners had to purchase their own sets from retail catalogues or via their families. This instigated a view that association television was only for 'lower class' inmates with few outside resources. Communal viewing thus exemplified institutional dependency in its starkest form (Lindlof 1987), a belief that was reinforced by the fact that, on many occasions, inmates would have to leave the TV room for lock-up before the end of the programme or sports event they were watching. Now, inmates have to rent prison-issue sets and, although there was much disquiet about the unfairness of this initiative, the standardisation of television sets did at least ensure that most people who were eligible could have one, and that competitiveness over who watched which television was reduced.

Not all prisoners have in-cell television though and, although most prisons provide multiple sets on each wing (usually at least three: one for BBC1, one for ITV and one for BBC2, Channel 4 and Channel 5), I heard several accounts suggesting that if a television set becomes damaged or broken, it may take an extremely long time to repair, leaving inmates with a diminished range of viewing choices. Furthermore, at Stocken, not every eligible prisoner wanted to subscribe to in-cell TV. Reliant on the TV association rooms, they were angered to find they were reduced to only one TV per wing, as the only other television room was being used as a locked storeroom for the personal sets that had been confiscated. Unsurprisingly, this caused friction and, like family viewing, dependence on one communal television presented an opportunity for some individuals to impose their will on others. In all prisons with association televisions, some prisoners find themselves either conforming to the media patterns of the dominant group (or a dominant individual) in order to 'fit in' or otherwise withdrawing from the inmate culture as a means of avoiding potential conflict:

I was in Highpoint in the seventies in a dormitory of about sixty people. Television rooms were real problems then – lots of scuffles – so you had to be very selective about what you went in to watch. Everyone used to go in to watch *Top of the Pops*, but that was about it (David).

I don't like the TV room. I never go in there. Too noisy, too rowdy, too smoky. Dangerous too. The thing that happened last night when someone got a pool cue in their face and ended up in the hospital – that originally started in the association room. Probably a row about which side the TV should be on (Kelly).

As these quotations illustrate, those inmates who *do* use association rooms may need to re-learn subcultural rules for the situation of media use. Several prisoners confirmed Cohen and Taylor's (1972) finding that association rooms are one of the few areas of the prison where inmates can withdraw temporarily from the structural demands that incarceration places upon them and obtain some degree of protection from official surveillance. However, this inevitably means that weaker or more vulnerable inmates will fall prey to aggressive or more dominant individuals. Not only does the open group aspect of it offer no protection against noise or undesired interactions (I heard many accounts of how terrified inmates would watch television at the back of the room, literally with their backs to the wall), but the potential for violent conflict in the TV rooms led one ex-prison governor to describe them as one of the greatest 'flashpoints' in the prison system.[6]

In a reminder of the findings of the media reception studies, several inmates mentioned that some prisoners watch television from their 'own' chair in association rooms. Of course, the marking out of personal territory and the jealous guarding of informal privileges are entirely understandable in the status-deprived world of the prison. But such unilateral decisions can be a further source of conflict, and at Ashwell the removal of armchairs and the installation of metal benches that were bolted to the floor were evidence of the inherent tensions that can develop in such situations. None of the association rooms I saw had the kinds of comforts one usually associates with recreational television use, but Ashwell's TV rooms (with the exception of those in the 'Super-Enhanced' unit) were arguably the worst:

I hate the seats they have in there. I never go in there for that reason. They're like the seats you get in bus stations. Can you imagine being able to sit comfortably on one of those things for the duration of a film? No way. But I suppose it's another way they get people to cough up for in-cell television (Steve).

One final point of interest in relation to the ways in which prisoners use media as a means of organising their social affiliations and disengagements is that personal media, especially in-cell television, often provide closure on an inmate career as release date approaches. This phenomenon was noted by Lindlof (1987: 190–91) in his study of an American correctional institution and was most emphatically illustrated to me by Matt, who was nearing the end of a four-year sentence:

> I just want to keep my head down and stay out of trouble. I've been in bother before and had days added. In fact in the old days I'd have been prepared to lose a year of my life not to play their game. But now I can see my release day ahead of me, so I'm just seeing out the last few weeks, not getting into any bother. It's quite hard because there's always someone ready to wind you up, but I just stay in my pad, watch TV all day and sleep as much as possible.

Television viewing thus not only consumes large blocks of time for the impatient prisoner anticipating his release, but it also provides a means of disengaging from the inmate culture and keeping away from potential trouble.

The use of media in this way may be linked to the finding that typical patterns of behaviour change over the course of a prison career. Like other interactionist studies (Adler and Adler 1983; Shover 1983) my research uncovered evidence of shifts in perceptions of self – resulting in different identities and coping strategies being adopted – at different points over the duration of a sentence. Most commonly, these changes of perception were brought about by temporal contingencies: an awareness of the passing of time and of time being an exhaustive resource (Shover 1983), and a general alertness to the processes of ageing and maturing, often accompanied by a growing impatience towards the activities and attitudes of younger inmates. It is possible, then, that the usefulness of personal media resources to inmates forms a U-shaped curve similar to Wheeler's (1961) characterisation of prisonisation, with radio, television, and other personal media being most needed at the point of entry into the institution as a source of continuity with the inmate's pre-prison life, and as a facilitator of the socialisation skills necessary to adapt to the inmate culture, and then at the end, as a means of closing out the sentence and anticipating life on the outside.

In conclusion to this chapter, I hope that the discussion of meso levels of social practices has highlighted some of the most significant dimensions of media use as it pertains to the demands on inmates' identities inflicted by the social and cultural milieu of the prison. My research uncovered a variety of ways in which media resources are interpreted, used and shaped in order to satisfy the needs of individuals and groups in this most highly regulated and bounded of environments. A pivotal resource in aiding inmates' responses to the pains of confinement, media are instrumental in the formation of collective identities, social networks and dyadic friendships in the meso, or intermediate, realms of subcultures, social networks, association activities and semi-structural arenas such as Prison Dialogue, debating societies and discussion groups. Media content provides patterns of thought, activity and talk. It provides material for learning and enacting roles, and can inspire performance. It is assimilated into discourse and provides the basis for defining relationships. It may ease the processes of acclimatisation, socialisation and colonisation, and can give two or more inmates a sense of common identity. It encourages affiliation and permits disengagement. It provides continuity with one's former life and gives a sense of control over one's environment. Little wonder, then, that Lindlof (1987: 195) concludes that 'few social settings offer more compelling evidence of the pragmatics of media exposure than the total institution'.

Notes

[1] The tensions between micro–macro and structure–agency relations are arguably best resolved in the studies of subcultures conducted in the 1970s (e.g. Willis 1977) and in more recent studies that have applied Giddens' theory of structuration to conditions such as unemployment (e.g. Burman 1988). Both successfully address the tensions between structural constraints and microsocial politics within the realms of community and culture.

[2] The argument that the more prisonised an inmate becomes, the less conventionally socialised he will be, supports Wheeler's (1961) argument that socialisation takes the form of a 'U-shaped curve'. Schmid and Jones (1991) come to a similar conclusion, arguing that the inmate enters prison with an outsider's perception of what it will be like. By the middle of his sentence, he comes to adopt an insider's perspective on the prison *world*, only to revert to the outsider's view in the final months of his sentence.

[3] A similar finding was noted in an American study which reported that nine out of ten prisoners had 'learned new tricks and improved their criminal expertise by watching crime programs [*sic*]' (Hendrick, G.H. (1977) When television is a school for criminals. *TV Guide* 29 January, quoted in Meyrowitz, 1985: 118). Hagell and Newburn (1994) note that young offenders also report watching *The Bill* for this reason, and Daniels (1997) makes a similar discovery in her study of media use at HMP Sudbury.

[4] A quarterly newspaper for prisoners that carries reports of changes in prison rules and legislation affecting them.

[5] Once more, parallels can be found in Willis' (1977) study of the ways in which lower working-class boys prepare for the dull repetition of unskilled labour in adult life.

[6] The emphasis that was placed on television rooms being potential trouble-spots by numerous prison officers, governors, governor grades and Home Office personnel, together with the prevailing view that in-cell television encourages passivity rather than discontent, makes it all the more surprising that so many prison researchers who have purported to be investigating matters of order and control in prisons have marginalised or ignored the presence of media, seeing it as incidental rather than central to the maintenance or disruption of order. Very brief references to incidents that have occurred in association TV rooms can be found in Toch (1992: 283) and Sparks *et al* (1996: 240).

Chapter 6

The macrosocial institutional sphere

It is rare to find an environment where media proliferate yet are as highly regulated as in prisons. This chapter will explore this dichotomy further, examining the extent to which – despite the differential levels of freedom and constraint that media consumption can facilitate at individual and social levels – media resources act as a locus of power for the prison authorities. In most studies of media reception, the structure – agency dynamic features only in terms of either the interplay between media industries and their audiences (in other words, the relationship between production and consumption), or the micropolitical dynamics that shape media use within private domains (text and context). But in this analysis, it is another dimension of power – the macro levels of government, Home Office, prison service, governors, officers and other staff who use media to regulate and control inmates' behaviour – that is of interest.[1]

Giddens' theory of structuration, which has been used critically throughout this study, has been censured for understating the extent to which hierarchically organised social structures limit the agency of individuals (Vaughan 2001). Mindful of this criticism, this chapter will discuss the extent to which, in the prison society, identity is shaped and autonomy constrained by structural imperatives, and whether the issue of media availability in prisons is determined by the requirements of the institution or the needs of inmates. In their efforts to regulate the actions of those under their supervision, prison authorities employ a range of techniques which might appear to be beneficial to inmates, but may in fact be primarily or solely designed to serve the interests of the prison and prison service. At the core of such decision-making lies the crucial distinction between what prisons are for, and how prisons should be run. Before considering the specific reasons behind the implementation of media into prisons it is first necessary to consider what purposes prisons serve, and then explore how policies regarding media fit into the overall

161

rationale. Adler and Longhurst (1994) argue that the history of British prisons hinges on three key moments of transformation constructed around justifications for imprisonment following the decline of principles of reform. They are rehabilitation, normalisation and control, and what follows is a brief historical outline of each approach, accompanied by an attempt to uncover the discursive strategies behind the implementation of media resources, and their consequences, intended and unintended, for these three 'purposes' (or 'ends', as Adler and Longhurst term them) of imprisonment.

Reform and rehabilitation

One of the foundations of public concern about media in prisons, which has been crystallised in the debate about whether in-cell television should be allowed, is that watching television appears to undermine one of the fundamental principles on which the modern prison system was established: that prisons should be places of reform. In the early nineteenth century prisons became places of moral education, social improvement and religious piety, all of which were designed to allow the criminal to contemplate his wrongdoing, and repent. The prison was thus transformed from simply a place of pretrial detention into one where criminals could be excluded, differentiated, made self-conscious of their misdemeanours and rationally controlled (Muncie 2001). In short, prisons became the *punishment* for crime. The nineteenth-century zeal for reform was tempered in the twentieth century when the emergence of Darwinism and the development of disciplines such as criminology, psychology and psychiatry resulted in reformism being superseded by rehabilitation, at least within official, hegemonic discourses. No longer was there an over-riding belief in the criminal as someone who actively chooses to commit crime, and can similarly exert his or her autonomy in deciding to repent and reform. Rather, a model of criminality was developed which stressed the deviance of the offender. Far from being seen as rational traits to be reversed by the individual concerned, crime and deviance were conceived as pathological malfunctions to be treated by skilled practitioners (Adler and Longhurst 1994; Muncie 2001).

As a broad ideal determining penal policy, the rehabilitation or 'treatment' model fell out of favour to be replaced by a conclusion that 'nothing works' (Lipton *et al* 1975) and that the central pillar of the criminal justice system should be justice rather than crime control. However, a modified rehabilitative approach remains central to much prison policy and practice, and efforts to devise effective treatment programmes targeted at specific types of offender are prevalent in today's prison system. But my research indicated that, far from enabling inmates to make positive life choices and assert their autonomy in meaningful ways, such programmes were universally derided as a waste of time and money. Many vocational courses and treatment programmes had long waiting lists, and several inmates serving relatively short sentences felt they had little chance of making it to the top of the list before their parole date. For those serving long or life sentences, however, there was an added pressure in that one of the major release criteria is that the individual has successfully addressed his offending behaviour. These inmates were wise to the fact that in the under-resourced prison system, their chances of release at the end of their tariff would be enhanced not only by attending the courses that were available, but by simply showing willing and putting their names down for them. Their understanding of the collusion that is required of them in managing their own prison sentences by demonstrating a willingness to attend classes and treatment programmes hardly makes it any more palatable to them. But being able to see through the institutional ideology at least gave my respondents some sense of inverting macrosocial processes, even though their responses were largely passive and enforced.

Unfortunately for inmates, if they are not wholly compliant in the procedures that assess, process and classify them, they are often stereotyped as 'awkward'. Burman (1988: 76) provides a useful analogy in relation to the resistances of the unemployed to government agencies and counsellors:

> [F]rom a system point of view . . . 'awkward' meant an eruption of individual agency cutting against the bureaucratic grain. Here the . . . self was reaching for the authorial pen and trying to 'write' his or her own practices. These struggles, though painful, were synergistic responses to a domination which was experienced as unfair. At their best . . . they knowledgeably penetrated the mystique and professional pretensions of that system.

Many of my respondents had indeed penetrated the mystique and pretensions of the prison and probation systems, and prided themselves on having insight into macrosocial processes and ideologies that were meant to remain hidden from them. They implicitly understood that the system which subjects them to marginalisation, classification, surveillance and the pejorative judgements of prison staff and the wider society was itself not beyond censure:

The screws treat us like scum, but they're just the same as us. Most of them operate on a system of bribery – or worse (Del).

The public class us as animals, but they're the animals that put us in here (Jamie).

Ironically, given the prison system's (and arguably, the wider public's) apparently weak commitment to rehabilitation, it is fears about the nature and potentially harmful influences of electronic media that may underlie its delayed and restricted implementation. The question of whether people are sent to prisons *as* punishment or *for* punishment is still central to discussions about what prisoners have a right to expect in terms of basic minimum standards of living, and in popular discourses on the purposes of imprisonment, arguments for rehabilitation are sometimes (and arguably increasingly) overshadowed by notions of reform and retribution. Consequently, it is of little surprise to witness evidence of hostility among the general public towards in-cell television, which is seen as both a high-status commodity that has no role in a place of austerity, and as a potentially corrupting influence that might undermine efforts to 'treat' the individual. *The Independent* (30 November 1997) summed up the prevailing view in an editorial under the heading 'Television – a force for good in our nation's prisons':

> Prison, eh? Nice cosy beds, good food, gyms, libraries . . . More like Butlins than a punishment. It'll be colour televisions next. The right-wing tabloids will be in full cry, no doubt, as will some backbenchers. Michael Howard will lose no opportunity to remind us that he rejected the idea, and to mock Jack 'tough on crime' Straw for his wet liberalism in this regard. Nor will the reaction be confined to politicians and editorialists. The verb 'to cosset' will be vigorously conjugated in the snug bars and Happy Eaters of the nation. Many people will be genuinely outraged . . . It is a fundamental social trait to want to see the guilty suffer. All cultures provide for punishment and we are a very rare example in human history of a culture which doesn't kill at least some of its criminals. Here, and now, the instinct for retribution means support for tough and unpleasant prison conditions. If they are not to hang, or go hungry, then they should at least squirm a little – be bored and uncomfortable, not leisured and entertained.

Reform and rehabilitation are thus usually regarded as mutually exclusive goals, and claims that television undermines attempts to reform criminals play down its potential to aid offenders' rehabilitation back into society. Indeed, it is often precisely television's rehabilitative, democratising role that is at the heart of objections to media availability in prisons. Central to much political rhetoric and public discourse is the notion that retribution leads to deterrence, and should therefore be the primary task of the prison service. Mere loss of liberty is insufficiently powerful to accomplish these ends; the inmate must be made to suffer through a series of deprivations – including the deprivation of access to the medium of greatest penetration in the UK population as a whole – which will clearly demonstrate the advantages of remaining out of prison. This position dominates a great deal of the media coverage of prisons and is one that reflects the views of a sizeable proportion of the British population:

> The history of Britain's prisons since 1945 has not been a happy one. It is a story of many dedicated people trying to make things better, and continually trapped by what can only be called 'the system' – the system in which the sentencers produce a steadily rising prison population; the system that fears political embarrassment and revelations in newspapers about prisoners enjoying themselves watching colour videos more than it fears revelations about prisoners locked up for twenty three hours a day and having no access to sanitation (Stern 1987: 247).

But as *The Independent* editorial (30 November 1997) goes on to say, in most developed societies mass media technologies are taken utterly for granted and television, more than any other medium, is for the modern citizen the 'ubiquitous window on society, a prime source of thinking and information'. The view of rehabilitationists, then, is that one of the primary benefits of in-cell television is its capacity to allow prisoners to remain part of society even while they are formally segregated from the outside world:

> [Television] shapes us. Now, granted, prisoners are physically cut off from society. But that is as much for our safety as for their punishment. Assuming that we hold to the idea of rehabilitation and the return of prisoners to ordinary life after their sentences, then cutting them off from social trends, thinking, entertainment and news is pointless, even stupid. Prisoners who watch television for hours are not only likelier to be easier to guard and oversee; they are also likely to end up more like the rest of us (ibid.).

Among the British press, *The Independent* is unusual in presenting such a liberal view and the majority of newspapers have opposed the implementation of personal television sets in prisons. Opposition to television in prisons is arguably but one strand of a much wider anti-television sentiment in Britain, a hostility that has bordered on moral panic (Corner 1995). There is a pervasive feeling, probably derived from the Protestant work ethic, that watching television is unproductive, especially in comparison to other more 'worthy' activities. The appeal of TV as a way of filling time is seen to work against the pursuit of more creative activities, to erode family and community ties, and consequently to harm personal and social development. However, the notion of time being measured against value or usefulness presupposes the viewer has more purposeful alternative options available to him or her. Far from being a precious commodity, in prison, time can become an enemy, and media resources are frequently employed to fill 'weary time' and to facilitate the transcending of everyday life (Brunsdon 1990). A further argument against television is its representation as a cultural invader (Corner 1995), an anxiety that is part of a broader preoccupation with the globalisation of cultural forms and products and, in particular, the American origin of much popular global culture. Television is but one area of interest to critics who view anything American as intrinsically cheap, trashy and alien to British culture and identity, and a more widespread version of this trend is concern for a general debasement of taste (ibid.). Many high-profile commentators have alluded to what John Reith, the first Director General of the BBC, called the 'lowest common denominator' of public taste. Within the prison service, much is spoken about the potential of in-cell television to provide in-house channels of information and education, as if to provide justification for its implementation,[2] but the consumers are, like the rest of the population, generally more interested in being entertained, and it is sometimes the undemanding or sensationalised that best fulfils this need.

Another element of anti-television feeling is attitudinal influence. The claim here is increasingly used to sum up the 'problem' with television as a whole, but specifically it is believed that visual images are capable of exerting a negative influence upon the attitudes and behaviour of viewers. This influence is seen to be sufficiently pervasive and unassailable to have a general effect on social values and action, and criminal activity as learned behaviour is at the very heart of anti-TV sentiments. One of the most common versions of this concern is the 'copy-cat' theory of disorder, which is widely articulated in relation to prison disturbances. Within the prison service there is recognition that once in-cell television is installed, it is difficult for the prison governor to regulate or censor specific programme content. In the course of my research I encountered many prison officers and governors who expressed concern about what they perceived as television's capacity to blur fantasy and reality, but some went further, noting that it could be especially problematic in relation to specific prison populations:

> Sex offenders who have [in-cell television] may have their cognitive deficiencies reinforced and thus undermine the offending behaviour work they have participated in (Governor, in response to questionnaire).

> The watershed issue is a real issue for Juvenile Centres. A policy of what time the TV goes off needs to be established which takes account of what is on (Governor of YOI, in response to questionnaire).

> In general I don't see there being a need to regulate or censor in-cell TV – it would be virtually impossible to do so, in fact. But there *are* potential issues that may need to be addressed in relation to vulnerable or violent inmates, in terms of television feeding their imaginations and perhaps intensifying, even supporting, their fantasies in some way (Governor, in conversation).

Related to this fear of unhealthy influence is the perceived link between television viewing and cognitive impairment. Usually advanced by reference to psychological data, this argument sees cultural deterioration as a consequence of eroded mental capacities and is frequently used to illustrate claims of falling educational standards (Corner 1995). Although there is no conclusive evidence to support this view, it has entered the public consciousness and may partially explain why some long-sentence prisoners – fearing mental deterioration – favour reading, writing or pursuing hobbies to watching television.

It is clear, then, that the overtly moralistic and class-tinged bias inherent in much anti-media sentiment dovetails neatly with the traditions and ethos of the prison service. Put simply, the arguments are that media in general, and television in particular, hinder the criminal's inclination to reform, do nothing to reduce the likelihood of him reoffending and reward him for his deviant behaviour. Even though in most prisons in-cell television is part of the Incentives and Earned Privileges scheme and is therefore only available to those who have earned the right to have it, for many people its enduring status as luxury goods preclude it from being an option for convicted prisoners. This sentiment pervades even among senior prison service staff:

> I don't agree with them having personal televisions, I think it's morally objectionable. To put it in perspective, I had a relative in hospital recently for a major operation. She was going to be in for quite a long time, and obviously we wanted to make her as comfortable as possible, so we signed up to 'hospitelly' as they call it. It cost us £10 a day for the same service they get in here for £1 a week. It really gets up my nose to hear them complaining that they don't get this, that and the other in here. They get so much more than they would on the outside (Governor Grade, in conversation).

> I do have a problem with it [in-cell television] to be honest with you. It's just another little thing, isn't it . . . another little perk that swings the pendulum their way (Senior Officer, in conversation).

Even the claim that it is rehabilitative is unproven. In fact, many of the senior prison service personnel who responded to my questionnaire concurred with the views of inmates noted earlier that in-cell television can diminish social skills:

> [In-cell television] reduces opportunities to socialise with other prisoners and the social benefits which 'sharing' a facility can confer – encourages greater selfishness (Governor, in response to questionnaire).

> As with 'dining in cell', now almost universally introduced, some social benefits will be lost (Governor, in response to questionnaire).

Among supporters of in-cell television, however, it is believed that not only does TV keep inmates in touch with an outside world to which they will eventually return but it also provides a means by which prisoners have to pay for something out of their prison earnings, and therefore teaches them responsibility. Furthermore, the flexibility of the IEP policy means that individual prison governors can decide how to use in-cell TV as part of their own control or rehabilitation strategies at a local level. What this means in respect to the latter is that, in most prisons, in-cell television is used as an incentive to get and keep inmates off drugs. For example, at Gartree, prisoners are only permitted in-cell television after they have had successive negative results in mandatory drugs tests for six months, while at Ashwell a rather different approach is taken with those who are deemed to be making strenuous efforts to beat their drug addictions being rewarded with in-cell TV, sometimes even at no cost.[3] It is widely acknowledged that drugs present contemporary prison governors and officers with one of the greatest threats to security and control, and for prison authorities to use whatever means available to minimise these problems is understandable. However, one governor's belief that he is replacing one addiction with another less harmful one is arguable. I saw little evidence to suggest that anyone was successfully refraining from taking drugs simply because they had a television. Indeed, some inmates felt in-cell TV creates the very environment which encourages recreational drugs use:

> I was in prison twenty years ago. The experience was completely different then, it's now much more civilised. It used to be three in a cell, pot under the bed. But in some ways things have got worse. They were far less security minded then. Everything revolves around security now. But there wasn't the common experience of heroin then, just cannabis and hooch. Now we have in-cell television, electricity . . . It's not the fault of the authorities but they've created the perfect environment for taking drugs with this in-cell TV (David).

Whatever the success of Ashwell's policy of using television to encourage people off drugs, it clearly demonstrates that the rehabilitative discourse persists in prisons. But while many prison spokespersons publicly acclaim the benefits of the in-cell TV scheme, there is still some residual doubt about its efficacy on the part of many prison staff and inmates. The dichotomies inherent in the system are clear to see. Many people believe television can aid the rehabilitation of offenders back into society, yet there is an underlying concern that it diminishes their chances of reform. Within the prison service, there are hopes in-cell television will enhance prison regimes by encouraging good behaviour, yet there are simultaneously fears it will be detrimental to regimes by reducing personal contact and interaction; it is commended as a means of communication with the outside world, but it has simultaneously been noted it reduces the channels of face-to-face communication within the prison walls and provides private, hidden contexts in which drug taking and other illegal activities can take place; while public statements are made about the potential of in-cell television to enhance educational opportunities, in reality it is curtailing association time, replacing some education provision and reducing attendance at the classes that remain.

Given all these considerations, it has to be assumed that the commitment to rehabilitating (or, for that matter, reforming) prisoners is being undermined by more paramount concerns.

Normalisation

Since the publication of the Woolf report, the prison service has addressed calls for prisons to be 'normalised' (Bottomley *et al* 1997), and media resources are a key component of this effort. The strategy of 'normalisation' has two elements. First, it is based upon the notion that prisoners are normal individuals who happen to have committed a crime, a premise that contrasts with rehabilitation discourse which maintains that crime is committed by maladjusted individuals who must be made 'better' in prison. The second aspect of normalisation is that the punishment component of imprisonment is the deprivation of liberty and that, aside from that, inmates should be able to live as 'normally' as possible within the constraints of confinement: in other words, the experience of the prison itself should not be punitive. The principle of normalisation is intrinsic to the notion of prisons providing 'humane containment', a central tenet of King and Morgan's evidence to the May committee, set up in 1978 to review the state of the prison services and to make recommendations for change. Lord Justice May rejected the normalising discourse of King and Morgan's report, but there has nevertheless been an increasing commitment to normalising the prison environment over the last two decades, most evident in improved living conditions. Although many argue that normalisation in British prisons does not go far enough, the changes that *have* taken place to make imprisonment more like life outside represent a significant development in attitude among prison authorities. In essence, the prison environment has historically been governed by a principle of deterrence known as 'less eligibility' whereby conditions in prisons must be no *better* than those experienced by the poorest sections of the working classes. However, with prisons under increasing scrutiny from government inspectors, academic researchers and prison reform groups, regimes are increasingly underpinned by efforts to ensure they are no (or not substantially) *worse* than those experienced by the equivalent population outside. It is from within this wider context of entitlement that the introduction of media resources into prisons must be regarded, for if the question of media access for inmates was simply one of less eligibility, personal television sets would have been introduced several years ago.

In-cell television raises many of the arguments previously rehearsed in relation to the introduction of in-cell radio in 1974 and the reasons for the delay in implementing the scheme are probably as complex as the rationales behind its introduction now.[4] In addition to historic notions of less eligibility, one of the latent concerns that may have impeded its progress is the belief that electronic media are fundamentally changing the nature of incarceration, eroding the 'totality' of total institutions and challenging traditional arguments about the purposes of imprisonment:

> Prisons were once more than places of physical incarceration; they were places of informational isolation as well. A prisoner was not only limited in movement but also 'ex-communicated' from society . . . Today, however, many prisoners share with the larger society the privileges of radio, television, and telephone . . . For better or worse, those prisoners with access to electronic media are no longer completely segregated from society. The use of electronic media has led to a redefinition of the nature of 'imprisonment' and to a *de facto* revision of the prison classification system: The communication variables of 'high information' prisons versus 'low information' prisons now have been added to the physical variables of 'high security' and 'low security' (Meyrowitz 1985: 117–18).

Although in-cell television is increasingly being seen as a key earnable privilege, the fact that not all prisons (nor all prison wings) can accommodate television sets for technical reasons means this aspect of a policy that was designed to eliminate some of the inconsistencies in prisoner entitlements – IEP – is perceived as grossly unfair by many inmates:

> Here [at Stocken] some wings have no TV, some have got in-cell TV, some have got in-cell TV *with* satellite. It creates a two-tier system within an already two-tiered system. I'm on Enhanced, yet I haven't got a TV. I feel like a second-class citizen (Rob).

> When in-cell TV was announced all inmates expected to get it immediately, but many will not do so for a number of years. Inmates will gain and lose as they move establishments (Governor, in response to questionnaire).

However, as Meyrowitz suggests, those prisoners who *do* have personal TVs are no longer excluded from participation in the public sphere and, in general, prisons today are far better integrated into the wider community than ever before. Two key points arise from this development. First, those 'on the outside' can no longer use television as a private forum in which to discuss the problems of crime and crime prevention since inmates can now 'enter' society via the fibre-optic cables of telecommunications (Meyrowitz 1985: 118).[5] Secondly, it is possible that as prisoners are increasingly able to monitor and interact with the larger environment informationally, they correspondingly increase their demands for greater physical access to the outside world and expect entitlements commensurate with those accorded the wider population. These two processes arguably create a shift in the balance of power, so that instead of normalisation happening at the pace at which the prison service think appropriate, inmates are themselves playing a role in change.

The prison authorities are thus faced with a dilemma. On the one hand, concerns about television constituting 'bad culture' have gained popular credence and are as intrinsic a part of everyday cultural currency as the related belief that prisoners must be subjected to sufficient deprivation in prison to deter them from ever reoffending again. Over the last fifty years, when much public attention has been focused on the erosion of traditional values and cultural ties (Corner 1995), television has provided a convenient scapegoat, and nowhere more so than in the frequent – if methodologically unsound – attempts to link media images with rising crime. Notions of prisoner empowerment therefore do not sit easily with modern political rhetoric which is arguably still more concerned with public perception than with prisoners' rights. Indeed, one of the aims of the IEP policy is to meet 'public expectations about what kind of place prison should be' (Liebling *et al*, 1997:x), and if the press are to be believed, the vast majority of the British public are not in favour of personal television sets in prisons.

On the other hand, the argument that television is a luxury that prisoners do not deserve is becoming increasingly hard to sustain. In the UK and America, 98.9per cent of households own at least one TV set, 75 per cent own two or more sets and one third of the population subscribe to cable or satellite. It is estimated that viewers in Britain watch an average of 24 hours per week, while an A. C. Nielsen report claims that, in the USA, TV sets are switched on for approximately 50 hours per week (quoted in Fowles 1992). As such, television in both countries (as in the rest of the developed world) is deemed far less a luxury than a public utility, and the provision of television sets in prisons is entirely consistent with normal life. Put simply, if the prison service adheres to the view that the vast majority of people in its institutions are not pathological but are 'normal' individuals who happen to have transgressed the consensual codes of society, it has to concede that prisoners have as much right as anyone else to watch television in whatever form and quantity they so desire, even if its normalisation of the prison environment leads to an escalation of prisoners' demands and expectations.

Control

From the discussion so far it can be inferred that any theoretical analysis of an environment where social control is a fact of everyday life must take account of Marxist theories of power relations. Critics argue that those with least power in society are over-represented in prisons, and that one of the primary functions of imprisonment has always been to regulate the behaviour of, and discipline, the least powerful strata of society (see, for example, Rusche and Kirchheimer 1939/68; Foucault 1977; Ignatieff 1983). This, then, raises an important issue relating to media that is rarely publicly voiced. Television and other media technologies are undoubtedly desirable commodities that improve the quality of everyday life for most prisoners, whatever view one takes of their entitlement to such privileges. But their capacity to serve the needs of officers, governors, the prison service, government and the wider realms of power is less frequently discussed. In an era when managerialism has emerged as an influential conceptual development in penal policy, the needs of the individual prisoner have become increasingly overshadowed by the requirements of rationality, efficiency, cost-effectiveness, accountability and organisation (Feeley and Simon 1992; Bottoms 1995). For example, in-cell television enshrines the principles of the three dimensions of managerialism (Bottoms 1995) that have dominated the criminal justice and penal systems over the last ten years. It is *consumerist* in that it appeals to liberal individualists as an important human rights development and pays lip-service to the notion of prisoners as possessors of entitlements. It has *systemic* characteristics in that it reduces out-of-cell activity, thus potentially cutting staff costs. It also offers an incentive for good behaviour, and potentially constitutes a policy that can be implemented consistently across the whole prison estate (although with variations being devised at a local level, and technical implementation problems at some prisons, this is not yet the case). Finally, it is *actuarial* in its capacity to occupy large numbers of potentially unruly prisoners while minimising interaction between them.

It has been noted that one of the most frequently expressed analogies in relation to television as a form of control is that it is a habit-forming addiction; a drug (Mander 1980; Postman 1985). The resemblance between the properties of drugs and those of television was not lost on a governor who described in-cell television to me as 'the multi-coloured narcotic', or the staff, one of whom commented: 'you should see them when *Neighbours* is on – it's like a tranquilliser.' The increasing reliance by prison authorities and staff on using television to occupy and pacify an otherwise potentially volatile population represents an important change in the philosophy and purpose of imprisonment. Where prison life in the past was structured around the production of discipline and the eradication of idleness (Foucault 1977), so that every minute of the day was used to its maximum efficiency, media are arguably rapidly replacing purposeful activity (work, association and so on) with non-purposeful (i.e. non-goal orientated) activity. Even within the modern rhetoric of the prison system, in-cell television appears to have conflicting purposes, for while it achieves one of the aims of 'Incentives and Earned Privileges' – to improve prisoner compliance through reward – it nevertheless seems to be at odds with another of IEP's primary intentions – to improve constructive occupation in prisons. The Marxist conclusion that decisions to introduce a particular incentive or punishment are generally underpinned not by considerations of the recipients' welfare, but by ideological and material interests on the part of those in power, would therefore seem convincing. The adoption of in-cell television in the majority of British prisons has coincided with a sharply rising prisoner population and a corresponding fall in work opportunities, which have combined to leave more inmates with longer periods of unstructured time to fill. Taken to an extreme, it might be argued that where prisons originally aimed to train and discipline the body in order to increase its capacities and improve its efficiency (Foucault 1977; Matthews 1999), they now fail adequately to occupy the body, but do go some way to occupy the mind, albeit in what many consider to be 'mind*less* activity'. Two inmates put their views strongly:

There's less resistance here [in Stocken] because there were TVs here already. People were conditioned. This is a very passive jail – it's a 'TV jail'. People are pacified because they won't want to lose their TV. It's not like a drug – it's even more powerful than that. I've got a friend in Bedford [Prison] who can't wait to get to a jail like this for the TV. Not just a TV. All that goes around the TV. Feet up, living a life of luxury. It's all that goes with it. It's not just a box in the corner. I mean, how easy can they make prison? (David).

This is a very petty jail and in-cell television is part of that. They're always putting up obstacles to test you. They can take it off you for the pettiest reason. It's all about the general public. In-cell television is good for new inmates but in a prison like this it creates a lazy environment. People don't do hobbies any more. Some of the young ones just watch television all day. 'Baby bird' we call it (Brian).

Yet to suggest that television is only useful in prisons as long as it performs the role of 'electronic babysitter' contradicts the findings of uses and gratifications-based audience research, and panders to what has been described as 'TV priggery' (Fowles 1992: ix). Unfortunately, however, many in the prison service voice privately – if not publicly – that the greatest advantage of in-cell television is to occupy the minds and senses of an otherwise fickle and unstable population. Conspiratorially minded critics have gone further, arguing that television prevents people from engaging in more serious political thought or activity (Eagleton 1991) and that throughout history, repressive regimes have sought to keep populaces passively entertained on a diet of cheap commercial television (Stevenson 1995). Although the prison service would not publicly acknowledge this is the case, they may tacitly believe that in-cell television is a useful safety valve for the system. Several wing officers told me that initially they had been extremely sceptical about the prospect of in-cell television because of the reduction in opportunities for social control strategies or 'dynamic security' that results. Most, however, were now entirely supportive of the initiative, at least in so far as it had reduced some of the inherent tensions and made aspects of their own work easier. For some, it had the advantage of giving them something to talk about with their inmate charges, but for most its function as a control mechanism was paramount. Several officers mentioned it had diminished opportunities for mischief-making and interpersonal violence, while some even suggested it had reduced incidents of self-harm and suicide. This senior officer's comment was typical:

I was very sceptical at first. It just didn't seem right that they should have their own television sets – it seemed we were rewarding them for their crimes. But although I still feel that it's *morally* wrong, I have to be honest and say that, as far as this prison's concerned, it's been a very good thing. There's less bullying now than there used to be and things are generally a lot quieter on the wings. I was a very loud and vocal critic of in-cell TV when we heard it was coming here, but I suppose I've been forced to eat my words.

But while the advantages to inmates are also acknowledged, there is little recognition of the hostility some prisoners feel knowing that, if it is not happening already, they may soon find themselves being locked up in their cells for longer periods and forgoing other previously enjoyed 'privileges' because it is assumed that in-cell TV guarantees compliance:

> TV has opened another gate – it's another little choice. But it means earlier and earlier bang-up. It locks you into a routine. If you're banged up at five o'clock at weekends, you'll start banging yourself up at five during the week. Also, when you had your own TV, there wasn't much they could do to you . . . now it's being used as part of the punishment regime. We've had them less than a week and already people have had their electricity cut off for having their TVs on too loud. It's an easy way for officers to get at you (Tim).

Of all the relationships that exemplify the unequal distribution of power and resources in prison it is the interface between inmates and officers which is most immediate and which is most strongly implicated in the flow of everyday life inside prisons. Officers perform several roles in relation to inmates: paternalistic guardians; rule enforcers; moral arbiters; and combatants with whom prisoners are engaged in perpetual mind games (McDermott and King 1988). What all these roles have in common, however, is that they might be more typically associated with the relationship between family members. It is therefore of little surprise to find that, when it comes to television viewing, many of the dynamics played out in living-rooms across the country have strong parallels within the prison community, and that as one of the most significant innovations in recent prison policy, in-cell television is frequently the conduit of authority (on the part of officers) and resistance (on the part of inmates). But there are numerous other, more subtle ways in which prisons are characterised by the patriarchal deployment of power (Mathiesen 1965). From the staff who deliberately allocate newspapers to the wrong inmates (for example, giving the *Telegraph* reader the *Mirror*, or the *Sun* reader a copy of the *Guardian*) to the officers who bring videos with a high sexual content for inmates to watch, as a 'wind-up' intended to irritate or humiliate their audience, media resources can provide a useful means of manipulating prisoners' emotions and reminding them of who is in charge.[6] Whether one should interpret such actions as mere mischief-making or something rather more sinister is debatable, but it is clear such conduct has a long history. Several research participants told me about the introduction of in-cell radio into prisons in 1974, when inmates had to have served at least four years and have a clean record of good behaviour before they were eligible for a radio set. Prior to this, the only form of communication in prisons was a radio controlled by officers, with loudspeakers positioned centrally on each landing. Inmates reported they struggled to hear the broadcasts, and would sit with their heads pressed up against their cell doors, straining to hear. Officers, mindful of their thirst for news of outside, would keep the volume at a level where the inmates could just make out odd words, but could not make complete sense of what was being reported. Other stories of this time told of how officers would refuse to put the radio on when requested to do so by inmates, and of how they would immediately switch it off if news came on about a criminal incident which might be of interest to the inmate audience. When questioned, one officer at Ashwell confirmed that the first prison radios were a powerful means of ensuring compliance: 'there was no better way of getting them all back in their cells after lunch than threatening not to turn the radio on.'

According to Vagg (1994), these kinds of stories epitomise not only the arbitrariness of officers' decision-making, but also demonstrate that prisoners are more interested in having access to media resources than they are in having greater rights in relation to other aspects of their treatment in prison. In the years prior to the introduction of in-cell television, Vagg notes that prisoners in The Netherlands reported being primarily interested in obtaining videos. Although this finding seems somewhat surprising, given the focus on prisoners' rights that is to be found in academic literature, Vagg believes there is some rationality to it. Prisoners' rights have guided inmates' expectations concerning their treatment in prison since the broad legal reforms of the 1960s and 1970s, when prisons – like other social institutions – became increasingly permeable to judicial, legal and other 'public' interventions, and notions of citizenship and civil rights entered penal discourses (Jacobs 1977). But at the time of writing, prisons in England and Wales are not especially politicised and, for most prisoners most of the time, 'rights' are background considerations to be referred to only on such rare occasions that demand it. Furthermore, at the stage at which a prisoner's rights become salient – for example, if he has attacked an officer – the outcome is usually clear cut and understandable (Vagg 1994). But at the routine level of whether one can take one's radio into the exercise yard, swap cassette tapes with another inmate, have more compact discs than is officially permitted, make a phone call outside the allotted time or request that a particular video is brought in, prisoners are reliant on the discretion and flexibility of their officers. For Vagg (ibid.: 83), these are the most important everyday issues for many inmates, yet their outcome rests upon a 'lurking unpredictability'. Consequently, while these issues may seem relatively trivial to the outsider, it is in such interactions that prison officers are able to reinforce where the power lies.

So, media resources clearly serve the purposes of the institution, offering a powerful incentive to good behaviour which, in turn, creates a calming influence on the regime, reduces staff costs and provides officers with a useful control mechanism. In an era when security and control have emerged as the dominant concerns directing prison policy – manifested in increased use of searching, mandatory drug testing, volumetric control of prisoners' possessions, reductions in temporary release and home leave, and many other restrictions (Liebling *et al* 1997) – media *may* be seen as an essentially democratising force, yet the extent of their ability to empower inevitably still depends on who is controlling access. Many critics are concerned that, despite ongoing discourses about rehabilitation and normalisation, it is security and control that remain at the root of the prison service's ideology and that continue to influence their media policy. Of course, some media are easier to regulate than others. Books and magazines are relatively simple to censor or to ban outright and, during my fieldwork, I came across several examples of literary material forbidden to prisoners, including hard-core pornography; texts – such as the fascist magazine *Bulldog* – which might incite racial violence; and educational material – such as science manuals instructing readers how to conduct potentially hazardous experiments – that could conceivably be used inappropriately. Prerecorded media texts are also relatively easy for the prison authorities to regulate and, while inmates are allowed to have a limited number of audio cassettes and compact discs in their possession, video tapes are usually only allowed into the prison if brought in by a *bona fide* member of staff.

In-cell television is, however, much more difficult to control. It can be prohibited to some inmates, or withdrawn as a punishment. But its content is virtually impossible to regulate other than by prescribing specific periods of time – for example, during working-hours or after 11 pm – when it must be switched off. Levels of literacy are much lower among prisoners than in the population as a whole, and audio-visual media therefore tend to be seen as a great leveller of inequalities. Computer technologies are arguably yet more democratising and, although many prison governors and Home Office officials reported they do foresee a day when the Internet will be used as routinely in prisons as it is outside, it is difficult to imagine at this point how the prison service would regulate the seemingly unregulateable flow of information which would inevitably result. Indeed, several of my inmate interviewees mentioned that restrictions on computer use had been severely tightened in the months preceding the introduction of in-cell television, and they viewed the confiscation of their personal computers – thought to be part of the overall drive to improve security – as being directly linked to the provision of personal TV sets, which was assumed to be intended as some sort of *quid pro quo* compensation. Most of these inmates, however, said they would rather have their computer back than have in-cell television.

Another factor concerning in-cell television that creates tension between prisoners and the prison authorities is the ownership and cost of the actual sets. Given that one of the factors which delayed the implementation of in-cell television in this country for so long was the widespread assumption it would be financed by the British tax-payer, some respondents have been angered by rumours that the television sets were purchased by the prison service in bulk from the high street retailer, Argos, at a discounted price of £44 per set. They were further aggrieved that they would be paying £1 per week rental which, as far as they were concerned, meant the scheme would very quickly be generating a steady source of income for the Treasury. On top of this, many were disappointed by the standard of the equipment. The prison service took the decision that the sets would not have remote controls because they could easily be lost, and because they might encourage inmates to leave the sets on standby which, it is argued, uses electricity and increases the risk of fire. Furthermore, prison-issue TV sets have no teletext facility, which angered many inmates who use the service for news and sports information.

But that loci of power rest in the micropolitical spheres of prison life 'on the ground', as well in the macro-structural dynamics above, is demonstrated by the fact that prisoners find ample opportunities to assert their agency and resist established forces and expectations. Reminiscent of Cohen and Taylor's (1972) street-wise and erudite prison respondents who mocked the lesser intelligence of their guards (an example being the 'thick screw' who thought it a compliment to be called an 'aggressive psychopath'; ibid.: 139), de Certeau (1984) characterises all social relations as being a conflict between the 'strategies' of the powerful – who are assumed to be cumbersome, unimaginative and bureaucratic – and the 'tactics' of the weak – who are, by contrast, nimble, creative and flexible. For de Certeau – and here his theory bears similarities to that of Giddens – institutions constitute one of the places where the powerful construct and exercise their power, but the weak create their own 'spaces' within those places; making them temporarily their own as they occupy and move through them. De Certeau uses the language of warfare to describe these processes, arguing that subordinates are like guerrillas, appropriating space as a means of resistance. This metaphor seems particularly apt in relation to my observations of the spaces connecting the different wings at HMP Ashwell. Known to inmates as 'the streets' these long, narrow corridors that run past the association rooms were out of the sight of staff in the wing offices and, during association time, groups of inmates would congregate to replicate some of the activities that might be encountered among such groups of young men on the 'real' streets outside. Given the opportunities these locations provided for inmates to mingle out of sight of any authorities, it seemed possible it was not just banter that was exchanged in these corridors. In fact, Ashwell's governor asked me to try to find out why so many inmates (in particular, those who did not have in-cell television) eschewed the association rooms with their TV sets and pool tables, and instead loitered in the corridors outside, but I found no evidence of any illegal activity. It may simply be that, like the adolescent youths encountered by Corrigan (1975), these prisoners were actively engaged in the social practice of 'doing nothing' except marking their 'patch'. More specifically, they had found a way of using the imposed system of 'association activity' and creating a territorial space reminiscent of those they would have on the outside. The fact it involved a stubborn resistance of an activity designated a 'privilege' (television), and was invisible to the wing officers, added to the sense of 'foiling the other's game' and enhanced the 'pleasure in getting around the rules of a constraining space' (de Certeau 1984: 18).

Individuals thus use media technologies as a source of empowerment – by rejecting them – in order to resist dominant ideologies. Most prisoners I spoke to think that in-cell TV is one of the best innovations they have seen in prison, yet many subscribed to in-cell television with extreme reluctance, and frequently only after a significant period of refusing it:

> Most of us are glad to have it, although I must admit that I held out for a while as a protest about the way it's been handled. [At Stocken] we were told we could buy our own TVs, so we had to lose ten weeks private cash to buy them, and then we're told we have to have *their* TVs. Basically, we're paying £1 a week to have something taken off us. They'll use it as a punishment as well. Instead of days remission we'll lose twenty-eight days TV (Bill).

> I didn't want in-cell TV, but in the end I had to have it because I'm on Enhanced. I can't pretend I don't watch it now that I've got it, but I held out as long as I could. I enjoyed my eight months here without it though (Andrew).[7]

Others flatly rejected in-cell television, principally because to do so demonstrates their individual strength of character and their refusal to toe the institutional line:

It's all carrot dangling in here. Well I refuse to bite the carrot. I'd like television but I'm not going to go down on my knees and grovel for it. Call it resistance, if you like. When you face institutional racism all you can do is resist . . . I refuse to buy into their way of doing things, especially as it's them who will reap the benefits (Paul).

It's a two-tier situation here. We're being bullied, intimidated and dictated to about what we can spend our money on. Jobs are scarce here and if you're unemployed, you're on £2.50 a week. They're saying we have to pay £1 of that for TVs. Well, I'm not having one. I've refused to pay. Nine people on this wing have refused in-cell television because of the £1 per week and because of the situation with the old TVs. In-cell television was never meant to be a privilege. When it was introduced it was a scheme . . . Prisons now have a monopoly. It costs them £44 a set, so in the first year they've already made £12 out of me. The TVs don't have remote controls, they don't have Ceefax which I used to keep up with world news, and we can't take them with us when we get out of here. I don't see why I should be bullied into paying £1 a week for something I don't have full use of. Argos have made money out of this, this prison will make a fortune from it . . . They won't give me a bill of sale for it, so I'm taking them to court (Billy).

As these examples illustrate, many prisoners believe it is not prisoners' rights or even the control factor that are of primary interest to the prison authorities, but financial considerations. At all the prisons I studied, questions about the cost of in-cell television to the institution and to individual prisoners were paramount. Many believed that after such a long period during which it was talked about, planned and not implemented, the only possible reason for its introduction now must be to make money from them. However, the belief that the prison service primarily views them, not as unique flesh-and-blood human beings but as units of cost within an over-bureaucratised framework of policy, simply gives inmates greater scope for resistance. Such protests undermine the often taken-for-granted assumption that human beings are passively compliant when faced with behaviour-linked rewards and punishments. Several inmates reported they had previously deliberately stayed on Basic regime as a sign of protest; others who were on Standard entitlements had no inclination to go any further; and others still who enjoyed Enhanced privileges mocked the Super Enhanced prisoners in Ashwell and Stocken's self-contained Scandinavian units.

In its discussion of macro structures and processes, this chapter has focused on the roles of prison officers, governors, the prison service, the Home Office and the wider public in implementing or endorsing prisoners' access to media. It was more difficult to research 'upwards' decisions taken regarding media policy than it was to research 'downwards' the opinions and feelings of inmates, but the accounts of many prison officers and governors I spoke to suggested there had been significant differences of opinion on policy between the Home Office and prison service personnel in the Michael Howard era of the mid-1990s which lingered on into the period when I was doing my fieldwork. These clashes of opinion were most manifestly an issue at those prisons that already had in-cell television prior to Howard's appointment as Home Secretary, where the success of the scheme (as perceived by inmates, staff and governors) was constantly undermined by the threat from above that it would be withdrawn. Howard's legacy appears to be that official opinion on prisoners' access to personal media remains guarded. The conclusion to be drawn from this discussion, however, is that although macro structures and processes permeate all areas of policy development, loci of power and control exist at all levels of the prison culture. Even where inmates have little choice, compliance implies resigned acceptance rather than dumb acquiescence. Indeed, negotiations between prisoners and prison governors regarding the origin, availability and cost of in-cell TV sets have provided a classic hegemonic site of struggle wherein the disempowered can engage in contested relations with the authorities that attempt to subordinate them. Far from lacking an understanding of economic drives, many inmates recognise that the struggle is not simply the product of an unequal relationship between themselves and the prison governor, but that the dominant interests extend far beyond the prison service into the realms of government and society.

At the beginning of this chapter I noted it is unusual to come across a setting where media proliferate yet are so highly regulated as the prison. Most British prisons are now relatively 'media-rich' institutions. Wherever I went in all the prisons I studied, I heard music from radios and stereo systems, encountered inmates voraciously reading newspapers and magazines and was confronted by the flickering images of television monitors. Media resources are everywhere: in cells, workshops, gyms, staff offices, wing offices and in officers' cafeterias and relaxation areas. Yet the carrot which is dangled to encourage good behaviour can very quickly turn into the stick which is used to punish, and in-cell television's status as reward/punishment is frequently ambiguous. As a senior manager put it: 'In-cell TV is a real and tangible reward which most prisoners want to have. It therefore forms an appropriate and visible part of IEP. Removal of TV is a very direct sanction which aids control of prisoners' (Head of Lifer Management Unit, in response to questionnaire).

Furthermore, despite the proliferation of media technologies, the most striking impression formed during my fieldwork was of how *total* these 'total institutions' seemed. All the prisons I spent time in are situated in remote locations, physically removed from the rest of the community. Most inmates are not from the immediate vicinity and, for many, their homes, families and identities are firmly tied to an entirely different part of the country (or, increasingly, to a different part of the world). But more elementary even than that, a prison is a closed, sequestered and usually almost entirely self-sufficient world. Despite being confronted by a volume of media technologies far exceeding that of any other kind of institution I have worked in, at no time previously had I felt so cut off from the world than I did during my field research. It was easy, then, to relate to the inmates who described their sense of removal from reality, the 'fuzziness' that tinged their perception of events on the outside or even the pointlessness of using media to keep abreast of world events. Media resources have undoubtedly had a profound impact upon prisoners' experiences of confinement and, as the previous two chapters demonstrated, are crucial to prisoners' sense of agency and autonomy, and to the preservation of a stable social identity amid seemingly overwhelming structural constraints. But for many inmates – particularly those serving long or life sentences – the permanent and pervasive impression of being confined within a closed and highly managed environment is barely alleviated by the presence of media, and many reported experiencing a profound sense of dislocation from the 'real world'.

Macro forces have combined in recent years to ensure a rising prison population whose numbers must be managed, controlled and rationalised. Initial consultations and debates by the prison service about the viability of personal media were overshadowed by an era of unprecedented government involvement in the prison service, characterised by authoritarian management and austerity. Even though the current government have permitted the introduction of personal media into most prisons in England and Wales, the possible reasons for the decision are many and varied, and may serve the requirements of institutions and prisoners in very different, and frequently conflicting, ways. As this chapter has demonstrated, the decision to extend prisoners' access to media has been driven by the advantages they offer to staff and governors as incentives for good behaviour. To some extent the 'carrot and stick' ideology underpinning the rules by which media initiatives (like other earnable privileges) are enforced and endorsed is made possible by the attitudes of the wider society which, by and large, fails to see prisoners as subjects, actively 'making a difference' in their individual and collective lives. Even academic research – which, in the sociological tradition, has resorted to reductive typologies of social behaviour, and in psychology has found imprisonment to have minimal effects on identity and behaviour – has been of limited usefulness in this respect. The net result of all this is that the pains of imprisonment have been 'strangely forgotten' (Mathiesen 1990) or 'tragically underestimated' (Liebling 1999a).

Notes

[1] In addition to the views of inmates, this chapter draws on information gathered from a questionnaire I administered to seventeen senior personnel working in various capacities within the prison service and/or with prisoners. The questionnaire focused specifically on the introduction into prisons of in-cell television, and respondents numbered among them ten prison governors (including one manager of a privately run prison), one head of a lifer management unit, two management consultants, one personnel manager, one head of regimes, a senior research associate in criminology and a lecturer in law. With the exception of the two university staff, all the respondents were studying for an MSt degree at the University of Cambridge, and were approached when I gave a class to them on theoretical and methodological issues arising from my research.

[2] At present only HMP Garth operates an internal channel for the communication of information and education, although plans are under consideration to extend the facility to all prisons with the technological capability to have it.

[3] The governor at Ashwell told me he allows prisoners who he perceives to be making a concerted effort to free themselves of drugs a few months of in-cell TV *gratis* as a sign of good faith and encouragement. Some inmates, however, have interpreted this as a sign that drugs-users are being rewarded for their habit.

[4] A number of other European countries preceded Britain in introducing in-cell television; for example, it was installed in French prisons in 1985 (Vagg 1994).

[5] Meyrowitz suggests that the example of prisons is extreme, although he emphasises that the impact of media on prisons and the resulting inclusion of prisoners in the public sphere are simply the latest development in a long history of gradual democratisation via the mass media, whereby previously marginalised or formally isolated groups – women, children, the poor, the disabled, ethnic minorities and homosexuals – have had access to, and been included, in all spheres of public participation.

[6] The range of *legitimate* controls at a prison officer's disposal may be exhausted, as Sykes (1958) suggests, but for Mathiesen (1965), all matters legitimately or non-legitimately controlled and distributed by staff are effective because they are related to power.

[7] At Ashwell all Enhanced and Super Enhanced accommodation comes with a television, so prisoners who achieve this level of entitlements and privileges *have* to subscribe to in-cell TV and be prepared to pay for it. The governor's view is that if an inmate is on Enhanced, but chooses not to have a TV, he is denying someone else the privilege of having it.

Conclusion: the paradoxical power of media in prisons

The social practices that shape identity, power and gratification through media consumption among prison inmates have been underpinned in this study by a dialectic of choice and constraint, and have been organised around the microsocial sphere of individuals, friends, partners and families; the intermediate mesocultural sphere of semi-formal and informal groups and networks; and the macrosocial sphere of government, society, the prison service, governors and prison staff. Like other prison sociologies this study represents a picture of prisons at a particular point in time; a snapshot of the everyday lived experiences of inmates as – at the beginning of a new millennium – a specific nexus of macro-political and social forces impact upon, and intersect with, the cultural imperatives of an underclass of men as they struggle to maintain a sense of who they are, and who they have been, in the face of innumerable stigmatising and dehumanising processes.

Giddens' structuration theory and Bourdieu's notion of habitus provided me with an 'orienting device' (Layder 1998) by which I was able to develop my ideas about how power, legitimacy, control, pain, and identity are mediated in men's prisons. The 'dialectic of control' that is central to Giddens' theory alerted me to the fact that even though prisons are very evidently structured by strict adherence to formal rules and by compliance in the face (or facelessness) of official hierarchies, the balances of power within them are neither fixed nor necessarily obvious to the casual observer. The synthesis of Bourdieu's concept of habitus within Giddens' theory gave structuration a more easily identifiable cultural dimension enabling me to explore the use of media resources as a means of expressing agency, affecting behaviour and constructing identities (thereby maintaining, nurturing or even entirely stepping out of one's usual habitus) among both the dominant and the dominated. This

185

approach offered an illuminating insight into the social and cultural life of prisons, although it is important to note that media are but one important resource that individuals in prisons have at their disposal when conducting their day-to-day relations with others who share their social world.

There may, then, be other informal, social conduits that act as 'third parties' in relationships of power and subordination, and that shape identity and responses to pain in prisons in similar ways. This study has demonstrated that media resources direct – indeed, mediate – flows of power between officers and inmates, and between inmates and other inmates, and I hope the interweaving of micro and meso frames of analysis has shed new light on the decisions, choices and actions that prisoners struggle with every day of their incarcerated lives. At the meso level of social practices, it has been demonstrated that the psychological survival of prison inmates depends largely upon their adoption, collectively or individually, of identities that enable them to adapt to their lives inside, or at least to cope with the stresses of confinement with a degree of success. Although solidarity is rare, pressure to conform is strong. Indeed, absorption into one or other of the subcultures in prison, and the resulting sense of 'belonging' to a group with a strong collective identity (whether the primary identification is based on ethnicity, political or criminal ideologies, access to contraband economies or some other variable) may provide a partial explanation for high rates of recidivism. The custodial experience provides a highly structured environment which – if one adheres to the inmate rules – can provide, for some inmates, ontological security based on mutual support and camaraderie. This cohesive structure among similarly disadvantaged social 'misfits' may compensate for the bleaker aspects of prison life (Hood and Sparks, 1970) although the notion that some inmates cope better with prison than with 'freedom' is problematic (Liebling 1999b). But given that many lower-class males in society at large get their most profound sense of self from group loyalties based on excessive displays of manliness, it is unsurprising that the hierarchies of power found in men's prisons relate directly to various concepts of masculinity (Fishman 1934; Sykes 1958; Irwin 1970). The forms and codes of masculine behaviour that charact-erise the inmate culture are likely to have been learned in response to the imperatives of masculinity in working-class culture, which act back on, shape and ultimately reproduce the need for prisons. The capacity of some inmates to resist their ascribed identities of 'prisoner' with all its connotations of weakness, conformity and the relinquishing of power, is testimony to the masculine hegemony that is so embedded in the hierarchy of the prison world.

However, as has been demonstrated, the removal of autonomy, choice and responsibility, and all the implications therein, *can* lead to anxieties concerning the deterioration of one's psychological and physical well-being and serve to negate the sense of manliness which is at the core of most prisoners' identities. Not all prisoners can 'do masculinity' in the ways prescribed by the prison hierarchy. For those who are defined by their peers as embodying a subordinate masculinity and who accept this characterisation of themselves, prison can become a terrifying ordeal. It is perhaps for these prisoners that media resources are most valuable in helping them to 'carve out a solitary space' (Radway 1984: 211) and construct identities that run counter to the dominant masculine ideals. In the relatively recent days of association TV, when inmates had to share viewing and negotiate access to media among relatively large numbers, patterns of family viewing were frequently replicated, whereby the content, manner and viewing context of television consumption were commonly determined by the biggest, strongest, loudest or most intimidating members of the group. Now that in-cell television has arrived, most prisons enjoy – for the time being, at least – a quieter, more acquiescent regime.

Meso and micro processes and pleasures associated with consuming media originate from both the form and content of media resources. At a general level, media use might be habitual, time-consuming, provide companionship and so on, but the programme or text-specific content of any particular medium will also provide an important source of gratifications of various kinds. Consequently, the benefits to inmates of having relatively unrestricted access to the forms of media which most of us in everyday life take for granted should not be underestimated. To recapitulate just a few examples: media have a structural capacity; they regulate patterns of activity and talk, and provide inmates with a means of filling, structuring and 'marking' time. They are relational, providing common ground for conversation and offering topics and illustrations on which people 'peg' opinions. They encourage affiliation with others and can provide a sense of common identity and shared fanship. Media encourage performance and spectacle, providing material for the construction or enhancement of masculine identities and encouraging the construction of identities based on popular cultural heroes and role models. They have the potential to increase social learning and develop various aspects of socialisation, and may advance cultural competence, extending the social dominance of some individuals over others. They can also provide a means of avoidance of other people, allowing some individuals (perhaps notably, vulnerable prisoners) to 'tune out' of the prison culture. They deny present realities and provide material for escapist or romantic fantasies, evoke memories and allow inmates to transcend the confines of time and space. They reinforce a sense of humanity, uniting the prison population with the wider society in common experience. They diminish the sense of being marginalised, of being an undeserving underclass. They act as the filter through which localised practices define and shape external structural forms into concrete personalised experiences. Finally, media technologies act as a source of resistance; inmates who reject in-cell TV are seeing through dominant ideologies and rejecting the ethos that behaviour is linked to reward and punishment.

I hope this book has made a valuable contribution to both the new generation of sociological prison research and to recent endeavours to understand how we construct self and identity in a mediated world. The bringing together of two bodies of research that have been previously disconnected and the integration of theory and practice have been important features of this study, and I hope such interdisciplinary, theoretically informed and empirically supported approaches will continue to guide prison research in the future. This study has provided a detailed description of a unique environment and given voice to people whose opinions are rarely sought, about subjects that are of intrinsic importance to them, and it has done so from within intellectual and theoretical frameworks that have aimed to develop our understandings of broader social phenomena. In its descriptive accounts of everyday life, supported by the personal stories of the people who live in confinement, it has hopefully succeeded in what it set out to achieve; that is, to attest to the legitimacy – indeed exigency – of media consumption and culture as sites of pleasure, reflexivity and ontology to the stigmatised, marginalised underclass who dwell in our prisons. With the introduction of the media of mass communications into prisons, inmates are undoubtedly enjoying unprecedented access to information and entertainment. And not only can media mitigate some of the pains of incarceration, and provide the material out of which identities are constructed, but they can also grant prisoners a semblance of public participation and return to them membership of some of society's democratic processes.

Yet it is hard to avoid the conclusion that media are being used undemocratically within the walls of many prisons. Media – especially personal media – are highly effective devices of social and behavioural control. Even family viewing is governed by rules, both implicit and explicit, and is used as a reward or punishment, as a bartering tool and as a conduit of power, so it is not difficult to imagine how in the prison environment the introduction of personal media – like letter writing and visits in an earlier phase – has become part of the state's armoury in the struggle to maintain order and achieve compliance in prisons (Scraton *et al*, 1991). The belief that TV viewing is an *in*activity underpins the prevailing idea among prison staff and authorities that personal television will result in passivity becoming the prison norm rather than discontent. Thus, whatever pleasures are to be found in media forms and content will always be tempered by the demands of the institution, to the extent that the incentive-driven implementation of media into prisons may be interpreted, not only as a lever for securing compliant behaviour, but as a means of undermining the individual inmate in relation to structural power. Perversely, the introduction of media resources into prisons may consequently be reproducing disadvantage and deprivation. As earlier lock-up times are introduced, as opportunities for inmates to interact with others are reduced and as some inmates are effectively coerced into having – and paying for – in-cell television if they are to enjoy other privileges associated with the 'enhanced' status ascribed to them, it is difficult to avoid the Foucauldian conclusion that personal media have one great, unspoken advantage as far as prison authorities are concerned, and that is to normalise the regulation and surveillance of inmates. In other words, in-cell television – for all its acknowledged advantages to inmates – is being used as the 'sweetener' which is intended to mask, or compensate for, the situational control measures that are creeping back into the logic of imprisonment (Morgan 1997). For the prison service then, the media's capacity to 'normalise' everyday life inside prisons may simply serve to ensure that the embedded practices of imprisonment – however undemocratic, unpopular or unpleasant – are accepted as natural to inmates over time.

One of this study's key findings is that power is not unidirectional, but flows in and through prisons in multifarious and complex ways. Media – in their role as both a resource and a constraint – have altered the delicate balance of power within prisons and continue subtly to change and shift relations of dominance and subordination. An understanding of this paradox – that media are used both as a source of empowerment by prison inmates and, at the same time, as a means of control over them – enables us to begin to address some important questions that remain at the heart of much prison literature; namely, why is it that when prisoners apparently enjoy greater standards of living than formerly, are more integrated into the world beyond the prison walls than ever before, and are enjoying greater civil and legal rights than their predecessors, do their personal testimonies indicate they may be experiencing a greater depth and weight of imprisonment than at any time previously? How is it that prisons seem – on the surface at least – more humane and yet at the same time are more punitive? It is these paradoxical questions that future prison research might usefully address in order to extend our understanding of the complexities of the social world of prisons.

References

Abercrombie, N. and Longhurst, B. (1998) *Audiences*. London: Sage.

Adam, B. (1995) *Timewatch: The Social Analysis of Time*. Cambridge: Polity Press.

Adams, C. (2000) Suspect data: arresting research. In R. King and E. Wincup (eds.) *Doing Research on Crime and Justice*. Oxford: Oxford University Press.

Adler, J. (1996) *Incidence of Fear in Prisons*. London: Prison Reform Trust.

Adler, J. and Longhurst, B. (1994) *Discourse, Power and Justice: Towards a New Sociology of Imprisonment*. London: Routledge.

Adler, P. and Adler, P. (1983) Relations between dealers: the social organisation of illicit drug transactions. *Sociology and Social Research* 67(3): 260–78.

Alasuutari, P. (ed.) (1999a) *Rethinking the Media Audience*. London: Sage.

Alasuutari, P. (1999b) Cultural images of the media. In P. Alasuutari (ed.) *Rethinking the Media Audience*. London: Sage.

Allor, M. (1988) Relocating the site of the audience. *Critical Studies in Mass Communication* 5(3): 217–33.

Altheide, D. L. and Snow, R. P. (1979) *Media Logic*. Thousand Oaks, CA: Sage.

Ang, I. (1985) *Watching Dallas: Soap Opera and the Melodramatic Imagination*. London: Methuen.

Ang, I. (1991) *Desperately Seeking the Audience*. London: Routledge.

Appadurai, A. (1993) Disjuncture and difference in the global cultural economy. In B. Robins (ed.) *The Phantom Public Sphere*. Minneapolis, MN: University of Minnesota Press.

Banister, P. A., Smith, F. V., Heskin, K. J. and Bolton, N. (1973) Psychological correlates of long-term imprisonment. I. Cognitive variables. *British Journal of Criminology* 13: 312–22.

Berger, A. A. (1998) *Media Research Techniques* (2 edn). Thousand Oaks, CA: Sage.

Best, S. and Kellner, D. (1991) *Postmodern Theory: Critical Interrogations.* London: Macmillan.

Bocock, R. and Thompson, K. (eds.) (1992) *Social and Cultural Forms of Modernity.* Cambridge: Polity Press.

Bondeson, U. (1989) *Prisoners in Prison Societies.* New Brunswick, NJ: Transaction Books.

Bostyn, A. M. and Wight, D. (1987) Inside a community: values associated with money and time. In S. Fineman (ed.) *Unemployment: Personal and Social Consequences.* London: Tavistock.

Bottomley, K., James, A., Clare, E. and Liebling, A. (1997) *Monitoring and Evaluation of Wolds Remand Prison.* London: Home Office Publications.

Bottoms, A. E. (1995) The philosophy and politics of punishment and sentencing. In C.M.V. Clarkson and R. Morgan (eds.) *The Politics of Sentencing Reform.* Oxford: Clarendon Press.

Bottoms, A. E. (1999) Interpersonal violence and social order in prisons. In M. Tonry and J. Petersilia (eds.) *Prisons. Crime and Justice, Volume 26.* Chicago, IL: University of Chicago Press.

Bottoms, A. E. (2000) The relationship between theory and research in criminology. In R. King and E. Wincup (eds.) *Doing Research on Crime and Justice.* Oxford: Oxford University Press.

Bottoms, A. E., Hay, W. and Sparks, R. (1990) Social and situational approaches to the prevention of disorder in long-term prisons. *Prison Journal* 70: 83–95.

Bourdieu, P. (1977) *Outline of a Theory of Practice.* Cambridge: Cambridge University Press.

Bourdieu, P. (1984) *Distinction: A Social Critique of the Judgement of Taste.* Cambridge, MA: Harvard University Press.

Bourdieu, P. (1996) Understanding. *Theory, Culture and Society* 13(2): 17–36.

Bowker, L. (1977) *Prisoner Subcultures.* Toronto: Lexington.

Boyle, J. (1977) *A Sense of Freedom.* London: Pan Books.

Boyne, R. (1991) Power-knowledge and social theory: the systematic misrepresentation of contemporary French social theory in the work of Anthony Giddens. In C. Bryant and D. Jary (eds.) *Giddens' Theory of Structuration: A Critical Appreciation.* London: Routledge.

Brittan, A. (1977) *The Privatised World.* London: Routledge.

Brittan, A. (1989) *Masculinity and Power.* Oxford: Blackwell.

Brod, H. (1990) Pornography and the alienation of male sexuality. In J. Hearn and D. Morgan (eds.) *Men, Masculinity and Social Theory.* London: Allen & Unwin.

Brunsdon, C. (1990) Problems with quality. *Screen* 31, Spring.

Bryant, C. and Jary, D. (eds.) (1991) *Giddens' Theory of Structuration: A Critical Appreciation.* London: Routledge.

Buckingham, D. (1993a) *Children Talking Television: The Making of Television Literacy.* London: Falmer Press.

Buckingham, D. (1993b) Boys' talk: television and the policing of masculinity. In D. Buckingham (ed.) *Reading Audiences: Young People and the Media.* Manchester: Manchester University Press.

Bukstel, L. H. and Kilmann, P. R. (1980) Psychological effects of imprisonment on confined individuals. *Psychological Review* 88: 469–93.

Burman, P. (1988) *Killing Time, Losing Ground: Experiences of Unemployment.* Toronto: Wall & Thompson.

Caird, R. (1974) *A Good and Useful Life: Imprisonment in Britain Today.* London: Hart-Davis.

Charlesworth, S. (2000) *A Phenomenology of Working Class Experience.* Cambridge: Cambridge University Press.

Clarke, J. (1975) The skinheads and the magical recovery of community. In S. Hall and T. Jefferson (eds.) *Resistance Through Rituals: Youth Subcultures in Post-War Britain.* London: Hutchinson.

Clemmer, D. (1958) *The Prison Community* (2 edn). New York: Holt, Rinehart & Winston.

Cockburn, C. (1983) *Brothers: Male Dominance and Technological Change.* London: Pluto Press.

Cockburn, C. (1986) *Machinery of Dominance.* London: Pluto Press.

Coffey, A. (1999) *The Ethnographic Self: Fieldwork and the Representation of Identity.* London: Sage.

Cohen, A. (1955) *Delinquent Boys: The Culture of the Gang.* New York: Free Press.

Cohen, S. (1983) Social control talk: telling stories about correctional change. In D. Garland and P. Young (eds.) *The Power to Punish: Contemporary Penalty and Social Analysis.* London: Heinemann.

Cohen, S. and Taylor, L. (1972) *Psychological Survival: The Experience of Long-Term Imprisonment.* Harmondsworth: Penguin Books.

Cohen, S. and Taylor, L. (1977) Talking about prison blues. In C. Bell and H. Newby (eds.) *Doing Sociological Research.* London: Allen & Unwin.

Connell, R. W. (1987) *Gender and Power.* Cambridge: Polity Press.

Connell, R. W. (1995) *Masculinities.* Cambridge: Polity Press.

Corner, J. (1995) *Television Form and Public Address.* London: Arnold.

Corrigan, P. (1975) Doing nothing. In S. Hall and T. Jefferson (eds.) *Resistance Through Rituals: Youth Subcultures in Post-War Britain.*

London: Hutchinson.

Corrigan, P. (1979) *Schooling the Smash Street Kids.* London: Macmillan.

Coyle, A. (1994) *The Prisons we Deserve.* London: HarperCollins.

Craib, I. (1984) *Modern Social Theory.* Brighton: Harvester.

Craib, I. (1998) *Experiencing Identity.* London: Sage.

Daniels, A. (1997) What access do prisoners in English prisons have to the media of mass communications and what use do they make of them? Unpublished MA dissertation, Centre for Mass Communications Research, University of Leicester.

Deacon, D., Pickering, M., Golding, P. and Murdock, G. (1999) *Researching Communications.* London: Arnold.

de Certeau, M. (1984) *The Practice of Everyday Life.* Berkeley, CA: University of California Press.

DeNora, T. (2000) *Music in Everyday Life.* Cambridge: Cambridge University Press.

Douglas, M. (1966) *Purity and Danger: An Analysis of Concepts of Pollution and Taboo.* London: Routledge & Kegan Paul.

Downes, D. (1988) *Contrasts in Tolerance.* Oxford: Oxford University Press.

Dunbar, I. and Langdon, A. (1998) *Tough Justice: Sentencing and Penal Policies in the 1990s.* London: Blackstone.

Dunn, R. (1979) Science, technology and bureaucratic domination: television and the ideology of Scientism. *Media, Culture and Society* 1: 351–62.

Dunning, E., Murphy, P. and Williams, J. (1988) *The Roots of Football Hooliganism: An Historical and Sociological Study.* London: Routledge.

Eagleton, T. (1991) *Ideology: An Introduction.* London: Verso.

Elliott, P. (1974) Uses and gratifications research: a critique and a sociological alternative. In J. Blumler and E. Katz (eds.) *The Uses of Mass Communications.* London: Sage.

Ericson, R., Baranek, P. and Chan, J. (1987) *Visualising Deviance: A Study of News Organisations.* Milton Keynes: Open University Press.

Feeley, M. and Simon, J. (1992) The new penology: notes on the emerging strategy of corrections and its implications. *Criminology* 30(4): 452–74.

Fineman, S. (ed.) (1987) *Unemployment: Personal and Social Consequences.* London: Tavistock.

Fishman, J. (1934) *Sex in Prison.* New York: National Library Press.

Fiske, J. (1987) *Television Culture.* London: Methuen.

Fiske, J. (1989) *Understanding Popular Culture.* London: Routledge.

Fiske, J. (1992) Popularity and the politics of information. In P. Dahlgren and C. Sparks (eds.) *Journalism and Popular Culture*. London: Sage.

Fiske, J. (1994) Audiencing: cultural practice and cultural studies. In N. Denzin and Y. Lincoln (eds.) *Handbook of Qualitative Research*. Thousand Oaks, CA: Sage.

Flanagan, T. (1982) Lifers and long-termers: doing big time. In R. Johnson and H. Toch (eds.) *The Pains of Imprisonment*. London: Sage.

Foucault, M. (1977) *Discipline and Punish: The Birth of the Prison*. London: Penguin Books.

Foucault, M. (1980) *Power/Knowledge: Selected Interviews and Other Writings 1972–1977*. Brighton: Harvester.

Fowles, A. (1992) *Why Viewers Watch: A Reappraisal of Television's Effects* (revised 2 edn). London: Sage.

Fryer, D. and McKenna, S. (1987) The laying off of hands: unemployment and the experience of time. In S. Fineman (ed.) *Unemployment: Personal and Social Consequences*. London: Tavistock.

Gaes, G., Flanagan, T., Motiuk, L. and Stewart, L. (1999) Adult correctional treatment. In M. Tonry and J. Petersilia (eds.) *Prisons. Crime and Justice, Volume 26*. Chicago, IL: University of Chicago Press.

Galtung, J. (1961) Prison: the organization of dilemma. In D. Cressey (ed.) *The Prison: Studies in Institutional Organization and Change*. New York: Holt, Rinehart & Winston.

Garland, D. (1990) *Punishment and Modern Society*. Oxford: Oxford University Press.

Gauntlett, D. (1995) *Moving Experiences: Understanding Television's Influences and Effects*. Luton: John Libbey.

Gauntlett, D. and Hill, A. (1999) *TV Living: Television, Culture and Everyday Life*. London: Routledge.

Gelsthorpe, L. and Morris, A. (eds.) (1990) *Feminist Perspectives in Criminology*. Milton Keynes: Open University Press.

Genders, E. and Player, E. (1995) *Grendon: A Study of a Therapeutic Prison*. Oxford: Clarendon Press.

Gergen, K. (1991) *The Saturated Self: Dilemmas of Identity in Contemporary Life*. New York: Basic Books.

Gibbs, J. (1982) The first cut is the deepest. In R. Johnson and H. Toch (eds.) *The Pains of Imprisonment*. London: Sage.

Giddens, A. (1976) *New Rules of Sociological Method*. London: Hutchinson.

Giddens, A. (1977) *Studies in Social and Political Theory*. London: Hutchinson.

Giddens, A. (1979) *Central Problems in Social Theory*. London: Macmillan.

Giddens, A. (1984) *The Constitution of Society*. Cambridge: Polity Press.

Giddens, A. (1990) *Consequences of Modernity*. Cambridge: Polity Press.

Giddens, A. (1991a) *Modernity and Self-Identity*. Cambridge: Polity Press.

Giddens, A. (1991b) Structuration theory: past, present and future. In C. Bryant. and D. Jary (eds.) *Giddens' Theory of Structuration: A Critical Appreciation*. London: Routledge.

Gilmore, T. (1990) *Manhood in the Making*. New Haven, CT: Yale University Press.

Giroux, H. (1983a) *Theory and Resistance in Education*. London: Heinemann.

Giroux, H. (1983b) Theories of reproduction and resistance in the new sociology of education: a critical analysis. *Harvard Educational Review* 53: 257–93.

Goffman, E. (1959) *The Presentation of Self in Everyday Life*. New York: Anchor.

Goffman, E. (1961a) On the characteristics of total institutions: the inmate world. In D. Cressey (ed.) *The Prison: Studies in Institutional Organization and Change*. New York: Holt, Rinehart & Winston.

Goffman, E. (1961b) *Asylums: Essays on the Social Situation of Mental Patients and Other Inmates*. London: Penguin Books.

Golding, P. and Murdock, G. (1990) Screening out the poor. In J. Willis and T. Wollen (eds.) *The Neglected Audience*. London: British Film Institute.

Gramsci, A. (1971) *Selections from Prison Notebooks*. London: Lawrence & Wishart.

Grapendaal, M. (1990) The inmate subculture in Dutch prisons. *British Journal of Criminology* 30: 341–55.

Gray, A. (1987) Behind closed doors: women and video. In H. Baehr and G. Dyer (eds.) *Boxed In: Women On and In Television*. London: Routledge.

Gray, A. (1992) *Video Playtime: The Gendering of a Leisure Technology*. London: Routledge.

Grodin, D. and Lindlof, T. (1996) *Constructing the Self in a Mediated World*. Thousand Oaks, CA: Sage.

Hagell, A. and Newburn, T. (1994) *Young Offenders and the Media*. London: Policy Studies Institute.

Hall, S. (1980) *Drifting into a Law and Order Society*. London: Cobden Trust.

Hall, S. (1992) The question of cultural identity. In S. Hall, D. Held and T. McGrew (eds.) *Modernity and its Futures*. Cambridge: Polity Press.

Hall, S. (ed.) (1997) *Representation: Cultural Representations and Signifying Practices*. London: Sage.

Hall, S., Held, D. and McGrew, T. (eds.) (1992) *Modernity and its Futures*. Cambridge: Polity Press.

Hansen, A., Cottle, S., Negrine, R. and Newbold, C. (1998) *Mass*

Communication Research Methods. Basingstoke: Macmillan.

Hearn, J. and Morgan, D. (eds.) (1990) *Men, Masculinity and Social Theory.* London: Allen & Unwin.

Hebdige, D. (1979) *Subculture: The Meaning of Style.* London: Routledge.

Hebdige, D. (1989) After the masses. *Marxism Today* January: 48–53.

Held, D. and Thompson, J. B. (eds.) (1997) *Social Theory of Modern Societies.* Cambridge: Cambridge University Press.

Her Majesty's Prison Service (2000) *Annual Report and Accounts, April 1999–March 2000.* London: HMSO.

Hermes, J. (1995) *Reading Women's Magazines: An Analysis of Everyday Media Use.* Cambridge: Polity Press.

Hermes, J. (1999) Media figures in identity construction. In P. Alasuutari (ed.) *Rethinking the Media Audience.* London: Sage.

Herzog, H. (1944) What do we really know about daytime serial listeners? In P. F. Lazarsfeld (ed.) *Radio Research 1942–3.* New York: Duell, Sloan & Pearce.

Hey, V. (1986) *Patriarchy and Pub Culture.* London: Tavistock.

Himmelweit, H. and Swift, T. (1976) Continuities and discontents in media taste. *Journal of Social Issues* 32(6): 135–56.

Hobson, D. (1982) *Crossroads: The Drama of a Soap Opera.* London: Methuen.

Hodge, B. and Tripp, D. (1986) *Children and Television.* Cambridge: Polity Press.

Höijer, B. (1990) Studying viewers' reception of television programmes: theoretical and methodological considerations. *European Journal of Communication* 5(1): 29–56.

Hood, R. and Sparks, R. (1970) *Key Issues in Criminology.* London: Weidenfeld & Nicolson.

Horowitz, R. (1986) Remaining an outsider: membership as a threat to research support. *Urban Life* 14: 409–30.

Horton, D. and Wohl, R. (1956) Mass communication and para-social interaction. *Psychiatry* 19: 215–19.

Howard, M. (1993) Speech to the Conservative Party conference, 6 October, London.

Howe, A. (1994) *Punish and Critique.* London: Routledge.

Hunt, J. (1989) *Psychoanalytic Aspects of Fieldwork.* London: Sage.

Ignatieff, M. (1978) *A Just Measure of Pain.* London: Penguin Books.

Ignatieff, M. (1983) State, civil society and total institutions: a critique of recent social histories of punishment. In S. Cohen and A. Scull (eds.) *Social Control and the State.* London: Martin Robertson.

Irwin, J. (1970) *The Felon.* Englewood Cliffs, NJ: Prentice-Hall.

Irwin, J. (1980) *Prisons in Turmoil*. Chicago, IL: Little, Brown.

Irwin, J. and Cressey, D. (1962) Thieves, convicts and the inmate culture. *Social Problems* 10(1): 142–55.

Jacobs, J. (1977) *Stateville: The Penitentiary in Mass Society*. Chicago, IL: Chicago University Press.

Jacobs, J. (1983) *New Perspectives on Prisons and Imprisonment*. Ithaca, NY: Cornell University Press.

Jefferson, T. (1997) Masculinities and crimes. In M. Maguire, R. Morgan and R. Reiner (eds.) *The Oxford Handbook of Criminology* (revised 2nd edn). Oxford: Oxford University Press.

Jenkins, R. (1996) *Social Identity*. London: Routledge.

Jensen, K. B. and Rosengren, K. E. (1990) Five traditions in search of an audience. *European Journal of Communications* 5: 207–38.

Jewkes, Y. (2001) Listen without prejudice: exploring the role of Prison Dialogue. *Prison Service Journal* 36: 59–62.

Johnson, R. and Toch, H. (eds.) (1982) *The Pains of Imprisonment*. London: Sage.

Johnson, T., Dandeker, C. and Ashworth, C. (1984) *The Structure of Social Theory*. London: Macmillan.

Jones, K. and Fowles, A. (1984) *Ideas on Institutions: Analysing the Literature on Long-Term Care and Custody*. London: Routledge.

Jupp, V. (1989) *Methods of Criminological Research*. London: Routledge.

Kalinich, D. (1980) *Power, Stability and Contraband: The Inmate Economy*. Chicago, IL: Waveland Press.

Katz, E., Blumler, J. G. and Gurevitch, M. (1974) Utilization of mass communication by the individual. In J. G. Blumler and E. Katz (eds.) *The Uses of Mass Communication*. Beverly Hills, CA: Sage.

Kellner, D. (1995) *Media Culture*. London: Routledge.

Kilminster, R. (1991) Structuration theory as a world view. In C. Bryant. and D. Jary (eds.) *Giddens' Theory of Structuration: A Critical Appreciation*. London: Routledge.

Kimmel, M. (1990) After fifteen years: the impact of the sociology of masculinity on the masculinity of sociology. In J. Hearn and D. Morgan (eds.) *Men, Masculinity and Social Theory*. London: Allen & Unwin.

King, M. (1992) Male sexual assault in the community. In G. Mezey and M. King (eds.) *Male Victims of Sexual Assault*. Oxford: Oxford University Press.

King, R. (2000) Doing research in prisons. In R. King and E. Wincup (eds.) *Doing Research on Crime and Justice*. Oxford: Oxford University Press.

King, R. and Elliott, K. (1977) *Albany: Birth of a Prison – End of an Era*.

London: Routledge.

King, R. and McDermott, K. (1995) *The State of Our Prisons*. Oxford: Clarendon Press.

King, R. and Morgan, R. (1980) *The Future of the Prison System*. Farnborough: Gower.

King, R. and Wincup, E. (eds.) (2000) *Doing Research on Crime and Justice*. Oxford: Oxford University Press.

Laing, R. (1960) *The Divided Self*. Harmondsworth: Penguin Books.

Layder, D. (1994) *Understanding Social Theory*. London: Sage.

Layder, D. (1998) *Sociological Practice: Linking Theory and Social Research*. London: Sage.

Lefebvre, H. (1971) *Everyday Life in the Modern World*. London: Penguin Books.

Lefebvre, H. (1991) *Critique of Everyday Life*. London: Verso.

Liebling, A. (1992) *Suicides in Prison*. London: Routledge.

Liebling, A. (ed.) (1997) *Security, Justice and Order in Prison: Developing Perspectives*. Cambridge: University of Cambridge Institute of Criminology, Cropwood Conference Series.

Liebling, A. (1999a) Doing research in prison: breaking the silence? *Theoretical Criminology* 3(2): 147–73.

Liebling, A. (1999b) Prison suicide and prisoner coping. In M. Tonry and J. Petersilia (eds.) *Prisons. Crime and Justice, Volume 26*. Chicago, IL: University of Chicago Press.

Liebling, A. (2000) Prisons, criminology and the power to punish or a brief account of the state of the art in prison research. Paper presented to the British Criminology conference 2000, University of Leicester, July.

Liebling, A. and Krarup, H. (1993) *Suicide Attempts and Self-Injury in Male Prisons. Report for the Home Office Research and Planning Unit*. London: Home Office, September.

Liebling, A., Muir, G., Rose, G. and Bottoms, A. (1997) *An Evaluation of Incentives and Earned Privileges: Final Report to the Prison Service. Vol. 1*. London: Home Office, July.

Lindlof, T. (1987) Ideology and pragmatics of media access in prison. In T. Lindlof (ed.) *Natural Audiences: Qualitative Research of Media Uses and Effects*. Norwood, NJ: Ablex.

Lindlof, T. (1995) *Qualitative Communication Research Methods*. Thousand Oaks, CA: Sage.

Lindlof, T. and Meyer, T. P. (1987) Mediated communication as ways of seeing, acting, and constructing culture: the tools and foundations of qualitative research. In T. Lindlof (ed.) *Natural Audiences: Qualitative*

Research of Media Uses and Effects. Norwood, NJ: Ablex.

Lipton, D., Martinson, R. and Wilks, J. (1975) *The Effectiveness of Correctional Treatment: A Survey of Correctional Treatment Evaluations*. New York: Praeger.

Little, M. (1990) *Young Men in Prison*. Aldershot: Gower.

Livingstone, S. (1990) *Making Sense of Television: The Psychology of Audience Interpretation*. Oxford: Pergamon Press.

Lowenthal, D. (1985) *The Past is a Foreign Country*. Cambridge: Cambridge University Press.

Lull, J. (1980) The social uses of television. *Human Communication Research* 6(3): 198–209.

Lull, J. (1988) *World Families Watch Television*. London: Sage.

McClymont, K. (1993) *In Cell Television at HMP Stocken: An Initial Evaluation*. Stocken: HM Prison Service.

McDermott, K. and King, R. (1988) Mind games: where the action is in prisons. *British Journal of Criminology* 28(3): 357–78.

McKay, H., Jayewardene, C. and Reedie, P. (1979) *The Effects of Long-term Incarceration and a Proposed Strategy for Future Research*. Ottawa: Ministry of the Solicitor General of Canada.

McLaughlin, E. and Muncie, J. (1986) *Controlling Crime*. London: Sage.

McQuail, D. (1969) *Towards a Sociology of Mass Communications*. London: Collier-Macmillan.

McQuail, D. (1994) *Mass Communication Theory: An Introduction* (revised 3 edn). London: Sage.

McQuail, D., Blumler, J. and Brown, J. (1972) The television audience: a revised perspective. In D. McQuail (ed.) *Sociology of Mass Communications*. Harmondsworth: Penguin Books.

Mac an Ghaill, M. (ed.) (1996) *Understanding Masculinities*. Milton Keynes: Open University Press.

Mackay, H. (1997) *Consumption and Everyday Life*. London: Sage.

MacLeod, J. (1987) *Ain't No Makin' It: Leveled Aspirations in a Low-Income Neighborhood*. London: Tavistock.

Mander, J. (1980) *Four Arguments for the Elimination of Television*. Brighton: Harvester.

Mathiesen, T. (1965) *The Defences of the Weak: A Sociological Study of a Norwegian Correctional Institution*. London: Tavistock.

Mathiesen, T. (1990) *Prison on Trial*. London: Sage.

Matthews, R. (1999) *Doing Time: An Introduction to the Sociology of Imprisonment*. London: Macmillan.

Messerschmidt, J. (1986) *Capitalism, Patriarchy and Crime*. Totowa, NJ: Rowman & Littlefield.

Messerschmidt, J. (1999) Making bodies matter: adolescent masculinities, the body, and varieties of violence. *Theoretical Criminology* 3(2): 197–220.

Meyrowitz, J. (1985) *No Sense of Place: The Impact of Electronic Media on Social Behaviour*. Oxford: Oxford University Press.

Miedzian, M. (1991) *Boys Will Be Boys: Breaking the Link between Masculinity and Violence*. New York: Anchor.

Miller, T. and McHoul, A. (1998) *Popular Culture and Everyday Life*. London: Sage.

Millett, K. (1971) *Sexual Politics*. London: Hart-Davis.

Minsky, R. (1996) *Psychoanalysis and Gender: An Introductory Reader*. London: Routledge.

Minsky, R. (1998) *Psychoanalysis and Culture: Contemporary States of Mind*. Cambridge: Polity Press.

Morgan, R. (1997) Imprisonment: current concerns and a brief history since 1945. In M. Maguire, R. Morgan and R. Reiner (eds.) *The Oxford Handbook of Criminology* (revised 2 edn). Oxford: Oxford University Press.

Morley, D. (1980) *The* Nationwide *Audience*. London: British Film Institute.

Morley, D. (1986) *Family Television: Culture, Power and Domestic Leisure*. London: Comedia.

Morley, D. (1992) *Television Audiences and Cultural Studies*. London: Routledge.

Morley, D. and Silverstone, R. (1991) Communication and context: ethnographic perspectives on the media audience. In K. Jensen and N. Jankowski (eds.) *A Handbook of Qualitative Methodologies for Mass Communication Research*. London: Routledge.

Morris, T. and Morris, P. (1963) *Pentonville: A Sociological Study of an English Prison*. London: Routledge.

Muncie, J. (2001) Prison histories: reform, repression and rehabilitation. In E. McLaughlin and J. Muncie (eds.) *Controlling Crime* (2nd edn). London: Sage.

Murdock, G. (1997) Thin descriptions: questions of method in cultural analysis. In J. McGuigan (ed.) *Cultural Methodologies*. London: Sage.

Newburn, T. and Stanko, E. (eds.) (1994) *Just Boys Doing Business? Men, Masculinities and Crime*. London: Routledge.

Newton, C. (1994) Gender theory and prison sociology: using theories of masculinities to interpret the sociology of prisons for men. *Howard Journal of Criminal Justice* 33(1): 193–202.

O'Shea, A. (1989) 'Television as culture: not just texts and readers', *Media,*

Culture and Society, 11 (3).

O'Sullivan, T. (1991) Television memories and cultures of viewing 1950–65. In J. Corner (ed.) *Popular Television in Britain: Studies in Cultural History.* London: British Film Institute.

O'Sullivan, T., Hartley, J., Saunders, D., Montgomery, M. and Fiske, J. (1994) *Key Concepts in Communication and Cultural Studies* (2 edn). London: Routledge.

Patton, M. Q. (1990) *Qualitative Evaluation and Research Methods* (2 edn). Thousand Oaks, CA: Sage.

Philo, G. (1990) *Seeing and Believing: The Influence of Television.* London: Routledge.

Player, E. and Jenkins, M. (eds.) (1994) *Prisons after Woolf: Reform through Riot.* London: Routledge.

Postman, N. (1985) *Amusing Ourselves to Death: Public Discourse in the Age of Show Business.* London: Methuen.

Poulantzas, N. (1978) *State, Power, Socialism.* London: New Left Books.

Pratt, J. (2000) Emotive and ostentatious punishment: its decline and resurgence in modern society. *Punishment and Society* 2(3): 417–40.

Probyn, W. (1977) *Angel Face: The Making of a Criminal.* London: Allen & Unwin.

Pronger, B. (1990) *The Arena of Masculinity: Sports, Homosexuality and the Meaning of Sex.* New York: St Martin's Press.

Pursehouse, M. (1991) Looking at *The Sun*: into the nineties with a tabloid and its readers. In *Cultural Studies from Birmingham.* Birmingham: Department of Cultural Studies, University of Birmingham.

Radway, J. (1984) *Reading the Romance: Women, Patriarchy and Popular Literature.* Chapel Hill, NC: University of North Carolina Press.

Rawlinson, P. (2000) Mafia, methodology, and 'alien' culture. In R. King and E. Wincup (eds.) *Doing Research on Crime and Justice.* Oxford: Oxford University Press.

Remy, J. (1990) Patriarchy and fratriarchy as forms of androcracy. In J. Hearn and D. Morgan (eds.) *Men, Masculinity and Social Theory.* London: Allen & Unwin.

Ruggiero, V. (1991) The disrespect of prison. Paper presented at the 'Respect in prison' conference, Bishop Grosseteste College, Lincoln, July.

Rusche, G. and Kirchheimer, O. (1939) *Punishment and Social Structure* (reprinted 1968). New York: Columbia University Press.

Sapsford, R. (1983) *Life Sentence Prisoners: Reaction, Response and Change.*

Milton Keynes: Open University Press.

Scacco, A. M. (1975) *Rape in Prison*. Springfield, IL: Charles C. Thomas.

Scannell, P. (1996) *Radio, Television and Modern Life*. Oxford: Blackwell.

Schmid, T. and Jones, R. (1991) Suspended identity: identity transformation in a maximum security prison. *Symbolic Interaction* 14(4): 415–32.

Schroder, K. (1999) The best of both worlds? Media audience research between rival paradigms. In P. Alasuutari (ed.) *Rethinking the Media Audience*. London: Sage.

Scraton, P., Sim, J. and Skidmore, P. (1991) *Prisons under Protest*. Milton Keynes: Open University Press.

Segal, L. (1990) *Slow Motion: Changing Masculinities, Changing Men*. London: Virago.

Seidler, V. (1991) *Recreating Sexual Politics*. London: Routledge.

Serge, V. (1970) *Men in Prison*. London: Gollancz.

Shannon, T. and Morgan, C. (1996) *The Invisible Crying Tree*. London: Doubleday.

Shover, N. (1983) The later stages of ordinary property offender careers. *Social Problems* 31: 208–18.

Silverstone, R. (1994) *Television and Everyday Life*. London: Routledge.

Silverstone, R. (1999) *Why Study the Media?* London: Sage.

Sim, J. (1994) Tougher than the rest? Men in prison. In T. Newburn and E. Stanko (eds.) *Just Boys Doing Business? Men, Masculinities and Crime*. London: Routledge.

Simpson, P. (1984) One man and his dog show. In L. Masterman (ed.) *Television Mythologies*. London: Comedia.

Smith, C. and Wincup, E. (2000) Breaking in: researching criminal justice institutions for women. In R. King and E. Wincup (eds.) *Doing Research on Crime and Justice*. Oxford: Oxford University Press.

Smith, J. (1993) *Misogynies: Reflections on Myths and Malice*. London: Faber & Faber.

Snow, R. P. (1983) *Creating Media Culture*. Thousand Oaks, CA: Sage.

Somers, M. and Gibson, G. (1994) Reclaiming the epistemological 'other': narrative and the social constitution of identity. In C. Calhoun (ed.) *Social Theory and the Politics of Identity*. Oxford: Blackwell.

Sparks, R. (1971) *Local Prisons: The Crisis in the English Prison System*. London: Heinemann.

Sparks, R., Bottoms, A. E. and Hay, W. (1996) *Prisons and the Problem of Order*. Oxford: Oxford University Press.

Spigel, L. and Jenkins, H. (1991) Same Bat channel, different Bat times: mass culture and popular memory. In R. Pearson and W. Uricchio (eds.) *The Many Lives of the Batman*. New York: Routledge.

Spradley, J. P. (1979) *The Ethnographic Interview*. New York: Holt, Rinehart & Winston.

Stern, V. (1987) *Bricks of Shame: Britain's Prisons*. Harmondsworth: Penguin Books.

Stevens, D. J. (1994) The depth of imprisonment and prisonization: levels of security and prisoners' anticipation of future violence. *Howard Journal of Criminal Justice* 33(1): 137–57.

Stevenson, N. (1995) *Understanding Media Cultures: Social Theory and Mass Communication*. London: Sage.

Sykes, G. (1958) *The Society of Captives: A Study of a Maximum Security Prison*. Princeton, NJ: Princeton University Press.

Sykes, G. and Messinger, S. (1960) The inmate social system. In L. Radzinowicz and M. Wolfgang (eds.) *Crime and Justice. Vol. 3*. New York: Basic Books.

Thompson, J. B. (1989) The theory of structuration. In D. Held and J. B. Thompson (eds.) *Social Theory of Modern Societies*. Cambridge: Cambridge University Press.

Thompson, J. B. (1995) *The Media and Modernity: A Social Theory of the Media*. Cambridge: Polity Press.

Thurston, R. (1996) Are you sitting comfortably? Men's story-telling, masculinities, prison culture and violence. In M. Mac an Ghaill (ed.) *Understanding Masculinities*. Milton Keynes: Open University Press.

Toch, H. (1975) *Men in Crisis*. Chicago, IL: Aldine.

Toch, H. (1992) *Living in Prison: The Ecology of Survival* (2 edn). Princeton, NJ: Princeton University Press.

Tolson, A. (1977) *The Limits of Masculinity*. London: Routledge.

Tonry, M. and Petersilia, J. (eds.) (1999) *Prisons. Crime and Justice, Volume 26*. Chicago, IL: University of Chicago Press.

Tudor, A. (1979) On alcohol and the mystique of media effects. In J. Cook and M. Lewington (eds.) *Images of Alcoholism*. London: British Film Institute/Alcohol Education Centre.

Tulloch, J. and Jenkins, H. (1995) *Science Fiction Audiences: Watching Doctor Who and Star Trek*. London: Routledge.

Tulloch, J. and Moran, A. (1986) *A Country Practice: Quality Soap*. Sydney: Currency Press.

Tunstall, J. (1983) *The Media in Britain*. London: Constable.

Vagg, J. (1994) *Prison Systems: A Comparative Study of Accountability in England, France, Germany and The Netherlands*. Oxford: Clarendon Press.

Vaughan, B. (2001) Handle with care: on the use of structuration theory within criminology. *British Journal of Criminology* 41: 185–200.

von Hirsch, A. (1992) Proportionality in the philosophy of punishment. In M. Tonry (ed.) *Crime and Justice: A Review of Research. Vol. 16.* Chicago, IL: University of Chicago Press.

Walmsley, R., Howard, L. and White, S. (1991) *The National Prison Survey: Main Findings.* London: HMSO.

Ward Jouve, N. (1988) *The Street-Cleaner: The Yorkshire Ripper Case on Trial.* London: Marion Boyars.

Warren, C. (1988) *Gender Issues in Field Research.* London: Sage.

Weber, M. (1964) *The Theory of Social and Economic Organization.* New York: Free Press.

Weigert, A. (1981) *Sociology of Everyday Life.* New York: Longman.

Westwood, S. (1990) Racism, black masculinity and the politics of space. In J. Hearn and D. Morgan (eds.) *Men, Masculinity and Social Theory.* London: Allen & Unwin.

Wheeler, S. (1961) Socialization in correctional communities. *American Sociological Review* 26(5): 697–712.

Willis, J. and Wollen, T. (eds.) (1990) *The Neglected Audience.* London: British Film Institute.

Willis, P. (1974) *Symbolism and Practice: A Theory for the Social Meaning of Pop Music.* Stencilled Occasional Paper. Birmingham: Centre for Contemporary Cultural Studies, University of Birmingham.

Willis, P. (1977) *Learning to Labour.* Aldershot: Gower.

Willis, P. (1982) Male school counterculture. In *U203: Popular Culture.* Milton Keynes: Open University Press.

Wilson, W. J. (1987) *The Truly Disadvantaged: The Inner City, the Underclass and Public Policy.* Chicago, IL: University of Chicago Press.

Woodward, K. (1997) *Identity and Difference.* London: Sage.

Worrall, A. (2000) Life as a woman: the gendered pains of indeterminate imprisonment. Paper presented to the British Society of Criminology conference, University of Leicester, July.

Wrong, D. (1967) The oversocialised concept of man in modern sociology. In L. Coser and B. Rosenberg (eds.) *Sociological Theory: A Book of Readings.* London: Collier-Macmillan.

Zamble, E. and Porporino, F. J. (1988) *Coping, Behavior and Adaptation in Prison Inmates.* New York: Springer-Verlag.

Index